2010
FIFA WORLD CUP
SOUTH AFRICA™

OFFICIAL BOOK

This edition published in 2010

Copyright © Carlton Books Limited 2010

Carlton Books Limited
20 Mortimer Street
London W1T 3JW

A CIP catalogue record for this book is available from the British Library

10 9 8 7 6 5 4 3 2 1

ISBN: 978-1-84732-516-7

Project Art Editor: Katie Baxendale
Book Designer: Luke Griffin
Cover Designer: Darren Jordan
Editorial: Stephen Guise, Anton Rippon and John Behan
Picture Research: Paul Langan
Production: Kate Pimm
Project Director: Matt Lowing

Manufactured under licence by
Carlton Books Limited.

Printed in Spain

ABOUT THE AUTHOR

Keir Radnedge has been covering football for more than 40 years. He has written countless books on the subject,
from tournament guides to comprehensive encyclopedias, aimed at all ages. His journalism career included *The
Daily Mail* for 20 years, as well as *The Guardian* and other national newspapers and magazines in the UK and
abroad. He is a former editor of *World Soccer*, generally recognized as the premier English language magazine
on global football. In addition to his writing, Keir has been a regular analyst for BBC radio and television, Sky
Sports and the American cable news channel CNN. He also edited a tournament newspaper at the FIFA World
Cup™ tournaments of 1982, 1986 and 1990. He has scripted video reviews of numerous international football
tournaments. He is also the London-based editor of SportsFeatures.com, the football and Olympic news website.

2010 FIFA WORLD CUP SOUTH AFRICA™

OFFICIAL BOOK

Keir Radnedge

Contents

Introduction

The 2010 FIFA World Cup™ will be like no other FIFA World Cup™ in history. For the first time the greatest event in football, the most widely followed sporting extravaganza on the planet, is breaking new ground in Africa – more specifically, South Africa.

This is an exciting and dramatic era for the land of the Rainbow Nation which has made such enormous strides forward since the historic day in 1990 when Nelson Mandela walked out of the Victor Verster Prison and the challenging process of unification began.

Mandela defied doctors' orders to travel to Zurich in 2004 when FIFA's executive committee voted to hold the 2010 tournament in South Africa. Not only could the bidding triumph not have been achieved, it could not even have been undertaken without him. Only in 1991 had South Africa been welcomed back into the FIFA family after the segregationist policy of apartheid, which had left the country out in the sporting cold, was dismantled.

Now South Africa is preparing to welcome the world to a fascinating and unique country whose people have a passion and a pride in their sport which is equalled in few other nations.

Football has been played in what is now South Africa since the late 19th century and has always been the sport of the majority black population, even if the rest of the world remained for too long in ignorance of the fact.

Bafana Bafana (literally "the Boys, the Boys") exceeded even their own fans' dreams by reaching the semi-finals of the FIFA Confederations Cup, the eight-nation warm-up event staged in June of 2009. "The Boys" even threatened to beat European champions Spain before losing narrowly in the third-place play-off.

The match ticket application phases for the finals were massively over-subscribed by fans from all around the world who have been happily prepared to make whatever financial sacrifices have been necessary to beat the worldwide recession. They all knew they will be privileged witnesses to a unique event in the history of world sport – and in a country whose historical, cultural and tourist opportunities are like no other.

South Africa will welcome the world with song and dance and the unique chorus of the vuvuzela horns which invest the land's football stadiums with an atmosphere like that at no previous FIFA World Cup™.

RIGHT: Brazil's Kaka and Argentina's Javier Mascherano battle it out in qualifying. Both of the players' teams will be looking to triumph in South Africa.

BELOW: England and Holland both showed impressive form in qualifying. England's Wayne Rooney and Holland's Joris Mathijsen contest the ball in a friendly that ended 2-2.

WELCOME TO THE 2010 FIFA WORLD CUP™

Africa's footballers have long demanded and deserved a place on the world stage – and now they have it. On their own continent Africa's best can take on the rest of the world with a confidence drawn from their own soil.

South Africa gave the world a taste of the tournament to come by hosting an exhilarating FIFA Confederations Cup in 2009.

The FIFA World Cup™ Arrives in Africa

The dream of bringing the FIFA World Cup™ to Africa was sparked in 1994 when the United States played host for the first time. Finally, 16 years later, history will be made on June 11, 2010, at Soccer City in Johannesburg when these unique finals kick off.

The previous 18 FIFA World Cups™ have been shared around among Europe (10: Italy 1934 and 1990, France 1938 and 1998, Switzerland 1954, Sweden 1958, England 1966, West Germany 1974, Spain 1982 and Germany 2006), South America (four: Uruguay 1930, Brazil 1950, Chile 1962, Argentina 1978), Central America (two: Mexico 1970 and 1986), North America (one: United States 1994) and Asia (one: South Korea/Japan in 2002).

The first African nation to attempt seriously to host the FIFA World Cup™ finals was not South Africa but Morocco, which bid in vain for 1994, for 1998 and then again for 2006 when South Africa also joined the bidding contest for the first time.

South Africa very nearly won, too. Morocco and England were eliminated in the first two rounds of voting. Thus the last round matched South Africa against Germany. FIFA president Sepp Blatter would have the casting vote in the event of a tie and no one doubted that he would have decided in favour of South Africa.

However, on the morning of the vote Charles Dempsey, the president of the Oceania Football Confederation, flew out before the meeting began, out of concern for his and his family's safety. Dempsey had been expected to vote for South Africa. Without him, Germany won by 12 votes to 11 and Blatter's casting vote was not needed.

The Africans were furious. The world federation's solution for the next round of decision-making was to introduce a rotation system. Asia had played host in 2002 and Europe in 2006. So the FIFA executive decided – at Blatter's urging – in favour of African hosts in 2010 and South America in 2014. South Africa tried again, so did Morocco; so did Egypt, and so, jointly, did Libya and Tunisia.

There were no nasty surprises in the voting this time. The Libya/Tunisia co-host bid was barred on the grounds that credible single-nation bids were on the table, and one round of voting was enough: South Africa polled 14 votes, Morocco 10 and Egypt none.

But that was the easy part. The real challenge is turning into reality, in front of billions of worldwide television viewers, the dream shared by Nelson Mandela and Sepp Blatter and Danny Jordaan (the South African sports minister who led the successful 2010 FIFA World Cup™ bid) of staging "the best-ever FIFA World Cup™."

In South African eyes at least, this is about more than just football. As Jordaan says: "This FIFA World Cup™ is not only about football issues. This is the power of football which we in South Africa are seeking to use to re-engage with the world.

"Truly, we have had to face challenges that no other organisers of a FIFA World Cup™ have had to face but still we remain confident because we believe that, for the African continent, this is the Time of Football."

RIGHT: Nelson Mandela's personal support for South Africa's 2010 FIFA World Cup™ bid was an important factor in its ultimate success.

BELOW: The South Africa team receive superb support and fans will be hoping the team can recreate their fine form of the FIFA Confederations Cup 2009.

A Very Special FIFA World Cup™

This is only the fifth time the FIFA World Cup™ has been staged in the southern hemisphere. But project South Africa is different because this will be a tournament in winter weather.

South Africa is a nation moving away from a divisive past and constructing a new society on an economic fast-track: millions are being spent on urban highway creation, on airport redevelopment and on an ambitious regional passenger transit system in and around Johannesburg to help traffic congestion at the out-of-town Soccer City complex which is scheduled to host eight games including the opening match and the Final.

The statistics are sensational. The 2010 FIFA World Cup™ will attract some 450,000 foreign fans – out of a projected 21m visitors for the entire year – and more than £980m in broadcasting rights. Preparing for the finals and running them has created 150,000 new jobs and a profit is guaranteed despite massive expenditure, such as £55.5m on safety and security, some £1.2bn on stadium investment, £1.45bn on infrastructure and £800m on transport.

As organizing leader Danny Jordaan found on his travels around the world, security remained a major concern abroad. This is being met by an increase in policing numbers from 175,000 to 200,000 plus a reserve force of 70,000, supported by a vast increase in investment in helicopters, a variety of police control vehicles and mobile camera systems.

Jordaan says: "Security is the central issue underpinning the FIFA World Cup™. Everyone coming here must have a safe, secure time so that they will want to return. Manchester United, Barcelona, Milan and big teams like these have all come here without a single incident. This is our track record. If we can keep secure 1.2m tourists

in December, which is the major tourism period, why can we not keep 450,000 secure during the FIFA World Cup™?"

A network of "World Cup law courts" is being created. Troublemakers arrested in or around the stadiums will be taken to the nearest designated police station, held in separate cells from "ordinary" criminals, confronted by specially assigned prosecutors and – if necessary – put on flights out.

But one special exemption from the usual rules and regulations surrounding a major football tournament has been agreed. FIFA World Cup™ fans will be able to bring vuvuzela trumpets into the stadia to create the unique atmosphere which enlivens big matches in South Africa. Those trumpets could be a crucial "12th man" for the hosts. Managers of several of the top nations who contested the FIFA Confederations Cup in 2009 admitted that their superstar players were distracted and disorientated by the high-volume

chorus from all around the ground.

If nothing else, the confusion of some of the superstar visitors should enhance the smile on the face of Zakumi, the leopard character which is the 2010 FIFA World Cup™ Official Mascot. Of course, he may not be able to emulate World Cup Willie (England, 1966), Tip & Tap (West Germany, 1974), Gauchito (Argentina,1978) and Footix (France, 1998) and bring the hosts victory. But South Africa, like Zakumi, intends, at the very least, to offer the world a winning and welcoming smile.

RIGHT: Dramatically won by Brazil, the FIFA Confederations Cup 2009 was a triumph in both organizational and footballing terms.

BELOW, LEFT: Zakumi, the Official Mascot for the 2010 FIFA World Cup™, is set to become one of the world's most recognizable children's characters.

BELOW: South Africa's original 2010 FIFA World Cup™ bid poster.

© 2007 FIFA TM

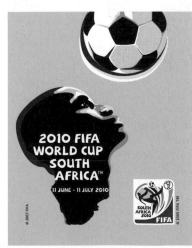

The Stadiums

South Africa is a land of excitement and surprise. The country at the foot of the African continent is three and a half times the size of France but with a population of 45million which is just two-thirds the number.

South Africans can boast about the world-class wildlife-watching and some remarkable natural landscapes ranging from Table Mountain to the Kruger National Park, from the snowy peaks of the Drakensberg Range to the temperate valleys of Western Cape.

This is also a nation with three capital cities – Tschwane/Pretoria (executive), Mangaung/Bloemfontein (judicial, legal) and Cape Town (legislative) – as well as 11 official languages.

Ensuring a fair balance of venues and matches has been a complex task, as has the attempt to settle on a fair standard ticket price.

The cheapest tickets at the finals are being sold only to South African residents. Their cost was set as low as US$20 for group matches and US$150 for the Final, the lowest prices since 1990. The cheapest tickets for overseas fans started at US$80 with a top price for the Final in Soccer City on July 11 of US$900.

The 2010 finals are being staged in 10 venues in nine cities spread across all points of South Africa's compass. Inevitably, the focus will be on Johannesburg: South Africa's largest city, the capital of the wealthiest province Gauteng, is the only one with two stadiums – Soccer City and Ellis Park.

Other venues, such as Pretoria and Rustenburg, and even Nelspruit and Polokwane, are within striking distance by car or bus. However, fans based in Johannesburg who intend to take in Cape Town and Port Elizabeth will probably want to study the flight schedules.

South Africa is bordered by Namibia, Botswana and Zimbabwe to the north and by Mozambique and Swaziland to the east while Lesotho is an independent country within a country.

Naturally, national and local authorities in South Africa hope that many of the football visitors will take time out or extend their stays to explore tourist attractions ranging from the southern coastline to the Kruger National Park.

Promoting the country is, after all, one of the reasons such immense effort has been put into bringing the FIFA World Cup™ to Africa for the first time.

This is one reason why the infrastructure development has included a significant upgrading of airports with a new terminal to welcome fans flooding into Johannesburg and an entirely new airport opening for business in Durban.

BELOW: Soccer City, Johannesburg, nicknamed the "Calabash" after the design of a traditional African brewing pot, will host the 2010 FIFA World Cup™ opening match and Final.

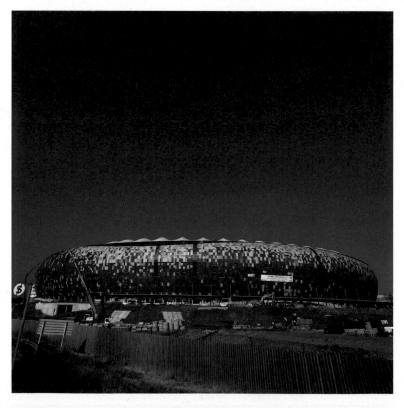

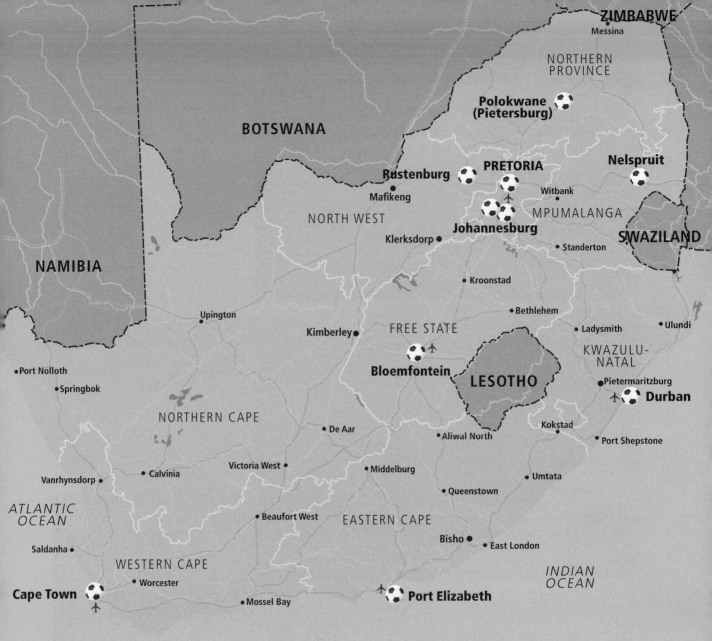

ZIMBABWE
Messina

NORTHERN PROVINCE

Polokwane (Pietersburg)

BOTSWANA

Rustenburg
Mafikeng

PRETORIA
Witbank

Nelspruit

NORTH WEST

MPUMALANGA

SWAZILAND

Klerksdorp
Johannesburg

Standerton

NAMIBIA

Kroonstad

Bethlehem
Ladysmith
Ulundi

Upington

Kimberley
FREE STATE

KWAZULU-NATAL

Bloemfontein

LESOTHO

Pietermaritzburg
Durban

Port Nolloth
Springbok

NORTHERN CAPE

De Aar

Aliwal North

Kokstad

Port Shepstone

Vanrhynsdorp
Calvinia
Victoria West

Middelburg

Umtata

ATLANTIC OCEAN

Queenstown

Saldanha
Beaufort West
EASTERN CAPE

INDIAN OCEAN

WESTERN CAPE
Worcester

Bisho
East London

Cape Town

Mossel Bay

Port Elizabeth

2010 FIFA WORLD CUP SOUTH AFRICA™

- ⚽ Stadium
- ✈ Airport
- – – – International border
- —— Provincial border
- —— Main road
- +++ Railway

BLOEMFONTEIN

FREE STATE STADIUM
Capacity: 45,368
Distance from Johannesburg:
270 miles (south)
Matches: 6 including one
second round

Bloemfontein, the "City of Roses," is the capital of Free State Province as well as the country's judicial capital. It is also known as Mangaung, which means the "place of cheetahs." June weather at 1,395m above sea level may mean freezing temperatures for night matches.

CAPE TOWN

CAPE TOWN STADIUM
Capacity: 63,691
Distance from Johannesburg:
900 miles (south-west)
Matches: 8 including one second round, one quarter- and one semi-final

This new stadium has a spectacular Table Mountain backdrop and usurps in status the Newlands rugby venue. Cape Town is South Africa's legislative capital, its second-largest city, capital of Western Cape Province and the country's most popular tourist destination.

DURBAN

MOSES MABHIDA STADIUM
Capacity: 70,000
Distance from Johannesburg:
375 miles (south-east)
Matches: 7 including one second-round and one semi-final

The Moses Mabhida Stadium boasts a spectacular arch which represents the unification of South Africa through sport. The stadium is the focus of the new Kings Park Sporting Precinct complex in what is the busiest port in Africa and the largest city in the province of KwaZulu-Natal.

JOHANNESBURG

SOCCER CITY
Capacity: 87,600
Matches: 8 including the opening match and the Final

Nicknamed the "Calabash", after the design of a traditional African brewing pot. Work began in February 2007 on the site of the old FNB Stadium adjacent to the South African FA's new office complex. Soccer City will be the focus of the world game on both June 11 and July 11.

JOHANNESBURG

ELLIS PARK
Capacity: 62,567
Matches: 7 including one second round and one quarter-final

Built in 1928 and named after a city councillor, Ellis Park was redeveloped in the early 1980s and again a decade later to host the final of the 1995 Rugby World Cup. Hosted the FIFA Confederations Cup 2009 Final in which Brazil defeated the United States.

NELSPRUIT

MBOMBELA STADIUM
Capacity: 45,014
Distance from Johannesburg: 210 miles (east)
Matches: 5

Nelspruit is the capital of the Mpumalanga Province, formerly Eastern Transvaal, and is located on the Crocodile River. It's also a main stopover point for tourists travelling to the Kruger National Park and to Mozambique.

POLOKWANE

PETER MOKABA STADIUM
Capacity: 45,553
Distance from Johannesburg:
210 miles (north-east)
Matches: 4 (all first round)

Polokwane is another city which benefits from a new stadium for the FIFA World Cup™, this one being named after a former leader of the African National Congress Youth League. Formerly Pietersburg, Polokwane is the capital of Limpopo Province and sits 1,230m above sea level.

PORT ELIZABETH

NELSON MANDELA BAY STADIUM
Capacity: 47,592
Distance from Johannesburg:
675 miles (south)
Matches: 8 including one quarter-final and the third-place play-off

Construction delays prevented the new stadium featuring in the FIFA Confederations Cup 2009 schedule. However, it will be ready to showcase the FIFA World Cup™ in Eastern Cape Province. Port Elizabeth sells itself to tourists as the country's watersport capital.

PRETORIA

LOFTUS VERSFELD STADIUM
Capacity: 49,598
Distance from Johannesburg:
40 miles (north-east)
Matches: 6 including one second round

Pretoria is the country's executive capital and one of its rugby heartlands – home to the Blue Bulls. The original stadium was created in 1906 and was named in 1932 after Robert Owen Loftus Versfeld, the founder of organised sports in Pretoria.

Performers arrange themselves in the shape of Africa at the start of the FIFA Confederations Cup 2009 Final between the USA and Brazil at Ellis Park.

RUSTENBURG

ROYAL BAFOKENG STADIUM
Capacity: 44,732
Distance from Johannesburg:
80 miles (north)
Matches: 5 including one
second round

The "Town of Rest" at the foot of the Magaliesberg mountain range in North West Province will welcome fans to an established stadium upgraded for the FIFA World Cup™. Some US$50m has been spent on one major new stand plus scoreboards, seating and floodlights.

A Unique Experience

Foreign fans streaming into South Africa will be familiar with the FIFA World Cup™ setting. But then, as they go inside to take their seats, they will find the atmosphere change as a unique African flavour is brought to the FIFA World Cup™.

The fans of clubs such as Kaizer Chiefs and Orlando Pirates will sing their songs, spontaneous dancing may erupt among the seating and in the gangways and then, linking it all, will be the instrument which brings a unique sound to the 2010 FIFA World Cup™ finals: the vuvuzela.

This cross between an air horn and a trumpet is a modern phenomenon. But the chorus of hundreds, even thousands, of vuvuzelas in a perpetual drone of ear-splitting noise could just provide the vital extra motivation which drives South Africa's own team to great deeds.

A year ahead of the FIFA World Cup™ and world governing body FIFA was being urged to ban the vuvuzela. Security experts said allowing them into the stadiums would contravene FIFA's own regulations about dangerous weapons. Several managers and players at last summer's FIFA Confederations Cup claimed that the cacophonous crescendo of sound put their teams off their game.

Dunga of Brazil and Bert Van Marwijk of Holland were among visiting coaches who criticised the "distracting sound" of the vuvuzelas. Maybe they were just worrying about results. After all, the distinctive chorus of the vuvuzelas – which became popular locally in the 1990s – helped fire hosts South Africa to the last four of the FIFA Confederations Cup.

But FIFA president Sepp Blatter came to the rescue, saying: "How can FIFA hold special events to combat discrimination if we discriminate against this expression of joy? It's a local sound and I don't know how it is possible to stop it. I always said that when we

decided to go to South Africa it was because we wanted to be in Africa – not western Europe.

"The vuvuzelas are noisy but the crowds here have energy, rhythm, music, dance, drums. This is Africa. We have to adapt a little. Every country's fans have their music. Come to Switzerland and you hear the fans ring cowbells. Maybe the vuvuzelas are louder but the principle is the same."

Visiting fans will not only hear the sound of African football but also see its face as portrayed on the official bid poster – a striking representation of the African continent forming a man's profile as he heads a football. The design was chosen after a nationwide public vote in South Africa.

FIFA president Blatter unveiled the poster in Durban on the eve of the

preliminary-round draw in late 2007. He said: "This picture invites the world to join in the celebration of the greatest football event on earth. It represents the African dream come true."

Imaginative architects have brought that dream to life in some remarkable designs for the new stadia – such as the 'giraffes' which support the roof in Nelspruit and the dramatic arch which will soar over the fans in Durban.

LEFT: Dressing up for the game, local songs and spontaneous dancing will be on display at the 2010 FIFA World Cup™ courtesy of the local fans.

BELOW: The sound of the fans' vuvuzela horns had been criticised for their "distracting noise" but they are at the heart of the African game and will bring a unique local sound to the FIFA World Cup™.

THE ROAD TO SOUTH AFRICA

No fewer than 200 nations set out on the road to the 2010 finals – including South Africa. They were the first hosts since Italy in 1934 to contest the preliminaries but only because their continental section was also the qualifying event for the 2010 African Cup of Nations. South Africa failed to reach the final group stage. This did not, of course, affect their FIFA World Cup™ status.

Slovenia's Zlatko Dedic celebrates his team's victory over Russia in the qualification play-offs and their place at the 2010 FIFA World Cup™.

How They Qualified

The 2010 FIFA World Cup™ will end on July 11 in front of more than 80,000 in Soccer City and a worldwide television audience to be counted in billions. Yet it began in front of just 60 fans on the Pacific island of Samoa on August 25, 2007, when the hosts lost 4-0 to Vanuatu.

In between kick-off that day and the final whistle of the concluding qualifying play-off in which Uruguay drew 1-1 with Costa Rica on November 18, 2009, FIFA's worldwide membership played 853 games.

These featured 2,344 goals which both thrilled and depressed, by turn, a record "live" turn-out of more than 20m fans, an average of almost 23,000 per match.

In fact, qualifying matches had begun five months before FIFA president Sepp Blatter oversaw the formal draw for the preliminaries in Durban in December 2007.

Africa has never had so many representatives at the finals. The six comprise South Africa and five qualifiers: Algeria, Cameroon, Ghana, Ivory Coast and Nigeria. Notable absentees, however, are record African champions Egypt. They lost 1-0 to Algeria in a dramatic, high-tension play-off in Sudan after both teams had finished with identical records in their final group.

Even more disappointing were Morocco and 2006 FIFA World Cup™ finalists Togo who struggled badly in Group A where Cameroon came through late for an African record sixth appearance in the finals.

In Asia, the highlight of the draw was the presence, for the first time, of Australia, who had "just arrived" from Oceania. They turned on the style in the climactic group stage, winning six and drawing two of their eight games to head Japan into the finals.

North and South Korea emerged from the other group after the usual political wrangles over venues and refereeing.

They both compete at the same finals for the first time.

Bahrain surprisingly beat Saudi Arabia in a play-off to earn the right to another play-off. Here, however, New Zealand called on experience partly gathered in last year's Confederations Cup to return to South Africa.

This is only the All Whites' second finals and the first time both they and Australia have been present simultaneously after earlier years of qualifying rivalry.

United States, Mexico and Honduras came through from Central, Caribbean and North America region though the Mexicans risked an early exit after struggling under ex-England boss Sven-Goran Eriksson. His replacement by 2002 boss Javier Aguirre kick-started a successful revival.

Last-minute drama across the group saw luckless Costa Rica edged out into fourth spot and condemned to their vain play-off against Uruguay.

The Uruguayans, 1930 and 1950 FIFA World Cup™-winners, missed out on one of the four guaranteed South American slots after losing their last game 1-0 in front of their own furious fans to Lionel Messi and Argentina. Earlier the Argentinians had feared they might need the play-off option themselves after Diego Maradona's men suffered a humiliating six-goal thrashing by Bolivia at altitude in La Paz.

A more relaxed Argentinian was

BELOW: Russia's Vasily Berezutskiy and Germany's Miroslav Klose challenge for the ball during their FIFA World Cup™ Group 4 qualifying match in Dortmund, Germany, in October 2008.

Marcelo Bielsa who guided Chile through to the finals for the first time in 12 years behind group pace-setters Brazil and Paraguay.

Group draws for major tournaments are notorious for bringing recent rivals together once more and, in Europe, this FIFA World Cup™ proved no exception. In Group Six, Croatia again faced England, whom Slaven Bilic's men had just beaten at Wembley in Euro 2008 qualification. An extra twist in the group was its further inclusion of dangerous outsiders Ukraine.

However, this England, now under Italian Fabio Capello, proved a very different prospect to the team who had stumbled up a Euro qualifying cul-de-sac under Steve McClaren. They won nine of their 10 games, losing only in Ukraine when it no longer mattered, and were the European section's 34-goal top scorers.

Spain won all 10 of their games in Group Five while the Netherlands won all eight matches in five-nation Group Nine. FIFA World Cup™ holders Italy, back under the management of 2006 FIFA World Cup™ winning coach Marcello Lippi, came through comparatively comfortably (Group Eight). So, in the end, did Denmark (Group One), Switzerland (Group Two) and Serbia (Group Seven).

Slovakia surprised their crisis-hit Czech neighbours in Group Three to reach the finals for the first time in their modern independent history, while Germany rose to the occasion on demand in Group Four to win decisively both home and then away against Russia.

This left the stage clear for four play-offs between the best eight second-placed teams and even greater drama.

Portugal, having only just sneaked up into runners-up spot in Group One at the last moment and missing injured Cristiano Ronaldo, eased through with home and away wins over Bosnia-Herzegovina. Simultaneously Greece, surprisingly, outwitted 2006

quarter-finalists Ukraine by winning the second leg away after being held to a goalless draw at home. Dimitrios Salpingidis struck the all-important goal in Donetsk.

An even greater surprise was Slovenia's success in shocking ambitious, over-confident Russia and their Dutch master coach Guus Hiddink. The Russians had only themselves to blame after falling asleep in defence in the closing minutes of the first leg in Moscow. That offered newly arrived Slovene substitute Necj Pecnik the chance to grab what proved the crucially decisive away goal.

Greatest drama of all the 853 qualifying games was reserved for the showdown between France and the Republic of Ireland in the Stade de France in Saint-Denis.

The Irish were angry from the outset that FIFA, at a late stage, had invoked a seeding system for the play-off draw. Their anger intensified when they were drawn against the most powerful opposition possible in Les Bleus.

France won the first leg 1-0, with a late Nicolas Anelka strike, at Croke Park in Dublin. The Irish, fired by their sense of injustice, responded by playing

the game of their lives in the Stade de France. A goal from skipper Robbie Keane secured extra time with a penalty shoot-out looming.

Then, with 17 minutes remaining, Thierry Henry controlled a through ball not once, but twice, with his left hand before crossing – William Gallas duly headed France level on the night and, ultimately, into the finals thanks to a 2-1 aggregate scoreline.

Swedish referee Martin Hansson and his assistant were possibly the only two people on planet football unsighted when France skipper Henry capitalised in what came to be headlined, notoriously, as La Main de Dieu, a nod to Diego Maradona's equally famous Hand of God.

Henry owned up only after the match. By then it was too late. Ireland were out and France were heading for the finals . . . where every step they take will be followed as closely in Dublin as in Paris.

BELOW: New Zealand's goalscorer Rory Fallon celebrates his team's 1-0 win over Bahrain in the qualifying play-off second leg which meant that the Oceania team reach the FIFA World Cup™ for the first time since 1982.

AFRICA

1st round

Madagascar bt **Comoros** 6-2, 4-0 (10-2 agg)
Sierra Leone bt **Guinea-Bissau** 1-0, 0-0 (1-0 agg)
Djibouti bt **Somalia** 1-0 (single game)

2nd round

Group 1

	P	W	D	L	F	A	Pts
Cameroon	6	5	1	0	14	6	16
Cape Verde Islands	6	3	0	3	7	8	9
Tanzania	6	2	2	2	9	6	8
Mauritius	6	0	1	5	3	17	1

Group 2

	P	W	D	L	F	A	Pts
Guinea	6	3	2	1	9	5	11
Kenya	6	3	1	2	8	5	10
Zimbabwe	6	1	3	2	4	6	6
Namibia	6	2	0	4	7	12	6

Group 3

	P	W	D	L	F	A	Pts
Benin	6	4	0	2	12	8	12
Angola	6	3	1	2	11	8	10
Uganda	6	3	1	2	8	9	10
Niger	6	1	0	5	5	11	3

Group 4

	P	W	D	L	F	A	Pts
Nigeria	6	6	0	0	11	1	18
South Africa	6	2	1	3	5	5	7
Sierra Leone	6	2	1	3	4	8	7
Equatorial Guinea	6	1	0	5	4	10	3

Group 5

	P	W	D	L	F	A	Pts
Ghana	6	4	0	2	11	5	12
Gabon	6	4	0	2	8	3	12
Libya	6	4	0	2	7	4	12
Lesotho	6	0	0	6	2	16	0

Group 6

	P	W	D	L	F	A	Pts
Algeria	6	3	1	2	7	4	10
Gambia	6	2	3	1	6	3	9
Senegal	6	2	3	1	9	7	9
Liberia	6	0	3	3	4	12	3

Group 7

	P	W	D	L	F	A	Pts
Côte d'Ivoire	6	3	3	0	10	2	12
Mozambique	6	2	2	2	7	5	8
Madagascar	6	1	3	2	2	7	6
Botswana	6	1	2	3	3	8	5

Group 8

	P	W	D	L	F	A	Pts
Morocco	4	3	0	1	11	5	9
Rwanda	4	3	0	1	7	3	9
Mauritania	6	0	0	6	3	19	0

Group 9

	P	W	D	L	F	A	Pts
Burkina Faso	6	5	1	0	14	5	16
Tunisia	6	4	1	1	11	3	13
Burundi	6	2	0	4	5	9	6
Seychelles	6	0	0	6	4	17	0

Group 10

	P	W	D	L	F	A	Pts
Mali	6	4	0	2	13	8	12
Sudan	6	3	0	3	9	9	9
Congo	6	3	0	3	7	8	9
Chad	6	2	0	4	7	11	6

Group 11

	P	W	D	L	F	A	Pts
Zambia	4	2	1	1	2	1	7
Togo	4	2	0	2	8	3	6
Swaziland	4	1	1	2	2	8	4

Group 12

	P	W	D	L	F	A	Pts
Egypt	6	5	0	1	13	2	15
Malawi	6	4	0	2	14	5	12
Congo DR	6	3	0	3	14	6	9
Djibouti	6	0	0	6	2	30	0

3rd round

Group A

	P	W	D	L	F	A	Pts
Cameroon	6	4	1	1	9	2	13
Gabon	6	3	0	3	9	7	9
Togo	6	2	2	2	3	7	8
Morocco	6	0	3	3	3	8	3

Group B

	P	W	D	L	F	A	Pts
Nigeria	6	3	3	0	9	4	12
Tunisia	6	3	2	1	7	4	11
Mozambique	6	2	1	3	3	5	7
Kenya	6	1	0	5	5	11	3

Group C

	P	W	D	L	F	A	Pts
Algeria	7	5	1	1	10	4	16
Egypt	7	4	1	2	9	5	13
Zambia	6	1	2	3	5	5	5
Rwanda	6	0	2	4	1	8	2

Group D

	P	W	D	L	F	A	Pts
Ghana	6	4	1	1	9	3	13
Benin	6	3	1	2	6	6	10
Mali	6	2	3	1	8	7	9
Sudan	6	0	1	5	2	9	1

Group E

	P	W	D	L	F	A	Pts
Côte d'Ivoire	6	5	1	0	19	4	16
Burkina Faso	6	4	0	2	10	11	12
Malawi	6	1	1	4	4	11	4
Guinea	6	1	0	5	7	14	3

Qualified: South Africa (hosts), Cameroon, Tunisia, Algeria, Ghana, Côte d'Ivoire

Cameroon's Rigobert Song trips while challenging Togo's Alexys Romao during an African Cup of Nations and FIFA World Cup™ Africa qualifier match 2009. Togo defeated Cameroon 1-0.

ASIA

1st round

Tajikistan bt Bangladesh 1-1, 5-0 (6-1 agg)
Thailand bt Macau 6-1, 7-1 (13-2 agg)
United Arab Emirates bt Vietnam 1-0, 5-0 (6-0 agg)
Syria bt Afghanistan 3-0, 2-1 (5-1 agg)
Singapore bt Palestine 4-0, 3-0 (7-0 agg)
Lebanon bt India 4-1, 2-2 (6-3 agg)
Oman bt Nepal 3-0, 2-0 (4-0 agg)
Yemen bt Maldives 3-0, 0-2 (3-2 agg)
Turkmenistan bt Cambodia 1-0, 4-1 (5-1 agg)
Jordan bt Kyrgyzstan 0-2, 2-0 (2-2 agg, 6-5 pens)
North Korea bt Mongolia 4-1, 5-1 (9-2 agg)
Hong Kong bt Timor-Leste 3-2, 8-1 (11-3 agg)
Qatar bt Sri Lanka 1-0, 5-0 (6-0 agg)
Bahrain bt Malaysia 4-1, 0-0 (4-1 agg)
China PR bt Myanmar 7-0, 4-0 (11-0 agg)
Iraq bt Pakistan 7-0, 0-0 (7-0 agg)

2nd round

Thailand bt Yemen 1-1, 1-0 (2-1 agg)
Singapore bt Tajikistan 2-0, 1-1 (3-1 agg)
Syria bt Indonesia 4-1, 7-0 (11-1 agg)
Turkmenistan bt Hong Kong 3-0, 0-0 (3-0 agg)

3rd round

Group 1

	P	W	D	L	F	A	Pts
Australia	6	3	1	2	7	3	10
Qatar	6	3	1	2	5	6	10
Iraq	6	2	1	3	4	6	7
China PR	6	1	3	2	3	4	6

Group 2

	P	W	D	L	F	A	Pts
Japan	6	4	1	1	12	3	13
Bahrain	6	3	2	1	7	5	11
Oman	6	2	2	2	5	7	8
Thailand	6	0	1	5	5	14	1

Group 3

	P	W	D	L	F	A	Pts
South Korea	6	3	3	0	10	3	12
North Korea	6	3	3	0	4	0	12
Jordan	6	2	1	3	6	6	7
Turkmenistan	6	0	1	5	1	12	1

Group 4

	P	W	D	L	F	A	Pts
Saudi Arabia	6	5	0	1	14	5	15
Uzbekistan	6	5	0	1	15	7	15
Singapore	6	2	0	4	7	16	6
Lebanon	6	0	0	6	3	14	0

Group 5

	P	W	D	L	F	A	Pts
Iran	6	3	3	0	7	2	12
UAE	6	2	2	2	7	7	8
Syria	6	2	2	2	7	8	8
Kuwait	6	1	1	4	8	12	4

4th round

Group 1

	P	W	D	L	F	A	Pts
Australia	8	6	2	0	12	1	20
Japan	8	4	3	1	11	6	15
Bahrain	8	3	1	4	6	8	10
Qatar	8	1	3	4	5	14	6
Uzbekistan	8	1	1	6	5	10	4

Group 2

	P	W	D	L	F	A	Pts
South Korea	8	4	4	0	12	4	16
North Korea	8	3	3	2	7	5	12
Saudi Arabia	8	3	3	2	8	8	12
Iran	8	2	5	1	8	7	11
UAE	8	0	1	7	6	17	1

Qualified: Australia, Japan, South Korea, North Korea

Play-offs: Bahrain, Saudi Arabia

CONCACAF

(Confederation of North, Central American and Caribbean Association Football)

1st round

Barbados bt Dominica 1-1, 1-0 (2-1 agg)
St Lucia bt Turks & Caicos 1-2, 2-0 (3-2 agg)
Bermuda bt Cayman Islands 1-1, 3-1 (4-2 agg)
Antigua & Barbuda bt Aruba 3-0, 1-0 (4-0 agg)
Belize bt St Kitts & Nevis 3-1, 1-1 (4-2 agg)
Bahamas bt British Virgin Islands 1-1, 2-2 (3-3 agg, away goals)
Puerto Rico bt Dominican Rep. 1-0 (single game)
Grenada bt US Virgin Islands 10-0 (single game)
Surinam bt Montserrat 7-1 (single game)
El Salvador bt Anguilla 12-0, 4-0 (16-0 agg)
Netherlands Antilles bt Nicaragua 1-0, 2-0 (3-0 agg)

2nd round

United States bt Barbados 8-0, 1-0 (9-0 agg)
Guatemala bt St Lucia 6-0, 3-1 (9-1 agg)
Trinidad & Tobago bt Bermuda 1-2, 2-0 (3-2 agg)
Cuba bt Antigua & Barbuda 4-3, 4-0 (8-3 agg)
Mexico bt Belize 2-0, 7-0 (9-0 agg)
Jamaica bt Bahamas 7-0, 6-0 (13-0 agg)
Honduras bt Puerto Rico 4-0, 2-2 (6-2 agg)
Canada bt St Vincent & Grenadines 3-0, 4-1 (7-1 agg)
Costa Rica bt Grenada 2-2, 3-0 (5-2 agg)
Surinam bt Guyana 1-0, 2-1 (3-1 agg)
El Salvador bt Panama 0-1, 3-1 (3-2 agg)
Haiti bt Netherlands Antilles 0-0, 1-0 (1-0 agg)

3rd round

Group 1

	P	W	D	L	F	A	Pts
United States	6	5	0	1	14	3	15
Trinidad & Tobago	6	3	2	1	9	6	11
Guatemala	6	1	2	3	6	7	5
Cuba	6	1	0	5	5	18	3

Group 2

	P	W	D	L	F	A	Pts
Honduras	6	4	0	2	9	5	12
Mexico	6	3	1	2	9	6	10
Jamaica	6	3	1	2	6	6	10
Canada	6	0	2	4	6	13	2

Group 3

	P	W	D	L	F	A	Pts
Costa Rica	6	6	0	0	20	3	18
El Salvador	6	3	1	2	11	4	10
Haiti	6	0	3	3	4	13	3
Surinam	6	0	2	4	4	19	2

4th round

	P	W	D	L	F	A	Pts
United States	10	6	2	2	19	13	20
Mexico	10	6	1	3	18	12	19
Honduras	10	5	1	4	17	11	16
Costa Rica	10	5	1	4	15	15	16
El Salvador	10	2	2	6	9	15	8
Trinidad & Tobago	10	1	3	6	10	22	6

Qualified: United States, Mexico, Honduras

Play-offs: Costa Rica

South Korea's Ji-Sung Park battles for the ball against Iran's Hossein Kaebi in their FIFA World Cup™ qualifying match.

EUROPE

Group 1

	P	W	D	L	F	A	Pts
Denmark	10	6	3	1	16	5	21
Portugal	10	5	4	1	17	5	19
Sweden	10	5	3	2	13	5	18
Hungary	10	5	1	4	10	8	16
Albania	10	1	4	5	6	13	7
Malta	10	0	1	9	0	26	1

Group 2

	P	W	D	L	F	A	Pts
Switzerland	10	6	3	1	18	8	21
Greece	10	6	2	2	20	10	20
Latvia	10	5	2	3	18	15	17
Israel	10	4	4	2	20	10	16
Luxembourg	10	1	2	7	4	25	5
Moldova	10	0	3	7	6	18	3

Group 3

	P	W	D	L	F	A	Pts
Slovakia	10	7	1	2	22	10	22
Slovenia	10	6	2	2	18	4	20
Czech Republic	10	4	4	2	17	6	16
Northern Ireland	10	4	3	3	13	9	15
Poland	10	3	2	5	19	14	11
San Marino	10	0	0	10	1	47	0

Group 4

	P	W	D	L	F	A	Pts
Germany	10	8	2	0	26	5	26
Russia	10	7	1	2	19	6	22
Finland	10	5	3	2	14	14	18
Wales	10	4	0	6	9	12	12
Azerbaijan	10	1	2	7	4	14	5
Liechtenstein	10	0	2	8	2	23	2

Group 5

	P	W	D	L	F	A	Pts
Spain	10	10	0	0	28	5	30
Bosnia-Herzegovina	10	6	1	3	25	13	19
Turkey	10	4	3	3	13	10	15
Belgium	10	3	1	6	13	20	10
Estonia	10	2	2	6	9	24	8
Armenia	10	1	1	8	6	22	4

Group 6

	P	W	D	L	F	A	Pts
England	10	9	0	1	34	6	27
Ukraine	10	6	3	1	21	6	21
Croatia	10	6	2	2	19	13	20
Belarus	10	4	1	5	19	14	13
Kazakhstan	10	2	0	8	11	29	6
Andorra	10	0	0	10	3	39	0

Group 7

	P	W	D	L	F	A	Pts
Serbia	10	7	1	2	22	8	22
France	10	6	3	1	18	9	21
Austria	10	4	2	4	14	15	14
Lithuania	10	4	0	6	10	11	12
Romania	10	3	3	4	12	18	12
Faroe Islands	10	1	1	8	5	20	4

Group 8

	P	W	D	L	F	A	Pts
Italy	10	7	3	0	18	7	24
Republic of Ireland	10	4	6	0	12	8	18
Bulgaria	10	3	5	2	17	13	14
Cyprus	10	2	3	5	14	16	9
Montenegro	10	1	6	3	9	14	9
Georgia	10	0	3	7	7	19	3

Group 9

	P	W	D	L	F	A	Pts
Netherlands	8	8	0	0	17	2	24
Norway	8	2	4	2	9	7	10
Scotland	8	3	1	4	6	11	10
FYR Macedonia	8	2	1	5	5	11	7
Iceland	8	1	2	5	7	13	5

Qualified: Denmark, Switzerland, Slovakia, Germany, Spain, England, Serbia, Italy, Netherlands

Play-offs: Portugal, Greece, Slovenia, Russia, Bosnia-Herzegovina, Ukraine, France, Republic of Ireland

OCEANIA

1st round

Group 1

	P	W	D	L	F	A	Pts
Fiji	3	2	1	0	9	1	7
New Caledonia	3	2	1	0	5	1	7
Tahiti	3	1	0	2	1	5	3
Tuvalu	0	0	0	0	0	0	0
Cook Islands	3	0	0	3	0	8	0

Tuvalu are Associate Members, therefore results not included as part of 2010 FIFA World Cup South Africa™ qualifying.

Group 2

	P	W	D	L	F	A	Pts
Solomon Islands	4	4	0	0	21	1	12
Vanuatu	4	3	0	1	23	3	9
Samoa	4	2	0	2	9	8	6
Tonga	4	1	0	3	6	10	3
American Samoa	4	0	0	4	1	38	0

Final round

Group 3

	P	W	D	L	F	A	Pts
New Zealand	6	5	0	1	14	5	15
New Caledonia	6	2	2	2	12	10	8
Fiji	6	2	1	3	8	11	7
Vanuatu	6	1	1	4	5	13	4

Play-offs: New Zealand

SOUTH AMERICA

Group 1

	P	W	D	L	F	A	Pts
Brazil	18	9	7	2	33	11	34
Chile	18	10	3	5	32	22	33
Paraguay	18	10	3	5	24	16	33
Argentina	18	8	4	6	23	20	28
Uruguay	18	6	6	6	28	20	24
Ecuador	18	6	5	7	22	26	23
Colombia	18	6	5	7	14	18	23
Venezuela	18	6	4	8	23	29	22
Bolivia	18	4	3	11	22	36	15
Peru	18	3	4	11	11	34	13

Qualified: Brazil, Chile, Paraguay, Argentina

Play-offs: Uruguay

PLAY-OFFS

Asia
Bahrain bt **Saudi Arabia** 0-0, 2-2 (2-2 agg, away goals)

Asia v Oceania
New Zealand bt **Bahrain** 0-0, 1-0 (1-0 agg)

S America v CONCACAF
Uruguay bt **Costa Rica** 1-0, 1-1 (2-1 agg)

Europe
Greece bt **Ukraine** 0-0, 1-0 (1-0 agg)
Portugal bt **Bosnia-Herzegovina** 1-0, 1-0 (2-0 agg)
France bt **Republic of Ireland** 1-0, 1-1 (2-1 agg)
Slovenia bt **Russia** 1-2, 1-0 (2-2 agg, away goals)

LEFT: Portugal's Deco dribbles past Bosnia-Herzegovina's Samir Muratovic in their qualifying match.

ABOVE: New Zealand's Chris Killen and Bahrain's Mohamed Ahmed Salmeen in their qualifying play-off second leg match in Wellington.

Final Draw for the 2010 FIFA World Cup South Africa™

Soccer City on July 11: the place and date uppermost in the minds of the 32 FIFA World Cup™ finalists. who start out in eight groups of four. Winning is important for cash reasons, too. The winners will collect $30m and the losing finalists $24m.

History was both made by the draw for the 2010 finals and then retold as the renewals of great rivalries surfaced: England against the United States, Portugal against both Brazil and North Korea . . . and a repeat of the 1966 first round when the hosts faced Mexico, Uruguay and France.

The FIFA World Cup™ draw is always carefully stage-managed and Cape Town's version was no different.

South Africa benefited from the host's right to be among the top eight seeds along with record five-times champions Brazil, holders and four-times winners Italy, three-times winners Germany, double winners Argentina, 1966 champions England, double runners-up the Netherlands and European title-holders Spain.

FIFA general secretary Jerome Valcke and Oscar-winning South African actress Charlize Theron oversaw the draw ceremony. This allocated the 32 finalists into their eight groups to be played in 10 venues in nine cities.

However, the draw was not too kind to South Africa who will open up against Mexico, always awkward opponents at a FIFA World Cup™; next opponents Uruguay always defend their status as twice winners with a fearsome physicality; and concluding rivals France boast far more quality than their contentious qualification suggests.

After the draw, European champions Spain were rated by the London bookmakers as favourites to win the FIFA World Cup™.

Manager Vicente Del Bosque was not unnerved by the draw and said: "We can't complain. We can't hide the fact we are one of the favourites to win. We will have had a long season but we will have plenty of time to rest and to prepare."

Argentina manager Diego Maradona felt good and bad omens as Argentina were drawn in Group B against South Korea, Nigeria and Greece. He played against South Korea in 1986 when Argentina went on to win the FIFA World Cup™ but, in 1994, failed a dope test against Nigeria and was kicked out of the finals.

England coach Fabio Capello was cautiously confident after the draw matched England with the United States, Algeria and Slovenia in Group C. He will not want history to repeat itself. Notoriously, England, joint favourites to triumph in their first FIFA World Cup™, slumped 1-0 to a hastily-assembled team of American part-timers in 1950. This time the Americans benefit from their experience of local conditions at the 2009 Confederations Cup.

Other under-pressure managers at the draw included Germany boss Joachim Low and the Netherlands' Bert Van Marwijk. They sought to defuse over-confidence among fans back home while Italy's Marcello Lippi and Brazil's Dunga feared complacency among their own players.

As Dunga said: "The toughest match is going to be the first one . . . then the second one . . . and then the third one. That is the way we think. It's the only way we know."

RIGHT: South Africa President Jacob Zuma and FIFA President Joseph Blatter during the 2010 FIFA World Cup™ draw ceremony.

BELOW: English footballer David Beckham, South African actress Charlize Theron and FIFA Secretary General Jerome Valcke take part in the 2010 FIFA World Cup™ draw.

2010 FIFA World Cup™ Progress Chart

GROUP A

Date	Time	Venue	Home	Score	Away
11-JUN-10	15:00 BST	JOHANNESBURG (JSC)	SOUTH AFRICA	1 - 1	MEXICO
11-JUN-10	19:30 BST	CAPE TOWN	URUGUAY	0 - 0	FRANCE
16-JUN-10	19:30 BST	PRETORIA	SOUTH AFRICA	0 - 3	URUGUAY
17-JUN-10	19:30 BST	POLOKWANE	FRANCE	0 - 2	MEXICO
22-JUN-10	15:00 BST	RUSTENBURG	MEXICO	0 - 1	URUGUAY
22-JUN-10	15:00 BST	BLOEMFONTEIN	FRANCE	1 - 2	SOUTH AFRICA

GROUP B

Date	Time	Venue	Home	Score	Away
12-JUN-10	12:30 BST	PORT ELIZABETH	SOUTH KOREA	2 - 0	GREECE
12-JUN-10	15:00 BST	JOHANNESBURG (JEP)	ARGENTINA	1 - 0	NIGERIA
17-JUN-10	12:30 BST	JOHANNESBURG (JSC)	ARGENTINA	4 - 1	SOUTH KOREA
17-JUN-10	15:00 BST	BLOEMFONTEIN	GREECE	2 - 1	NIGERIA
22-JUN-10	19:30 BST	DURBAN	NIGERIA		SOUTH KOREA
22-JUN-10	19:30 BST	POLOKWANE	GREECE	0 - 2	ARGENTINA

GROUP C

Date	Time	Venue	Home	Score	Away
12-JUN-10	19:30 BST	RUSTENBURG	ENGLAND	1 - 1	USA
13-JUN-10	12:30 BST	POLOKWANE	ALGERIA	0 - 1	SLOVENIA
18-JUN-10	15:00 BST	JOHANNESBURG (JEP)	SLOVENIA	2 - 2	USA
18-JUN-10	19:30 BST	CAPE TOWN	ENGLAND	0 - 0	ALGERIA
23-JUN-10	15:00 BST	PORT ELIZABETH	SLOVENIA	0 - 1	ENGLAND
23-JUN-10	15:00 BST	PRETORIA	USA	1 - 0	ALGERIA

GROUP D

Date	Time	Venue	Home	Score	Away
13-JUN-10	15:00 BST	PRETORIA	SERBIA	0 - 1	GHANA
13-JUN-10	19:30 BST	DURBAN	GERMANY	4 - 0	AUSTRALIA
18-JUN-10	12:30 BST	PORT ELIZABETH	GERMANY	0 - 2	SERBIA
19-JUN-10	15:00 BST	RUSTENBURG	GHANA	1 - 1	AUSTRALIA
23-JUN-10	19:30 BST	JOHANNESBURG (JSC)	GHANA	0 - 1	GERMANY
23-JUN-10	19:30 BST	NELSPRUIT	AUSTRALIA	2 - 1	SERBIA

ROUND OF 16

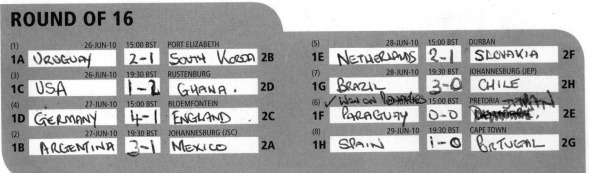

	Date	Time	Venue	Home	Score	Away	
(1) 1A	26-JUN-10	15:00 BST	PORT ELIZABETH	URUGUAY	2 - 1	SOUTH KOREA	2B
(3) 1C	26-JUN-10	19:30 BST	RUSTENBURG	USA	1 - 2	GHANA.	2D
(4) 1D	27-JUN-10	15:00 BST	BLOEMFONTEIN	GERMANY	4 - 1	ENGLAND .	2C
(2) 1B	27-JUN-10	19:30 BST	JOHANNESBURG (JSC)	ARGENTINA	3 - 1	MEXICO	2A
(5) 1E	28-JUN-10	15:00 BST	DURBAN	NETHERLANDS	2 - 1	SLOVAKIA	2F
(7) 1G	28-JUN-10	19:30 BST	JOHANNESBURG (JEP)	BRAZIL	3 - 0	CHILE	2H
(6) ✓ WON ON PENALTIES 1F		15:00 BST	PRETORIA	PARAGUAY	0 - 0	JAPAN	2E
(8) 1H	29-JUN-10	19:30 BST	CAPE TOWN	SPAIN	1 - 0	PORTUGAL	2G

GROUP E

Date	Time	Venue			
14-JUN-10	12:30 BST	JOHANNESBURG (JSC)	NETHERLANDS	2-0	DENMARK
14-JUN-10	15:00 BST	BLOEMFONTEIN	JAPAN	1-0	CAMEROON
19-JUN-10	12:30 BST	DURBAN	NETHERLANDS	1-0	JAPAN
19-JUN-10	19:30 BST	PRETORIA	CAMEROON	1-2	DENMARK
24-JUN-10	19:30 BST	RUSTENBURG	DENMARK	1-3	JAPAN
24-JUN-10	19:30 BST	CAPE TOWN	CAMEROON	1-2	NETHERLANDS

GROUP F

Date	Time	Venue			
14-JUN-10	19:30 BST	CAPE TOWN	ITALY	1-1	PARAGUAY
15-JUN-10	12:30 BST	RUSTENBURG	NEW ZEALAND	1-1	SLOVAKIA
20-JUN-10	12:30 BST	BLOEMFONTEIN	SLOVAKIA	0-2	PARAGUAY
20-JUN-10	15:00 BST	NELSPRUIT	ITALY	1-1	NEW ZEALAND
24-JUN-10	15:00 BST	JOHANNESBURG (JEP)	SLOVAKIA	3-2	ITALY
24-JUN-10	15:00 BST	POLOKWANE	PARAGUAY	0-0	NEW ZEALAND

GROUP G

Date	Time	Venue			
15-JUN-10	15:00 BST	PORT ELIZABETH	CÔTE D'IVOIRE	0-0	PORTUGAL
15-JUN-10	19:30 BST	JOHANNESBURG (JEP)	BRAZIL	2-1	NORTH KOREA
20-JUN-10	19:30 BST	JOHANNESBURG (JSC)	BRAZIL	3-1	CÔTE D'IVOIRE
21-JUN-10	12:30 BST	CAPE TOWN	PORTUGAL	7-0	NORTH KOREA
25-JUN-10	15:00 BST	DURBAN	PORTUGAL		BRAZIL
25-JUN-10	15:00 BST	NELSPRUIT	NORTH KOREA		CÔTE D'IVOIRE

GROUP H

Date	Time	Venue			
16-JUN-10	12:30 BST	NELSPRUIT	HONDURAS	0-1	CHILE
16-JUN-10	15:00 BST	DURBAN	SPAIN	0-1	SWITZERLAND
21-JUN-10	15:00 BST	PORT ELIZABETH	CHILE	1-0	SWITZERLAND
21-JUN-10	19:30 BST	JOHANNESBURG (JEP)	SPAIN	2-0	HONDURAS
25-JUN-10	19:30 BST	PRETORIA	CHILE		SPAIN
25-JUN-10	19:30 BST	BLOEMFONTEIN	SWITZERLAND	0-0	HONDURAS

QUARTER-FINALS

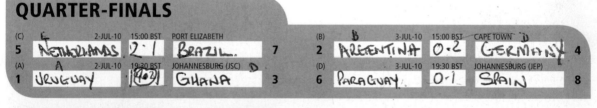

	Date	Time	Venue					
(C) 5	2-JUL-10	15:00 BST	PORT ELIZABETH	NETHERLANDS	2-1	BRAZIL	7	
(B) 2	3-JUL-10	15:00 BST	CAPE TOWN	ARGENTINA	0-2	GERMANY	4	
(A) 1	2-JUL-10	19:30 BST	JOHANNESBURG (JSC)	URUGUAY	1 (4-2)	GHANA	3	
(D) 6	3-JUL-10	19:30 BST	JOHANNESBURG (JEP)	PARAGUAY	0-1	SPAIN	8	

SEMI-FINALS

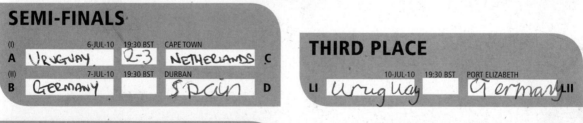

	Date	Time	Venue				
(I) A	6-JUL-10	19:30 BST	CAPE TOWN	URUGUAY	2-3	NETHERLANDS	C
(II) B	7-JUL-10	19:30 BST	DURBAN	GERMANY		SPAIN	D

THIRD PLACE

	Date	Time	Venue			
LI	10-JUL-10	19:30 BST	PORT ELIZABETH	URUGUAY		GERMANY LII

FINAL

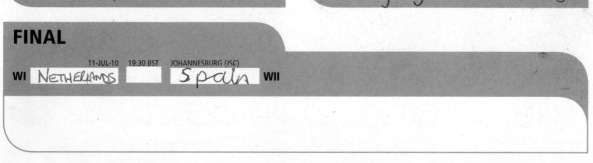

	Date	Time	Venue			
WI	11-JUL-10	19:30 BST	JOHANNESBURG (JSC)	NETHERLANDS		SPAIN WII

QUALIFYING TEAMS

Football history is represented by the 32 finalists in South Africa – who are, themselves, the first African hosts. All previous seven FIFA World Cup™ winners will be present – Brazil (five), Argentina (two) and Uruguay (two) from South America plus Italy (four), Germany (three), England (one) and France (one) from Europe. In addition, 15 of the 16 nations which have staged the finals are also present, Sweden being the only missing host nation.

Where each of the qualifying teams are hoping to be... Italy and France line up before the start of the 2006 FIFA World Cup™ final.

SOUTH AFRICA

BAFANA BAFANA

South Africa fans are relieved their team start automatically as hosts – because many fear they might have failed to qualify – and hope the return of Brazil's FIFA World Cup-winning coach Carlos Alberto Parreira will revive their 2010 hopes after months of despondency.

South Africa's fortunes have plummeted since they finished fourth in the Confederations Cup, on home soil in June 2009. They lost eight of their next nine games, finishing with 1-0 friendly defeats in Norway and Iceland, and the South African FA sacked coach Joel Santana.

Parreira's re-appointment was a controversial choice. He had taken charge in 2007, then returned to Brazil when his wife was diagnosed with cancer. Some critics doubted Parreira's commitment. Others argued that the job should have gone to a successful local coach. But Jomo Sono, Clive Barker and Gavin Hunt – asked by the SAFA to "advise" Santana while his regime fell apart – were all disregarded.

SAFA president Kirsten Nematandani says: "Time was against us, so we went with the coach who started the current process. These players are his players so we felt it was best to bring back the man who started the process."

Parreira says: "This is now about breaking our losing streak and building morale, because confidence is very low."

South Africa declined dramatically after the Confederations Cup. They lost 1-0 to eventual winners Brazil in the semi-finals. In the third place play-off, they led European champions Spain 1-0 – through Katelgo Mphela's goal – before sub Daniel Guiza scored for Spain in the 88th and 89th minutes. Mphela thumped home a stoppage time free kick to level. But Xabi Alonso hit Spain's winner in extra time.

South Africa goalkeeper Itumeleng Khune says: "We were devastated. We had a lot of chances to win, but we let them come back."

Santana had talked optimistically of a "promising future." Then South Africa suffered their worst run since they re-entered international football in 1992.

Skipper and centre back Aaron Mokoena said it had been "difficult for the players to take all these defeats", while former skipper Lucas Radebe became one of Santana's leading critics.

South Africa sides are measured against the squad that made a

COACH

CARLOS ALBERTO PARREIRA

Parreira's biggest coup was leading Brazil to FIFA World Cup™ victory in 1994. He turned down several offers to return as boss before taking them to the 2006 quarter-finals, where they lost 1-0 to France. The restored South Africa coach is heading for a record sixth FIFA World Cup™ finals. He also coached Kuwait (1982), United Arab Emirates (1990) and Saudi Arabia (1998). He took charge of South Africa for the first time in 2007. Parreira did not play professionally and took his first coaching job with Sao Cristavao in 1967. He steered Fluminense to the Brazilian championship in 1984. He also guided Fenerbahce to the Turkish title in 1996.

South Africa are hoping to make a good account of themselves at the 2010 FIFA World Cup™.

STAR MAN

STEVEN PIENAAR
Born: March 17, 1982
Club: Everton (England)

Playing for South Africa at Johannesburg's new Soccer City will fulfil a dream for Pienaar. He says: "Near my mother's home, you can see the new stadium. I used to dream of playing in the old one – so to play there in a FIFA World Cup™ finals would be something special."

Pienaar grew up in the township of Westbury, honed his skills at the local centre of excellence, then joined Ajax Capetown, a feeder club for the famous Dutch club. He won title medals with Ajax in 2002 and 2004 and spent an unhappy spell at Dortmund before reviving his career with Everton.

He has massive energy, combined with an eye for a pass. Everton use him on the left. South Africa may prefer him in a more central role.

SOUTH AFRICA AT THE FIFA WORLD CUP™

1930	did not enter
1934	did not enter
1938	did not enter
1950	did not enter
1954	did not enter
1958	did not enter
1962	did not enter
1966	suspended
1970	suspended
1974	suspended
1978	expelled from FIFA
1982	expelled from FIFA
1986	expelled from FIFA
1990	expelled from FIFA
1994	did not qualify
1998	1st round
2002	1st round
2006	did not qualify

ONES TO WATCH

BERNARD PARKER
Born: March 16, 1986
Club: FC Twente (Netherlands)

Parker is a pacy attacker who can play wide or through the middle. He netted both goals against New Zealand in South Africa's 2-0 Confederations Cup win and was named Man of the Match. Regular football in Europe has added to his sharpness. He was a successful young athlete and swimmer, but passed up both for football.

MATTHEW BOOTH
Born: March 14, 1977
Club: Mamelodi Sundowns (South Africa)

The 6ft 6in (1.98m) centre back is a cult figure with the fans, the only white player to be a regular starter. He laughs: "They sing 'Booth' when I'm on the ball – but some people from overseas have taken it as booing!"

He made his South Africa debut in 1999 but his international appearances were restricted by club commitments during his seven years playing in Russia.

Ex-Blackburn defender Mokoena, heading towards 100 caps, and centre back partner Matthew Booth supply experience. So do Sibaya and Maccabi Haifa attacker Thembinkosi Fanteni.

Attacker Bernard Parker spent a season with Red Star Belgrade and joined FC Twente in the summer of 2009.

But Parreira will look most of all to Everton midfielder Steven Pienaar, a 20-year-old hopeful in the 2002 squad. He has consistently shown skill and industry in the world's most high-profile league. Parreira hopes his influence will lift players around him, such as Fulham signing Kagisho Dikgacoi and the gifted but inconsistent Teko Modise.

The coach will pray for a prolific striker too. Parker and Mphela have both had their moments, but neither has scored consistently. Santana refused to consider a recall for McCarthy, but Parreira is a pragmatist. His decision on McCarthy's future may yet be crucial to South Africa's prospects.

significant impact after the end of the apartheid era. They won the African Nations Cup in 1996, were runners-up two years later and finished third in 2000. They also reached the FIFA World Cup™ finals in 1998 and 2002. Some stars of that period, such as defender Radebe, have retired. Others, such as Sibusiso Zuma, Siyabonga Nomvete and all-time top scorer Benni McCarthy, dropped out of Santana's plans.

Mokoena and Rubin Kazan midfielder Macbeth Sibaya are the only survivors from that old guard.

South Africa did not qualify for the 2006 finals. Now Parreira must succeed quickly where Santana failed, and rebuild the squad against a background of frustrated expectations. The South Africans were eliminated at the group stage of the 2008 African Nations Cup finals and failed to reach the 2010 finals.

MEXICO

EL TRI

Mexico recovered from a disastrous start to reach the 2010 FIFA World Cup™ thanks to an unbeaten six-game run – after Javier Aguirre had returned to replace Sven-Goran Eriksson as coach.

Aguirre revitalised the squad, even though his first game in charge ended with an embarrassing defeat in El Salvador.

As ever, the Azteca stadium in Mexico City proved a fortress for "El Tri." They won all five games there. But their most crucial victory was a 3-0 away win over Costa Rica.

Mexico qualified a point behind group winners United States. Their fans would happily have settled for that when their team had collected just three points after four matches. Ex-England coach Eriksson's side began with a 2-0 defeat in the US. They won 2-0 at home to Costa Rica, then slumped 3-1 in Honduras.

Eriksson was promptly sacked. Mexican FA president Justino Compean said: "We made the decision because we could not risk Mexico's participation in the FIFA World Cup™ finals."

Aguirre's experimental side then went down 2-1 in El Salvador. Four days later, Mexico beat Trinidad and Tobago 2-1 in the Azteca. That gave them the lift they needed.

Veteran forward Cuauhtemoc Blanco, who played at France 98, says: "I always believed that we'd go to the finals. After that win over Trinidad, I was convinced."

Miguel Sabah hit the goal which beat the US 2-1. The 30-year-old came off the bench to convert Efrain Juarez's pass, eight minutes from time. Sabah is a late developer, but may yet have a role to play. He says: "It was the most important goal of my career."

The next game sealed Mexico's progress. Giovani, Guillermo Franco and Andres Guardado scored as they won 3-0 away against qualifying rivals Costa Rica. Giovani's 30-yard spectacular turned the game, and he provided the assists for Franco and Guardado.

Juarez said: "We played a fantastic game. We were solid at the back and sharp in attack. That shows the positive spirit since Aguirre took over."

Home wins over Honduras and El Salvador clinched Mexico's place

COACH

JAVIER AGUIRRE

Aguirre is in his second spell as Mexico coach. He guided them to the last 16 in the 2002 FIFA World Cup™ finals, where they lost 2-0 to the United States. His takeover from Eriksson carries echoes of that tournament. He replaced Enrique Meza in 2001 after a run of poor results. He steered Mexico to the Copa America final that year – losing 1-0 to hosts Colombia – in addition clinching FIFA World Cup™ qualification.

Aguirre, an attacking midfielder, made 59 appearances for his country and scored 14 goals. He was one of the stars of the side that reached the 1986 FIFA World Cup™ finals but was sent off – for a second yellow card – in extra time against West Germany before Mexico lost the penalty shoot-out.

The return of coach Javier Aguirre has instilled a fresh confidence in the Mexico team.

STAR MAN

RAFAEL MARQUEZ
Born: February 13, 1979
Club: Barcelona (Spain)

National skipper Marquez is the only Mexican ever to have gained a European Champions League winner's medal – in Barcelona's win over Arsenal in the 2006 final. He was injured in the 2009 semi-final against Chelsea and needed knee surgery which kept him out of Barca's victory over Manchester United.

Marquez joined Barcelona from Monaco in 2003. He is the only one of ex-boss Frank Rijkaard's signings who still appears regularly for the European champions. He has played for them as a centre back and defensive midfielder; Mexico prefer him to stay in defence. He is a commanding figure, strong, determined and powerful in the air, a captain who leads by example. He has already won more than 80 caps and scored 10 goals.

MEXICO AT THE FIFA WORLD CUP™

1930	1st round
1934	did not qualify
1938	did not enter
1950	1st round
1954	1st round
1958	1st round
1962	1st round
1966	1st round
1970	quarter-finals
1974	did not qualify
1978	1st round
1982	did not qualify
1986	quarter-finals
1990	suspended
1994	2nd round
1998	2nd round
2002	2nd round
2006	2nd round

ONES TO WATCH

GUILLERMO OCHOA
Born: July 13, 1985
Club: America (Mexico)

The agile goalkeeper made his club debut for America, his only club, at 18 and was called into the national squad two years later. He has already earned more than 30 caps. He was one of the stars of Mexico's unbeaten run to qualification, conceding just four goals in five appearances. He is expected to move to Europe after South Africa 2010.

RICARDO OSORIO
Born: March 30, 1980
Club: Stuttgart (Germany)

Osorio was one of the stars of the Mexico side that reached the last 16 at Germany 2006. He joined German club Stuttgart for a £3m fee after the finals and helped them win the Bundesliga title in his first season. A regular in the national side since 2003, he has gained more than 70 caps.

with a game to spare.

Aguirre used experienced players. Skipper Rafael Marquez, defensive colleagues Carlos Salcido and Ricardo Osorio were regular choices. So were midfielders Gerrardo Torrado and Israel Castro. But he introduced players from Mexico's successful youth squads too, such as Giovani, defenders Juarez and AZ Alkmaar's Hector Moreno.

Midfielders Andres Guardado (of Deportivo de La Coruna) and Pablo Barrera followed. So did goalkeeper Guillermo Ochoa plus strikers Carlos Vela, Omar Arellano and Enrique Esqueda, who scored in Mexico's final 2-2 draw in Trinidad.

Guardado says: "Javier came to start a revolution in a group which was a little broken. What he transmits is his attitude. His will to win is so important because it removes our doubts."

Aguirre says: "We had to correct several things, starting with defensive mistakes. There were some difficulties. But when you achieve the goals you were hired to do, you feel satisfied."

This will be Mexico's 14th appearance in the finals. They have not failed to qualify since 1990, when they were disqualified for fielding an over-age player in a FIFA youth tournament. But they have never advanced beyond the quarter-finals – thanks to a 4-1 hammering by Italy on home soil in 1970 and a penalty shoot-out defeat by West Germany when Mexico were hosts again in 1986. The question though is: how competitive will they be in South Africa? Aguirre's defence is vulnerable in the air if crosses fly beyond Marquez and he lacks a dominant midfielder. Mexico are crying out for a prolific striker too. Blanco was their top scorer in qualifying with three goals, two of them penalties. Aguirre must pray that America's Esqueda – or Arsenal's Vela – can come good on the big occasion.

URUGUAY

LA CELESTE

Uruguay boast a proud FIFA World Cup™ tradition. They won the first-ever tournament, in 1930, beating Argentina in Montevideo, and 20 years later, they shocked hosts Brazil to lift the trophy again.

Now they look to attacking stars Luis Suarez and Diego Forlan to restore pride in South Africa after decades of disappointment. As coach Oscar Tabarez says: "The world is very different from when Uruguayan football enjoyed its greatest triumphs."

Uruguay reached South Africa only via a 2-1 aggregate win over Costa Rica in a play-off – the third time in a row they have faced such a showdown. "Here

We Go Again" read the newspaper headlines after they had lost 1-0 to Argentina and wasted the chance of automatic qualification.

Centre-back Diego Lugano forced home the only goal on the artificial turf away in San Jose and Uruguay held on for a 1-1 draw in Montevideo. Midfielder Diego Perez says: "We're used to suffering. It was no different this time around."

Suarez and Forlan offer hope. They shared 12 goals in the qualifiers. The dynamic Suarez opened the season with 15 in 11 games for Ajax and added two important strikes in his country's closing games. Forlan led Uruguay's scorers with seven goals, including the winner away against Ecuador in Quito.

Manchester United fans never saw the best of Forlan, but he has proved

himself at the top level, for his country and in Spain. Suarez's talent excites him. He says: "Luis has what it takes to succeed in La Liga and could easily follow me as a Golden Shoe winner."

Brazil and Argentina continue to dominate South American football since Uruguay lack their populations and resources, while local rivals, such as Chile and Paraguay, have also gained in strength. The FIFA World Cup™ finals have also become more intense. When Uruguay won in 1930, only 13 teams took part. In 1950, only 13 teams again contested the finals after a cursory set of qualifiers.

The Uruguayan stars of the 1950s – Juan Schiaffino, Alcides Ghiggia (who netted the 1950 FIFA World Cup™ Final winner), Jose Santamaria and Roque Maspoli – all developed

COACH

OSCAR TABAREZ

This will be the much-travelled Tabarez's second appearance at the finals. He steered Uruguay to the last 16 of Italia 90 when they lost 2-0 to the host country. He says: "What's changed since then? Well, I'm a bit bigger now!" Tabarez, nicknamed The Teacher or The Professor, also guided Uruguay's leading club Penarol to Copa Libertadores victory in 1987. He left his last club job, at Boca, in 2002 and became a TV analyst. He returned to take charge of the national side in March 2006 after Uruguay failed to qualify for the finals in Germany. He steered them to the Copa America semi-finals the following year where they lost to winners Brazil in a penalty shoot-out.

Winners in 1930 and 1950, Uruguay will see escaping the group stages as a sucess in South Africa.

STAR MAN

LUIS SUAREZ
Born: January 24, 1987
Club: Ajax (Netherlands)

Striker Suarez is the rising star of Uruguayan football. His scoring feats at Ajax have already made him a target for the top clubs in England and Spain. He is equally comfortable operating through the centre or drifting in from the wing. He netted five goals in the qualifiers and formed a dangerous partnership with Forlan. He was sent off for collecting a second yellow card – for dissent – on his international debut against Colombia in February 2007. But he has worked hard to improve his disciplinary record and received only two yellow cards in the qualifiers. The teenage Suarez helped Nacional win the Uruguayan title before leaving for Dutch side Groningen in 2006. Ajax signed him for £6m in August 2007.

URUGUAY AT THE FIFA WORLD CUP™

1930	champions
1934	did not enter
1938	did not enter
1950	champions
1954	4th place
1958	did not qualify
1962	1st round
1966	quarter-finals
1970	4th place
1974	1st round
1978	did not qualify
1982	did not qualify
1986	1st round
1990	2nd round
1994	did not qualify
1998	did not qualify
2002	1st round
2006	did not qualify

ONES TO WATCH

DIEGO FORLAN
Born: May 19, 1979
Club: Atletico Madrid (Spain)

Forlan is following in the footsteps of his father Pablo, who played for Uruguay at the 1974 finals. He has won more than 60 caps and netted more than 20 goals since his international debut in 2002. He has been prolific in Spanish football, twice finishing top scorer. He also won the Golden Shoe as Europe's top scorer in 2009, after sharing the award with Thierry Henry four years earlier.

CRISTIAN RODRIGUEZ
Born: September 30, 1985
Club: Porto (Portugal)

The tricky left-winger is one of the main supply routes for Suarez and Forlan. He is a fiery character too – he picked up one red card and five yellows in the qualifiers. He made his Uruguay debut at 18, and has gained more than 30 caps. As a teenager, he was offered a university place to study architecture, but chose to join Penarol instead and helped them to the Uruguayan title in 2003.

in their homeland. Now, promising youngsters such as Suarez move abroad as teenagers. Tabarez claims: "This lack of stability in our domestic game has a direct impact on the national team. That's why qualifying campaigns are such a traumatic experience for us."

A 3-1 home win over Colombia – when Suarez opened the scoring – gave Uruguay an opening. Suarez struck again at altitude in Ecuador and Forlan's stoppage-time penalty winner put his side's destiny in their own hands against Argentina. He says: "I don't know where I got the energy to take that kick."

Tabarez has a strong core of European-based stars: Gondin, Lugano, Perez, Suarez, Forlan, defenders Martin Caceres and Maxi Pereira, midfielders Sebastian Eguren and Walter Gargano, winger Cristian Rodriguez and veteran back-up striker Sebastian Abreu. He will need them all to stay fit and steer clear of cards at the finals.

Tabarez was in charge when Uruguay reached the last 16 at the 1990 FIFA World Cup™, losing 2-0 to the home nation Italy. They had gone through as one of the best third-placed teams. That is the only time since 1970 that they have advanced beyond the group stage. They did not even qualify in 1978, 1982, 1994 and 1998; or in 2006, when they lost a play-off shoot-out to Australia.

Uruguay had beaten the Australians 3-1 on aggregate to reach the 2002 finals. They lost their opening game 2-1 to Denmark, then drew 0-0 against France. They staged a thrilling comeback to draw 3-3 with eventual quarter-finalists Senegal, but still went home early.

Eight years later, Uruguayan fans will pin their hopes on Suarez and Forlan – and celebrate if their team survive the group stage.

FRANCE

LES BLEUS

Thierry Henry's double handball – which sent 2006 FIFA World Cup™ finalists France to South Africa – summed up their erratic qualifying campaign as a team of talented individuals which rarely realised their potential.

Les Bleus finished a point behind group winners Serbia then needed a dubious goal to advance via the play-offs at Ireland's expense.

Critics and fans alike questioned the future of Raymond Domenech, but the French federation kept faith with the controversial coach.

Domenech became notorious for proposing marriage to French TV presenter Estelle Denis in a live TV interview moments after Italy had knocked France out of Euro 2008. He is also a keen amateur astrologer,

adding to the air of eccentricity which surrounds him.

He has polarised opinion like no France coach since Aime Jacquet. The much-criticised Jacquet steered France to their first-ever FIFA World Cup™ victory then quit as a grateful nation said "sorry".

Domenech's opponents fear a South African re-run of the French nightmare under Jacquet's successor, Roger Lemerre, in 2002. France were eliminated at the group stage without scoring a goal, after losing to Senegal and Denmark and drawing with Uruguay.

Domenech received little credit for France's appearance in the 2006 Final. He had persuaded the great Zinedine Zidane, defender Lilian Thuram and midfield anchor Claude Makelele to come out of international retirement during the qualifiers. They – and stars such as Henry and Frank Ribery –

became France's heroes, not the coach.

David Trezeguet, who scored France's golden-goal winner at Euro 2000, quit the national team after their ignominious exit from Euro 2008. Domenech stayed, despite a national outcry. Trezeguet said: "What annoys me most is the reappointment of the coach."

There is no doubting the quality in France's squad: Hugo Lloris is an outstanding young goalkeeper; defender William Gallas offers vast experience; Patrice Evra is one of the world's top left backs; Lassana Diarra has made a name as a defensive midfielder; Yoann Gourcuff is the heir to Zidane; Henry remains a world great; Nicolas Anelka and Karim Benzema would walk into most countries' teams; and winger Ribery is coveted by the top clubs in England and Spain.

Yet France struggled through qualification. They opened with a shock

COACH

RAYMOND DOMENECH

Domenech was promoted from Under-21 boss to succeed Jacques Santini after France's disappointing performance at Euro 2004. He relied heavily on experience as France reached the 2006 FIFA World Cup™ Final, losing to Italy on penalties. He was fortunate to survive after France were eliminated at the group stage of Euro 2008 after defeats by Holland and Italy. He was under pressure from media and fans throughout the qualifying campaign as France trailed Serbia. He has tried to rebuild the squad, introducing players such as Lloris, Bacary Sagna, Lassana Diarra, Alou Diarra and Gourcuff. But he remains unpopular and probably needs a top-four finish in South Africa to keep his job.

Despite qualifying through the play-offs, the French team contains a number of world class players.

STAR MAN

THIERRY HENRY
Born: August 17, 1977
Club: Barcelona (Spain)

Henry is his country's all-time record scorer, the only Frenchman to net more than 50 international goals. He passed Michel Platini's previous record against Lithuania in October 2007. He made his France debut against South Africa in October 1997 and reached 100 caps against Colombia in June 2008. He scored three times at France 98, though he was an unused substitute for the Final victory over Brazil. He was one of the stars of France's Euro 2000 success, scoring three goals. But he was sent off against Uruguay as France were eliminated at the group stage of the 2002 FIFA World Cup™ Finals. He netted three times in the 2006 finals, including the quarter-final winner against Brazil. He was France's Player of the Year in 2000, 2003, 2004, 2005 and 2006.

FRANCE AT THE FIFA WORLD CUP™

1930	1st round
1934	1st round
1938	quarter-finals
1950	did not qualify
1954	1st round
1958	3rd place
1962	did not qualify
1966	1st round
1970	did not qualify
1974	did not qualify
1978	1st round
1982	4th place
1986	3rd place
1990	did not qualify
1994	did not qualify
1998	champions
2002	1st round
2006	runners-up

ONES TO WATCH

YOANN GOURCUFF
Born: July 11, 1986
Club: Bordeaux (France)

Attacking midfielder Gourcuff has become France's creative spark, just like former Bordeaux great Zidane. Typically, he scored his first international goal with a spectacular 30-yard shot to earn a 2-2 draw in Romania. He can also play as a support striker. Injuries cut short his time at Milan, but he starred in Bordeaux's 2009 title victory and was named France's Player of the Year.

HUGO LLORIS
Born: December 26, 1986
Club: Lyon (France)

Goalkeeper Lloris was France's find of the qualifying campaign. His predecessor for club and country, Gregory Coupet, calls him a "phenomenon". He made his competitive debut in the home qualifier against Romania and was outstanding in both games against the Republic of Ireland. He established himself as Nice's No. 1 at the age of 20 and joined Lyon for £8m in the summer of 2008.

defender Eric Abidal were other blows along the way. Ribery missed both play-off games against Ireland with knee trouble. Critics point to France's vulnerability in the air. Abidal, Escudé and Sebastien Squillaci all failed to convince, while Philippe Mexes started just one game, the defeat in Austria.

Other questions have concerned Domenech's decision to employ two defensive midfielders in Lassana Diarra and Jeremy Toulalan or Alou Diarra. His choice of Andre-Pierre Gignac for the closing games, ahead of Benzema and Florent Malouda, raised eyebrows too.

Yet France seemed in command after Anelka's deflected shot gave them the lead in the first leg of the play-off in Dublin. However, Robbie Keane's goal at the Stade de France set their nerves jangling. Then Henry took the ball out of the air, handled a second time, and crossed for Gallas to head France's extra-time winner. It was an inglorious way for a group of gifted players to reach South Africa.

3-1 defeat to Austria, who scored twice from high balls which the French defence failed to clear. Henry and Anelka scored in a 2-1 win over the Serbs in Paris. But Ribery and Gourcuff had to rescue a point after France trailed 2-0 in Romania after 16 minutes.

They dropped more points against the Romanians in Paris, when Julian Escudé conceded an own-goal seven minutes after Henry put France ahead. They needed to win in Belgrade. Henry's goal cancelled out Nenad Milijas's early penalty. But French hopes of pressing for victory were wrecked when Lloris was sent off for an alleged trip on Nikola Zigic. Replays suggested the keeper barely made contact with the tall Serbia striker.

Injuries to Ribery and Barcelona

ARGENTINA

WHITE AND SKY BLUES

Mario Bolatti's winner in Montevideo earned a last-minute FIFA World Cup™ reprieve for Argentina – and sent them and their controversial coach Diego Maradona back to the FIFA World Cup™ finals.

After six games of Maradona's reign, Argentina had been in danger of failing to reach the finals for the first time since 1970. A play-off loomed. Or, if results went the wrong way, they might even be eliminated. That was hardly the scenario Argentina's football bosses envisaged when they chose Maradona to succeed Alfio Basile in November 2008.

Basile, who steered Argentina to the 2007 Copa America final, quit after a 1-0 loss in Chile. The public reaction to Argentina's first competitive defeat by the Chileans had shocked him. Yet his side held the third automatic qualifying place with eight games left, ahead of Chile on goal difference.

Sergio Daniel Batista, who had led Argentina's Under-23 squad to Olympic gold in Beijing weeks before, seemed the obvious choice to succeed Basile. Other candidates included the successful ex-Boca Juniors coach Carlos Bianchi and Miguel Angel Russo of San Lorenzo.

But Maradona made his interest known. Noray Nakis, head of the selection committee, backed his candidature – and Argentine association president Julio Grondona confirmed him in the job. Had they been dazzled by Maradona's star quality?

Maradona was Argentina's greatest-ever player, but virtually untested as a coach. His last coaching job had been at Buenos Aires side Racing Club, which ended in 1995.

Appointing a playing legend had worked before for Argentina's old rivals West Germany. Their triumphant captain of 1974, Franz Beckenbauer, steered them to two FIFA World Cup™ finals, in 1986 and 1990. (Maradona's Argentina beat them 3-2 in 1986, but lost 1-0 four years later.)

By contrast, Maradona's reign has been a roller-coaster ride. One of his first acts was to oust 100-caps-plus veteran Javier Zanetti as captain and install Javier Mascherano even though the Liverpool midfielder said himself he lacked the "charisma" to do the job.

COACH

DIEGO MARADONA

Maradona was one of the greatest players of all time. His attacking genius inspired Argentina to FIFA World Cup™ victory in 1986 and carried a weaker side to the 1990 Final. His second goal in the 1986 quarter-final against England was voted Goal of the Century in a 2002 FIFA poll. He was a controversial figure too. He was banned from football for 15 months in 1991 after testing positive for cocaine. He was also sent home from the 1994 FIFA World Cup™ finals after testing positive for the stimulant ephedrine. His only previous coaching experience lasted barely a year, in the mid-90s.

The scare in nearly not qualifying may have given Argentina the wake up call they need.

STAR MAN

LIONEL MESSI
Born: June 24, 1987
Club: Barcelona (Spain)

The slight but lethal Messi is currently regarded as the world's top player. His dribbling skill, acceleration and clinical finishing were key factors in Barcelona's 2009 European Cup and Spanish "double" success. His contribution rewarded Barcelona's decision to bring him and his family to Catalonia in 2000 and pay for treatment to cure a growth hormone deficiency. Messi failed to find his best form consistently amid the turmoil of Argentina's qualifying campaign, but still netted four goals. He made his FIFA World Cup™ finals debut – eight days short of his 19th birthday – as a substitute in Argentina's 6-0 win over Serbia and Montenegro at Germany 2006 but sat out their quarter-final defeat by the Germans.

ARGENTINA AT THE FIFA WORLD CUP™

1930	runners-up
1934	1st round
1938	did not enter
1950	did not enter
1954	did not enter
1958	1st round
1962	1st round
1966	quarter-finals
1970	did not qualify
1974	2nd round
1978	champions
1982	2nd round
1986	champions
1990	runners-up
1994	2nd round
1998	quarter-finals
2002	1st round
2006	quarter-finals

ONES TO WATCH

JAVIER MASCHERANO
Born: June 8, 1984
Club: Liverpool (England)

Mascherano is one of the world's top defensive midfield players, expert at breaking up opponents' attacks. He is Argentina's skipper and has won more than 50 caps. He made his international debut in 2001 after starring in the FIFA World Under-17 championship. He won gold with Argentina at the Olympic football tournaments of 2004 and 2008.

SERGIO 'KUN' AGUERO
Born: June 2, 1988
Club: Atletico Madrid (Spain)

Aguero, who netted four goals in the qualifiers, is the youngest-ever player to appear in Argentina's top division. He was 15 years and 35 days when he made his debut for Independiente in 2003. He moved to Atletico in the summer of 2006 and won his first Argentina cap later that year. He was another member of the Argentina side which won the 2008 Olympic football tournament.

Maradona switched tactics to 3-4-3, using three small attackers, Lionel Messi, Carlos Tevez and Sergio Aguero, before reverting to 4-4-2.

Argentina used 49 players in qualifying, many of them in the latter stages as Maradona chopped and changed the personnel. He introduced promising youngsters from the domestic league such as Nicolas Otamendi and recalled old-stagers Juan Veron and Martin Palermo. His side crashed humiliatingly 6-1 in Bolivia, lost 2-0 in Ecuador and their place in South Africa came under serious threat after defeats by Brazil and Paraguay. The coach had to deny that he was about to resign.

Maradona gambled on internationally inexperienced centre backs Sebastian Dominguez and Otamendi at home to Brazil. Luisao and Luis Fabiano punished Argentina's vulnerability at dead-ball situations. They lost 3-1 despite a stunning long-range strike from Jesus Datolo. Zanetti says: "We paid very dearly for our lack of concentration at set pieces."

Maradona insisted there was "no cause for alarm." But worse followed in Paraguay: Argentina lost 1-0 and Veron was sent off.

They had to win their last two games to qualify automatically in fourth place. Palermo scrambled a 92nd-minute winner against Peru to give them hope. Old rivals Uruguay were their final group opponents.

A Uruguayan win would see them through instead of Argentina. Six minutes from time, substitute Bolatti scored the only goal.

For players, fans and media, joy mingled with relief. But Veron sums up the stiff task facing Maradona before the finals. He says: "We're through to South Africa. Now we have time for the coach to get to work and come up with a team that can please the fans."

Group B

NIGERIA

SUPER EAGLES

Nigeria's qualification for South Africa was greeted with an outpouring of relief rather than triumph. The celebrations were muted because – since 1994 – Nigeria expects its Super Eagles to play on the biggest stages – and they came so close to an early exit.

However, they staved off FIFA World Cup™ disaster, thanks to a decisive substitution which fuelled a second-half comeback while their main rivals suffered unexpected defeat. Obafemi Martins stepped off the bench to score twice in Nigeria's 3-2 win in Kenya, while group leaders Tunisia crashed 1-0 in Mozambique. So Nigeria topped the group by one point and reached South Africa despite the question-marks against them.

As that final qualifier approached, Nigerian fans had feared another let-down, to follow the Super Eagles' failure to qualify in 2006. That prospect was unthinkable.

Back then, Nigeria slid out after a shock 1-0 defeat against Angola, who went to Germany instead. This time, their future was in other hands too. But Dario's 83rd-minute winner for Mozambique gave the Nigerians a lifeline. Coach Shaibu Amodu gambled at half-time, with his side trailing 1-0 in Nairobi. He sent on Martins to play alongside Yakubu Aiyegbeni, the first time in the qualifiers he had used them as a twin spearhead. Martins levelled, Yakubu added a second – and Martins grabbed the winner nine minutes from time.

Former skipper Nwankwo Kanu knew how close the outcome had been. He says: "We all remember how Nigerians

felt, watching other African teams steal the show in Germany after we missed out. We couldn't afford another experience like that."

Amodu's job was on the line after Oussama Darragi snatched Tunisia's last-gasp equaliser in a 2-2 draw in Abuja, which left Nigeria needing to win their last two games. Martins and Yakubu, recovering from injuries, missed both draws against the Tunisians. Full-back Taye Taiwo says the players bore responsibility for the setback too: "We needed to play more as a unit. The forwards had to help more defensively and the defenders had to concentrate until the final whistle."

Meanwhile, Nigeria's build-up for the game was disrupted by a dispute between the coach and senior players over the omission of winger John Utaka. Even government officials were calling

COACH

SHAIBU AMODU

Amodu is in his fourth spell as Nigeria coach. He made his name as a coach with BCC Lions, steering them to Nigerian cup victory in 1990 and the African Cup Winners' Cup in 1991. He first took charge of the national team after the 1994 FIFA World Cup™ finals, when he succeeded long-serving Dutchman Clemens Westerhof for a year. He stepped in again before Philippe Troussier arrived to lead Nigeria at France 98. In his third spell, he guided them to the 2002 FIFA World Cup™ finals, but was replaced by Adegboye Onigbinde for the tournament. Amodu took over again in April 2008. Despite his side's qualification, many fans would prefer a more high-profile coach to lead them in the finals.

Nigeria will be looking to repeat their tournament best of reaching the second round in 1994.

STAR MAN

OBAFEMI MARTINS
Born: October 28, 1984
Club: Wolfsburg (Germany)

Martins is Nigeria's most prolific striker. He has averaged more than a goal every other game since his debut in 2004 and has his long-term sights on Yekini's national record of 37 goals. He joined Reggiana of Italy from Nigerian side Ebedei after a two-month trial in 2000 and moved to Internazionale a year later. Martins is a predator in the box, small, quick and effervescent. He often celebrates his goals with a trademark somersault. He brings huge top-level experience to the national team after regular Champions League appearance for Inter and with Wolfsburg in 2009–10. He was Africa's Young Player of the Year in 2003 and 2004.

NIGERIA AT THE FIFA WORLD CUP™

1930	did not exist
1934	did not exist
1938	did not exist
1950	did not enter
1954	did not enter
1958	did not enter
1962	did not qualify
1966	withdrew
1970	did not qualify
1974	disqualified
1978	did not qualify
1982	did not qualify
1986	did not qualify
1990	did not qualify
1994	2nd round
1998	2nd round
2002	1st round
2006	did not qualify

ONES TO WATCH

JOSEPH YOBO
Born: September 6, 1980
Club: Everton (England)

Centre-back Yobo has taken over from Kanu as Nigeria's skipper. He is their defensive organiser and a calming influence. Aerially strong and a model of consistency, he also adds vast experience of pressure games. He has made more Premiership appearances for Everton than any other overseas player – and has gained more than 60 caps for his country. He played in all three of Nigeria's games at the 2002 finals.

MIKEL JOHN OBI
Born: April 22, 1987
Club: Chelsea (England)

Forceful midfield anchor Mikel joined Ajax's South African offshoot from Nigerian club Plateau United. He was one of Nigeria's stars when they reached the World Under-20 Championship final in 2005. He was later the subject of a bitter transfer battle between Premiership giants Manchester United and Chelsea. He finally joined Chelsea in 2006 for a fee totalling £16m. He has played more than 20 times for Nigeria.

for Amodu's departure. But the Nigerian association stuck by him. Adeboye Onigbinde, Nigeria's 2002 FIFA World Cup™ coach, said that this was no time for "panic measures". Amodu's future was in even greater doubt as stoppage time loomed at home to Mozambique. Another substitute, Victor Obinna, saved him with the only goal, in the 93rd minute.

So Nigeria have another chance to add to their FIFA World Cup™ traditions. They reached the last 16 at France 98, losing 4-1 to Denmark. Four years later, they were eliminated from the "Group of Death" – led by England and Sweden – with Argentina going home early too.

But their best performance came on their first appearance, in 1994. By then, the Super Eagles' stars had made their names in Europe. Nigeria entered the finals as African champions. Their side included record scorer Rashidi Yekini, midfield general Jay-Jay Okocha and Sunday Oliseh. They led eventual finalists Italy 1-0 through Emanuel Amunike's goal until the 88th minute of their last-16 clash. Roberto Baggio levelled then hit an extra-time winner from the penalty spot. Amodu has Wolfsburg's Martins, Yakubu of Everton, Loko Moscow striker Peter Odemwingie and Malaga's Obinna to offer attacking aggression. Joseph Yobo has been a mainstay of the Everton defence for four seasons and he has built a solid partnership with Sion centre back Obinna Nwaneri. Chelsea's John Obi Mikel provides a formidable shield for the back four, while Seye Olifinjana adds midfield industry. But the lack of a playmaker like Okocha was apparent throughout the qualifying. That shows how much Nigeria's expectations have risen. Okocha and the stars of 1994 set the standard by which future generations will always be judged.

SOUTH KOREA

TIGERS OF ASIA

South Korea's comfortable qualification for the 2010 FIFA World Cup™ was a triumph for coach Huh Jung-Moo. His side eased through Asia's so-called "Group of Death" to reach South Korea's seventh FIFA World Cup™ finals – an Asian record.

The question now is: how far can he take them in the finals?

Every player in the South Korea squad knows they will be judged against the side of 2002, the only Asian team ever to reach the last four. They have historically struggled outside their homeland, from their 9-0 defeat by Hungary (and 7-0 by Turkey) in 1954, to their early elimination at Germany 2006.

Dutch master-coach Guus Hiddink was in charge in 2002. The Koreans were playing on home soil, in front of fervent crowds and they benefited from contentious decisions, both against Italy in the last 16 and then against Spain in the quarter-finals, before losing 1-0 to Germany.

Their performance at Germany 2006 under another Dutch coach, Dick Advocaat, was a failure by comparison. They went home early after a 2-0 defeat by Switzerland, despite a win over Togo and a draw with France.

Huh was a controversial choice when he was appointed in 2007, after former Republic of Ireland manager Mick McCarthy and ex-Liverpool and Lyons boss Gerard Houllier turned down the job. His brief was to qualify for the FIFA World Cup™ finals while developing young players to revitalise an ageing squad.

South Korea eased through pre-qualifying, along with their northern neighbours, from a group which also included Jordan and Turkmenistan.

But the North had much the better of a 1-1 draw in the opening game of the final qualifiers in neutral Shanghai. Huh was criticised for lack of organisation and tactical nous. He in turn pointed to the absence of important players because of European club commitments.

Star midfielder Park Ji-Sung and veteran defender Lee Pyong-Yo returned for the next game, a 4-1

COACH

HUH JUNG-MOO

Eyebrows were raised when Huh was appointed for his third spell as national coach in December 2007. He had just steered Chunnam Dragons to a mid-table slot in the K-League and critics wanted a bigger name. Huh first took charge in 1995, then again from 1998 to 2000 – when he was succeeded by Hiddink.

His recent task has been to guide South Korea to their seventh finals, while rebuilding the squad. He shrugged off criticism after the 1-1 draw with the North in Shanghai – and a run of four wins and a draw saw the team through with two matches to spare.

Huh will be the third South Korean to go to the finals as both player and coach. His colleagues at the 1986 finals, Cha Bun-Kun and Kim Pyung-Suk formed the management team in 1998.

South Korea will be looking to replicate their form of 2002 which saw them reach the semi-finals.

STAR MAN

PARK JI-SUNG
Born: February 25, 1981
Club: Manchester United (England)

Park's exploits with the national team, PSV and Manchester United have made him one of the world's most famous Koreans. The all-action midfielder starred in the South Korea side which reached the 2002 FIFA World Cup™ semi-finals on home soil. He later followed national coach Guus Hiddink to PSV. He may feel he has something to prove in South Africa, after South Korea's early elimination at Germany 2006. Park's return, after missing the opening final-group qualifier against North Korea, lifted the players around him. Huh made him captain and he led by example. He netted three times in the group, including one in each game against Iran. He is well on the way to passing 100 caps.

SOUTH KOREA AT THE FIFA WORLD CUP™

1930–50	did not enter
1954	1st round
1958	did not enter
1962	did not qualify
1966	did not enter
1970–82	did not qualify
1986	1st round
1990	1st round
1994	1st round
1998	1st round
2002	4th place
2006	1st round

win over the United Arab Emirates. Park scored the crucial second goal. That win gave Huh breathing space. One paper said: "They played as though they were dancing to a very swift rhythm."

The Koreans' 2-0 win in Saudi Arabia was a pivotal point. The dismissal of the Saudis' Naif Hazazi changed the game, Lee Keun-Ho netted first, and Park Chu-Young added a second in stoppage time. It was South Korea's first win over the Saudis for 19 years.

Park Ji-Sung hit an 81st-minute equaliser as South Korea drew 1-1 in Iran. Sub Kim Chi-Woo floated an 87th-minute free kick straight into the net to beat North Korea 1-0.

So Huh's team needed only to win in the UAE to clinch their finals place. They led 2-0 after 37 minutes through Park Chu-Young and Ki Sung-Yeung – and strolled though the rest of the game.

Huh started experimenting in home draws against Saudi Arabia and Iran and continued to do so in friendly wins over Paraguay and Australia. By now he had transformed the squad. As one Korean TV station

ONES TO WATCH

LEE PYONG-YO
Born: April 23, 1977
Club: Al-Hilal (Saudi Arabia)

The experienced left back is one of seven South Koreans who have passed 100 caps. He was another star of their run to the 2002 FIFA World Cup™ semi-finals – and also followed Hiddink to PSV. This will be his third finals appearance, after Germany 2006. He is not a regular starter now but is considered a valuable influence on his younger colleagues.

PARK CHU-YOUNG
Born: July 10, 1985
Club: Monaco (France)

The speedy attacker was once the bright young hope of South Korean football. He made his international debut as a teenager, against Uzbekistan in June 2005. Injuries and inconsistency hindered his progress, but he found his best form in the qualifiers. He can play as a support striker or winger. He scored twice in qualifying, in away wins over Saudi Arabia and the UAE.

said: "Huh has made a generational change in the line-up."

Goalkeeper Lee Woon-Jae, Lee Pyong-Yo and defender Kim Nam-Il are the only remnants of the old guard. Seol Ki-Hyeon and Ahn Jung-Hwan made early appearances then were discarded. Defender Oh Beom-seok, midfielders Ki Sung-Yeung, Lee Chung-Yong and Park Chu-Young and striker Lee Keun-Ho represent Huh's younger generation.

Park Ji-Sung says: "I think we're really coming together as a team. We're willing to make sacrifices for each other and that shows on the pitch. We're really focused."

Park Ji-Sung and Lee Keun-ho led the qualifying scorers with three apiece. Huh has been desperate to find a prolific striker. He will hope that Lee Keun-Ho can fill that role in South Africa.

GREECE

Greece head for the FIFA World Cup™ Finals for only the second time thanks to a historic goal from Dimitrios Salpingidis. His winner in Donetsk also saved coach Otto Rehhagel's job.

Questions were asked about Greece's German coach after their failure to qualify for Germany 2006 was followed by an early exit from the finals of Euro 2008, when they lost all three group matches.

Greece then finished second in European Group Two, after losing home and away to automatic qualifiers Switzerland. They had to beat Ukraine in a play-off to reach South Africa.

Rehhagel had been criticised for stubbornness, caution and allegedly outdated tactics. The criticism grew even louder after he played five at the back in the 0-0 first-leg draw in Athens. He claimed it was vital not to concede an away goal. The players believed him. Midfielder Kostas Katsouranis says: "Even though it was a goalless draw, we thought our hopes were still alive."

Rehhagel used a 5-4-1 formation in the return with two wide players, Salpingidis and Giorgios Samaras, breaking in support of striker Angelos Charisteas. After 31 minutes, a through ball from Samaras split the Ukraine defence and Salpingidis shot home. Then Italy-based centre-backs Vangelis Moras and Sokratis Papastathopoulos were outstanding as Greece held out under pressure.

Rehhagel was later asked if he would ever play an attacking game. He replied: "We will, when we have Lionel Messi, Kaka, Xavi and Andres Iniesta in our team."

He added: "We had to play on the break and that paid off. We had four defenders missing, so it was always going to be a struggle."

Rehhagel is used to the barbs. He pulled off perhaps the biggest shock in modern major tournaments when he steered unfancied Greece to victory at Euro 2004. Purists derided their approach – dogged defence and an emphasis on dead-ball moves. But they beat France in the quarter-finals, Czech Republic in the semis and hosts Portugal in the final, without conceding a goal. Their coach shrugged off the criticism and said he had simply made the best use of the players available.

He is a pragmatist. He created

COACH

OTTO REHHAGEL

This will be Rehhagel's first FIFA World Cup™ Finals appearance, though he has been in charge of Greece since 2001. His greatest triumph was guiding them to victory at Euro 2004. He was named "Greek of the Year" for that achievement, the first foreigner to win the award. He also turned down an offer later that summer to become Germany coach. Rehhagel made his name with Werder Bremen in the Bundesliga. He spent 14 years there, turning them from an unfashionable club into one of Germany's powerhouses. He led them to championship and cup successes and the European Cup Winners Cup in 1992. He also steered Kaiserslautern to the title in 1998.

In winning Euro 2004, Greece proved that the seemingly impossible is possible.

STAR MAN

THEOFANIS GEKAS
Born: May 23, 1980
Club: Bayer Leverkusen (Germany)

Gekas has been in and out of the Leverkusen side over the past two seasons. He even spent a brief loan spell in England with Portsmouth in the spring of 2009. But he has been a prolific scorer for Greece. Gekas has averaged almost a goal every other game since his debut against Albania in March 2005. He says: "The Greek system is geared towards my game." His most important contributions came in the last two group games. He netted four in Greece's 5-2 win over Latvia – after the Latvians led 2-1 at half-time – then scored the second goal in the 2-1 win over Luxembourg which clinched their play-off place.

GREECE AT THE FIFA WORLD CUP™

1930	did not enter
1934	did not qualify
1938	did not qualify
1950	did not enter
1954-90	did not qualify
1994	1st round
1998	did not qualify
2002	did not qualify
2006	did not qualify

ONES TO WATCH

ANGELOS CHARISTEAS
Born: February 9, 1980
Club: Nurnberg (Germany)

Charisteas was the hero of Greece's Euro 2004 victory, heading the lone winning goal against Portugal in the final in Lisbon. He also scored against Spain and France and was named in the UEFA Team of the Tournament. The tall, 1.91m (6ft 3in) striker usually plays as a target man. He netted four goals in the qualifiers. He has won more than 80 caps since scoring twice on his debut against Russia in February 2001.

GIORGIOS KARAGOUNIS
Born: March 6, 1977
Club: Panathinaikos (Greece)

Skipper Karagounis, one of Greece's most successful footballing exports, is another of the Euro 2004 heroes. He scored the first goal of the tournament in Greece's 2-1 group win over Portugal. He has won more than 90 caps since his debut in 1999. He is Greece's elder statesman, their midfield playmaker and dead ball expert. He returned to Panathinaikos from Benfica in 2007.

a vibrant team at Werder Bremen, featuring attacking stars such as Rudi Voller, Karlheinz Riedle and Mario Basler. Greece lack such quality. As Switzerland's German boss Ottmar Hitzfeld says: "He's a very clever coach who adapts to circumstances. Greece's strength is their defence and they have an abundance of strong, physical players."

They also have a penalty-box poacher in Theofanis Gekas. The Bayer Leverkusen striker finished top scorer in the European qualifiers with 10 goals. He was a tactical substitute in Donetsk but he is likely to start behind a target man in South Africa.

Samaras says: "It's great to have him in the team because, even if he doesn't touch the ball for a while, just give him one chance and he'll score you a goal."

Rehhagel has built the squad on a core of Panathinaikos stars – goalkeeper Alexandros Tzorvas, full-backs Nikos Spiropoulos and Lukas Vyntra, centre-back Giorgios Setaridis, skipper Giorgios Karagounis, Katsouranis and Salpingidis.

PAOK keeper Kostas Chalkias and Olympiakos defender Vasilis Torsidis are other home-based players likely to figure. The coach has blended them with Greece's foreign legion. Moras is with Bologna in Italy, Papastathopoulos with their Serie A rivals Genoa. Defender Sotirios Kyrgiakos is in his first season at Liverpool. Defensive midfielder Christos Pastazoglou turns out in Cyprus for Omonia Nicosia. Attackers Charisteas (Nurnberg) and Iannis Amanatidis (Eintracht Frankfurt) play in Germany.

Amanatidis says the coach knows Greece need a "Plan B" in South Africa. The striker adds: "Rehhagel refuses to be distracted by swings in attitude towards the team. He can only choose the tactics to suit the players he has available. But we're working hard to give ourselves alternatives."

Greece lost all their three group games the last time they reached the FIFA World Cup™ at USA 1994, and failed to score a goal. They will be a tougher proposition under Rehhagel.

ENGLAND

England want a FIFA World Cup™ double in 2010: victory on the pitch in South Africa and then, in December, success with their bid to host the finals in 2018. First, out on the pitch, comes a test of the turn-around accomplished under Italian manager Fabio Capello.

On September 6, 2008, England began their FIFA World Cup™ qualifying campaign with a stuttering 2-0 win over Andorra. Their travelling fans were starting to jeer when Joe Cole stepped off the bench to score twice.

Fast forward to September 9, 2009. England crushed Croatia 5-1 at Wembley to reach the finals with two games to spare. It was their eighth straight group win and they had scored 31 goals. They are counted among the leading contenders for South Africa 2010. That is a tribute to their transformation under Fabio Capello.

Perhaps the crucial game was England's 4-1 win in Croatia, four days after their struggles against Andorra. Skipper John Terry said beforehand that England would probably have accepted a draw. Instead, Capello unleashed the pace of (then) 19-year-old Theo Walcott, who scored a hat-trick. It was Croatia's first-ever competitive home defeat and raised confidence throughout the England ranks.

Capello had instilled discipline and organisation. He concentrated too on improving the players' self-belief, which had plummeted under his managerial predecessor Steve McClaren. His intensity began to rub off on the squad.

England scored three in the last 15 minutes to beat Kazakhstan 5-1. They survived a tricky opening half to win 3-1 in Belarus.

That was the game in which Capello showed how to combine Steven Gerrard and Frank Lampard for England. Lampard played through central midfield alongside Gareth Barry. Gerrard started on the left and often moved inside to link with Wayne Rooney.

Terry grabbed an 85th-minute winner against Ukraine. Gerrard says: "Eighteen months ago, we might have gone into our shell when Ukraine levelled, and played the last 20 minutes with fear. This was

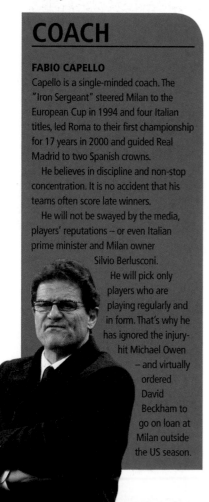

COACH

FABIO CAPELLO

Capello is a single-minded coach. The "Iron Sergeant" steered Milan to the European Cup in 1994 and four Italian titles, led Roma to their first championship for 17 years in 2000 and guided Real Madrid to two Spanish crowns.

He believes in discipline and non-stop concentration. It is no accident that his teams often score late winners.

He will not be swayed by the media, players' reputations -- or even Italian prime minister and Milan owner Silvio Berlusconi.

He will pick only players who are playing regularly and in form. That's why he has ignored the injury-hit Michael Owen -- and virtually ordered David Beckham to go on loan at Milan outside the US season.

ENGLAND v UKRAINE
Wednesday 1 April 2009, Wembley Stadium

Fabio Capello has moulded England into a side very few would like to face in South Africa.

STAR MAN

WAYNE ROONEY
Born: October 24, 1985
Club: Manchester United (England)

The dynamic Rooney has become Capello's attacking star. He poses England's biggest goal threat, scoring nine times in their opening eight qualifiers. He is powerful, pacy and capable of moments of brilliance. He operates as a second striker, sometimes drifting left so that Gerrard can check inside. He has benefited from starting in the middle for United this season after playing second fiddle to Cristiano Ronaldo. He has a point to prove at a major tournament too. He scored twice against both Switzerland and Croatia at Euro 2004 before limping out of the quarter-final against Portugal. Two years later, he was rushed back from a metatarsal injury and used as a lone striker. He was sent off for a stamp on Portugal defender Ricardo Carvalho in England's quarter-final defeat.

ENGLAND AT THE FIFA WORLD CUP™

1930	ineligible
1934	ineligible
1938	ineligible*
1950	1st round
1954	quarter-finals
1958	1st round
1962	quarter-finals
1966	champions
1970	quarter-finals
1974	did not qualify
1978	did not qualify
1982	2nd round
1986	quarter-finals
1990	4th place
1994	did not qualify
1998	2nd round
2002	quarter-finals
2006	quarter-finals

*England, though outside FIFA, rejected a late invitation to compete after the withdrawal of Austria

ONES TO WATCH

JOHN TERRY
Born: December 7, 1980
Club: Chelsea (England)

Terry is England's all-action defender, hurtling in to head the ball in either box, or laying himself on the line with block tackles. He is also one of Capello's leaders on the pitch. Injuries have slightly cut his pace over the past two years but he remains a physically imposing stopper – and a serious threat at corners and free kicks.

STEVEN GERRARD
Born: May 30, 1980
Club: Liverpool (England)

The mercurial Gerrard is enjoying his most consistent spell for England. He seemed baffled at first by Capello's decision to use him from the left but has since settled in the role. He has an excellent understanding with Rooney. He specialises in spectacular goals, often blasted from outside the box.

much more positive." Lampard adds: "You might not have seen that two years ago. Confidence has come from results and performances."

Capello has built the team around top scorer in qualification Wayne Rooney. The Manchester United man has revelled in his favourite role behind a powerful striker, such as Emile Heskey. Capello says Rooney can be as influential for England as the great

Raul has been for Real Madrid.

Centre backs Terry and Rio Ferdinand are a formidable partnership. Ashley Cole is one of the world's finest left backs. Winger Aaron Lennon tore Croatia's defence apart at Wembley. He, Walcott and striker Jermain Defoe can be used as "impact" substitutes too.

But Capello admits that the prospect of injuries concerns him in such a relatively short tournament. While Ferdinand has

had a series of knocks, Terry has suffered from back trouble – and the coach will pray that Rooney is fully fit, unlike in Germany four years ago.

Problem areas remain. Capello has tried Ben Foster, Robert Green and the veteran David James, yet England still lack a dominant goalkeeper. Enthusiastic attacking right back Glen Johnson has been caught out defensively. Heskey's scoring record is poor – just one goal, in the 4-0 win in Kazakhstan – during the qualifiers.

Yet Croatia coach Slaven Bilic believes England can win the FIFA World Cup™. So do many England fans, after the false dawns of 2002 and 2006. For Terry, it's a case of "peaking" at the right time in South Africa.

Capello's record suggests his teams are well equipped to do that. He knows the pitfalls too. He played for Italy when they went to the 1974 finals among the favourites – and were knocked out in the group stage.

UNITED STATES

The United States know all about causing a stir at a major tournament in South Africa. Last summer they led Brazil 2-0 at half-time in the FIFA Confederations Cup before eventually going down 3-2. A 2010 repeat would be historic.

In the Confederations semi-finals the Americans had ended Spain's 35-game unbeaten run with a shock 2-0 win thanks to goals from Jozy Altidore and Clint Dempsey. Then strikes from Dempsey and key man Landon Donovan gave them command by the 27th-minute against Brazil in the final.

Memories of the second half still haunt the US players. Donovan says: "We all know why Brazil are consistently one of the world's best. But, at 2-0 up, we should have been able to kill the game off. We weren't happy with just going that far in the final. We felt we had to demand more of ourselves."

Coach Bob Bradley believes that the match shows how much the US players had raised their standards – and expectations. He says: "That final appearance was an important step but it was not something that happened by chance. It was a result of lots of things happening in US soccer – such as Major League Soccer players deciding to go to Europe and our regular appearances at the FIFA World Cup™ finals across all the age groups."

Bradley's son Michael, an attacking midfielder with Borussia Moenchengladbach, adds: "We've definitely improved. If you look at our team and see who's playing for which clubs in Europe, then the outlook is very positive."

Claudio Reyna, Brian McBride and Eddie Pope led the exodus. Donovan has played for top Bundesliga sides Bayer Leverkusen and Bayern Munich. Tim Howard is Everton's first choice keeper. Captain Carlos Bocanegra is with Rennes after four years in the Premiership. Midfielder Dempsey is a firm favourite at Fulham, while West Ham full back Jonathan Spector is another Premiership regular. Centre backs Oguchi Onyewu (Milan) and Steve Cherundolo (Hannover) have established themselves in Europe too.

Bradley has successfully blended those overseas stars with youngsters such as striker Altidore and developing MLS talent, like Houston Dynamos' Ricardo Clark and Chivas USA defender Jonathan Bornstein.

The unfancied Americans' 1-0 win

COACH

BOB BRADLEY

Bradley has rebuilt his squad since the retirement of many of his 2006 generation. He says: "We've challenged the older guys to take roles leading the team and we've watched young players grow."

He was named as interim coach after the 2006 FIFA World Cup™ finals, an appointment made permanent five months later when the US federation's negotiations with Jurgen Klinsmann fell through.

He had been national coach Bruce Arena's assistant at Germany 2006. He was also Arena's No. 2 at MLS club DC United. He led Chicago Fire to the MLS Cup and US Open Cup double in 1998 and was named MLS Coach of the Year.

Solid performers such as Landon Donovan (10) and Clint Dempsey (8) will make the US tough opponents.

STAR MAN

LANDON DONOVAN
Born: March 4, 1982
Club: Los Angeles Galaxy (United States)

Donovan is probably the most outstanding of all the US stars. He was named Player of the Year for the sixth time in nine seasons in October 2009 and was also voted Player of the Decade. He is the only American to have won more than 100 caps and has scored more than 40 goals for his country, another record. He made his name as a 20-year-old, netting against Poland and arch rivals Mexico during the Americans' run to the 2002 FIFA World Cup™ quarter-finals.

Donovan joined Bayer Leverkusen in 1999 after starring in the US side that finished fourth in the 1999 World Under-17 Championship. He moved to LA Galaxy in 2005 but spent the early months of 2009 on loan with Bayern Munich in Germany.

USA AT THE FIFA WORLD CUP™

1930	semi-finals
1934	1st round
1938	did not enter
1950	1st round
1954	did not qualify
1958	did not qualify
1962	did not qualify
1966	did not qualify
1970	did not qualify
1974	did not qualify
1978	did not qualify
1982	did not qualify
1986	did not qualify
1990	1st round
1994	2nd round
1998	1st round
2002	quarter-finals
2006	1st round

ONES TO WATCH

JOZY ALTIDORE
Born: November 6, 1989
Club: Hull City (England, loan)

Altidore led the US scorers with five goals in qualifying, including a hat-trick against Trinidad and the winner at home to El Salvador. He also scored the opener in the Americans' Confederations Cup win over Spain. He made his Red Bulls debut as a 16-year-old. When he moved to Villarreal in June 2008, the fee of £7m was a record for a player from MLS.

CARLOS BOCANEGRA
Born: May 25, 1979
Club: Rennes (France)

US skipper Bocanegra has more than 70 caps and boasts six years' experience in Europe, four with Fulham in the English Premier League. He says it would be a "dream move" if he could play a season in Spain after his Rennes contract expires in 2011.

He is a wily, experienced centre back who chips in with goals such as his winner in the home qualifier against Honduras.

over England in the 1950 finals, thanks to Larry Gaetjens's goal, was one of the great shocks of FIFA World Cup™ history.

No one underestimates the Americans now. They qualified in 1990, hosted the finals in 1994, and have qualified for every FIFA World Cup™ finals since.

Their high point came in 2002, when they beat arch rivals Mexico 2-0 to reach the quarter-finals then went down 1-0 to eventual runners-up Germany.

This time around in qualifying they topped the final CONCACAF group, one point ahead of Mexico. They showed their mettle in their final match. They had already qualified yet came from 2-0 down to draw 2-2 with Costa Rica, thanks to Bornstein's equaliser in the fourth minute of stoppage time. They had also recovered from a two-goal deficit early in the qualifiers, when Frankie Hejduk's 88th-minute strike

clinched a 2-2 draw in El Salvador.

But the celebrations after the Costa Rica match were tinged with anxiety. Onyewu is racing against time to make the finals after suffering a knee injury which needed surgery. Before the game, striker Charlie Davies suffered serious injuries in a car crash. Coach Bradley says: "We had two days of tough news."

Two away wins effectively secured for the US their place in South Africa. Clark scored the only goal in Trinidad and Tobago. Then Donovan sealed a 3-2 win in Honduras after two Conor Casey goals.

Bocanegra says: "It's been a great team effort. We have a dynamic coach and we approach our games with the right mentality."

Howard adds: "We have a core of experienced players who push the youngsters in the right direction. We're a young team with a mixture of naivety and boldness. But what's happened over the last year has given us an edge."

ALGERIA

DESERT FOXES

Algeria are back at the FIFA World Cup™ finals after a wait of 24 years. Centre-back Antar Yahia's decisive volley clinched qualification and sank north African rivals Egypt in a play-off in Omdurman. Now they aim to reach the last 16 for the first time.

The Algerians still remember their first appearance at the finals with bitterness. They sprang one of the shocks of Spain 1982 in their opening group game – when Rabah Madjer and Lakhdar Belloumi scored in a 2-1 win over European champions West Germany.

Algeria next lost 2-0 to Austria. They made a flying start in their final match: Salah Assad netted twice and Tedj Bensouala added another to give them a 3-0 half-time lead over Chile. Then they relaxed. Chile pulled back to 3-2 – and Algeria were to be eliminated on goal difference after one of the most cynical contests in finals history.

West Germany took an early lead against Austria. The teams realised that, if the score stayed 1-0, both would advance at Algeria's expense. Critics at the time described the rest of the match as a "non-aggression pact". West Germany went on to reach the Final while Algeria went home early.

Four years later, present coach Rabah Saadane led them to the finals in Mexico. They were trapped in a "group of death" featuring Spain and Brazil and were eliminated after two predictable defeats plus a draw against Northern Ireland.

Algeria were one of Africa's powerhouses back then. Now Saadane has found a core of players who can compete again. He says: "We have progressed from a very tough group, because Egypt have for some time been the best African team at continental level. I'm a big believer in a settled unit. So I will trust this squad."

Algeria, who beat Egypt 3-1 at home in Blida, were unbeaten and led the final group by three points before their last game, in Cairo. The Algerian team bus was attacked on the way from the airport. Star striker Rafik Saifi was one of four players hurt.

Egypt then won 2-0 – thanks to sub Emad Mateab's goal five minutes into stoppage time – to match Algeria's record and force a play-off because the teams had finished joint top of the group with identical records.

The Algerians' anger might have boiled over. Instead, Saadane's low-key approach kept them focused. Skipper

COACH

RABAH SAADANE

Saadane is in his fifth term as Algeria coach. The former defender first took charge in 1981. He steered Algeria to the FIFA World Cup™ finals the following year, but was replaced by playing legend Rachid Mekloufi before the tournament in Spain. He returned to coach the squad in 1985 and stayed in charge for the 1986 finals. He stepped in again briefly in 1999 and 2003, then replaced French coach Jean-Michel Cavalli in October 2007 after Algeria failed to qualify for the 2008 African Nations Cup finals.

Algeria came through a difficult play-off with African rivals Egypt to seal their place in South Africa.

STAR MAN

RAFIK SAIFI
Born: February 7, 1975
Club: Al-Khor (Qatar)

Veteran attacker Saifi has become a national icon after more than a decade in the Algeria team. He has won more than 50 caps and was voted Algeria's Player of the Year in 2008. Saifi, who scored two important qualifying goals against Zambia, often appeared in struggling sides. Now he says: "It's time for Algeria to smile again after all these years." The FIFA World Cup™ Finals could provide the perfect finale to his long career. He helped MC Algiers win the national title in 1999 before moving to France later that year. He played more than 100 league games for Troyes and netted 25 goals in 90 league appearances for Lorient. He joined Al-Khor in August 2009.

ALGERIA AT THE FIFA WORLD CUP™

1930–62	did not exist
1966	withdrew
1970	did not qualify
1974	did not qualify
1978	did not qualify
1982	1st round
1986	did not qualify
1990	did not qualify
1994	did not qualify
1998	did not qualify
2002	did not qualify
2006	did not qualify

ONES TO WATCH

ANTAR YAHIA
Born: March 21, 1982
Club: Bochum (Germany)

The powerful centre-back became an instant hero after hitting the winner against Egypt. He made his international debut in January 2004 and has been a regular under Saadane. He made his name in France with Bastia after failing to break through at Internazionale in Italy. He moved to Nice in 2005, then to Bochum two years later. He was born to Algerian parents living in France.

KARIM ZIANI
Born: August 17, 1982
Club: Wolfsburg (Germany)

Attacking midfielder Ziani was also born in France to Algerian parents. He cost Marseille £8m in June 2007 and commanded a fee of £7m when he joined Wolfsburg in the summer of 2009. Small and skilful, he can operate through the middle, or as a winger. He is one of Algeria's dead-ball experts and their regular penalty taker. He made his debut in 2003 and has won more than 40 caps.

Yazid Mansouri says: "We showed that we can keep our heads."

Young keeper Fawzi Chaouchi, who played because of suspension, made important saves as Algeria defended their lead tenaciously. Saadane said they "had won with dignity". Defender Madjid Bougherra said they had gained "justice". Saifi says: "It meant so much to us. We wanted it even more than Egypt."

Saadane pinpointed two games which convinced him of Algeria's potential. The first came in the pre-qualifying group, when his side fought back from a 1-0 deficit to beat 2002 FIFA World Cup™ quarter-finalists Senegal 3-2. He says: "That was a test of character and ability. I thought then, maybe we'd made progress to compete for a FIFA World Cup™ place.

"Our 2-0 win in Zambia was another turning point because it put us top of the group and gave us momentum."

Saadane's squad features several players with European experience. Ex-Marseille midfielder Karim Ziani plays in Germany with Wolfsburg. Yahia and forward Karim Mantour are both Bundesliga regulars. Defender Nadir Belhadj has Premiership experience with Portsmouth. Centre back Bougherra plays for Scottish club Rangers. Rafik Halliche is with Nacional in Portugal.

Mansouri and fellow midfielder Yacine Bezzaz have built careers in France at Lorient and Strasbourg respectively. So did Saifi.

Ziani says: "We have good players playing at good clubs, so it's logical that we're making progress. This generation of players has got into the habit of playing together. The coach has kept the same core and that has paid off. Now there's a big wave of enthusiasm in our country."

Mansouri says: "We've slowly been realising that we can make a mark on our country's history. We doubtless won't be among the favourites, but surprises are what makes football great." As Algeria so nearly proved in 1982.

SLOVENIA

Slovenia sprang the surprise of the qualifying play-offs when they knocked out Russia to reach the FIFA World Cup™ finals for the second time – a major triumph for a small country which was once the northern-most province of the old Yugoslavia.

Zlatko Dedic's home winner in Maribor settled the tie on away goals after Slovenia had trailed 2-0 with time running out in Moscow. Then substitute Necj Pecnik had headed home an 88th-minute rebound off goalkeeper Igor Akinfeev. That gave Slovenia a vital away goal and tilted the balance of the tie.

Russia coach Guus Hiddink had cautioned his players not to underestimate the Slovenes. Russia's star, Andrey Arshavin, was fatally prescient when he warned: "In the play-offs, an accidental goal can change the situation completely."

Then Bochum striker Dedic turned in Valter Birsa's 44th-minute cross to send Slovenia to South Africa. Russia were furious with referee Terje Hauge, who sent off Alexander Kerzhakov for a challenge on keeper Samir Handanovic and later dismissed Yuri Zhirkov for a second yellow card. TV replays showed that Slovenia defender Bostjan Cesar hit Kerzhakov in the face and Handanovic also aimed a slap at the Russian.

But while the Russian media blamed their "weak-willed" team, Slovenia celebrated. Coach Matjaz Kek says: "It was a historic night. We've realised a dream: to be among the best teams in the world. It was a triumph for our determination and all our preparation."

Slovenia came good late in the qualifiers, when it mattered. The key results were their 3-0 home win over Poland and a surprise 2-0 victory over group winners Slovakia away in Bratislava. Auxerre midfielder Birsa put them ahead, and Pecnik, of Portuguese club Nacional, added a stoppage-time second.

Right-back Miso Brecko says: "We always felt we had a chance, provided we took something from that game. We were a bit surprised that Slovakia won their final game in Poland – but we'd made sure of second place at least."

A 3-0 victory in San Marino left Slovenia two points behind the Slovaks and clinched their play-off spot.

COACH

MATJAZ KEK

Kek has been internationally recognised since Slovenia's success against Russia. He has become famous for his planning and attention to detail. He made his name with Maribor, taking over as coach in 2000 after a season as assistant. He steered them to league titles in 2001 and 2003. He had won three Slovenian championships with them as a player. Kek then took charge of the Slovenia under-15 and under-16 teams in 2006. He succeeded Branko Oblak as national coach on January 3, 2007. Slovenia failed to qualify for Euro 2008, from a group dominated by Romania and Holland. But Kek repaid the association's faith in him by turning a young team into surprise FIFA World Cup™ qualifiers.

Few fancied Slovenia to overcome Russia in their play-off, yet they ultimately deserved to progress.

STAR MAN

ZLATKO DEDIC
Born: October 5, 1984
Club: Bochum (Germany)

Dedic secured his place in Slovene football folklore with the winner against Russia. That was his third goal for Slovenia, all coming in the qualifiers. He also opened the score in their 3-0 win over Poland and netted in the 1-1 opening draw in Wroclaw. The forward made his international debut in 2004 then finally established himself as a key player in the qualifying campaign. He had played only three league games in Slovenia before joining Italian side Parma in 2001. He spent much of his five years there on loan before joining second division Frosinone to earn a regular starting place. He moved to Bochum in the summer of 2009.

SLOVENIA AT THE FIFA WORLD CUP™

1930–90	did not exist
1994	did not enter
1998	did not qualify
2002	1st round
2006	did not qualify

Kirm of Wisla Krakow play more conservative roles.

Slovenia – inspired by their greatest-ever player Zlatko Zahovic – reached the 2002 FIFA World Cup™ finals, only to fall at the group stage. They lost to Spain, South Africa and Paraguay.

The new generation are confident they can do better. Novakovic and Radosavljevic are the only regulars aged over 30. Novakovic says: "We've worked hard for three years to reach where we are now. We have a strong spirit in the squad. The younger players have grown up together in the youth teams and the experienced guys, like Robert [Koren] and I, are ready to help out whenever we can."

Suler says: "The younger players listen to both of them and we've become very strong mentally."

Jokic adds: "We're a young team. We may not have any household names, but we're all playing for good clubs."

Suler is keen to make another point too. Zahovic's Slovenia of Euro 2000 and the 2002 FIFA World Cup™ were products of the old Yugoslav system, before the political federation split into its component parts.

He says: "We're the first generation to graduate from the Slovenian system rather than the Yugoslav system and that makes us very proud."

ONES TO WATCH

MILOVOJE NOVAKOVIC
Born: May 18, 1979
Club: Koln (Germany)

The tall, 1.92m (6ft 4in) striker led Slovenia's scorers in qualifying with five goals. He has won more than 30 caps. He left Olimpija Ljubljana in 2002 to play in Austria, but made his name after moving to Litex of Bulgaria. He joined Koln for 1.5m euros in August 2006. He was top scorer with 20 goals as they won promotion to the Bundesliga in 2008.

ROBERT KOREN
Born: September 20, 1980
Club: West Bromwich Albion (England)

The attacking midfielder skippered Slovenia through the qualifiers. He made his international debut in 2003 and has over 40 caps. He was regarded as one of the most gifted midfielders in Norway before joining West Bromwich on a "Bosman" free transfer in January 2007. While with Lillestrom he suffered a freak training ground injury later that year which caused loss of vision, but made a full recovery.

Their success was based on a mean defence – Koln's Brecko, Cesar of Grenoble, Gent's Marko Suler and Sochaux left-back Bojan Jokic – in front of Udinese keeper Handanovic. They conceded only six goals in 12 games. Defensive midfielder Birsa had a role to play too, screening the back line.

Striker Milivoje Novakovic says: "Sure, our rearguard is very strong.

But defending starts with the players up front. We all close down. That's what our system is based on."

Dedic and Koln's Novakovic were the only players to score more than twice though Pecnik, who broke into the squad during the qualifiers, threatened as an impact sub. He is likely to do that job again in South Africa, while Robert Koren, Tomsk's Alexander Radosavljevic and Andraz

GERMANY

DER MANNSCHAFT

No FIFA World Cup™ finals would be complete without Germany, the masters of tournament football. Their team may be exciting, like Franz Beckenbauer's 1974 FIFA World Cup-winners, or dour, like the 1982 finalists. But the Germans are always formidable.

Their qualification was typically thorough. Joachim Low's side polished off Liechtenstein, Azerbaijan and Wales, then won both games against their main rivals Russia. Lukas Podolski and skipper Michael Ballack scored in the 2-1 win in Dortmund while Miroslav Klose's 48th international goal clinched the 1-0 victory in Moscow which saw

Germany to South Africa with a game to spare. They survived the last 21 minutes with 10 men after defender Jerome Boateng was sent off for a second yellow card. Ballack says: "We showed nerves of steel that day."

The Germans are famous for such resilience. Full-back Philipp Lahm believes that mental strength is born of previous triumphs. He says: "We've been very successful in the past and that's an inspiration to the next generation.

"We won the FIFA World Cup™ in 1954, 1974 and 1990 and the European Championship in 1972, 1980 and 1996. We've made it through to finals at least as often. So we've grown up with the conviction that Germany are always good enough to reach the Final."

He adds: "Spain look very good, the English are strong and have a very good coach and no one can ever ignore

Brazil. But we're definitely among a group of countries with a chance of taking the trophy. We were third in 2006 and runners-up at Euro 2008, so we're ambitious for 2010."

Ballack says: "We have a lot of technical quality, allied to physical strength. That combination carried us to the Euro 2008 final."

Long-serving centre-back Christoph Metzelder agrees: "There are six or seven teams around the world who play better football than we do. So we need to bring other attributes into play. If we do that again, we'll be dangerous opponents."

Ballack insists Germany have top-class match-winners too. He says: "We have individual skills which can turn a game. Teams at the top are so well matched. That means an individual can make a difference."

Lahm is a brilliant attacking full-

COACH

JOACHIM LOW

Low was Jurgen Klinsmann's assistant at the 2006 finals and succeeded him as coach afterwards. He used a blend of technique and physical power to take Germany to the Euro 2008 final and he is likely to repeat the formula in South Africa. He has rebuilt the side over the past 18 months, despite criticism after home friendly defeats by England and Norway. He has introduced young players such as Ozil, Boateng, Thomas Muller and full back Andreas Beck. Low has proved his diplomatic skills by resolving an argument in the qualifier in Wales, when Podolski slapped Ballack. He has also shown his authority by ending striker Kevin Kuranyi's international career after a half-time walk-out.

Historically, Germany have been one of the FIFA World Cup's most consistent performers.

STAR MAN

MICHAEL BALLACK
Born: September 26, 1976
Club: Chelsea (England)

Ballack has skippered the German team since 2004 – when he took over from Oliver Kahn – and is approaching 100 caps. He hopes that South Africa 2010 will end the jinx that has cursed him in major finals. He was on the losing side in UEFA Champions League finals with Bayer Leverkusen (2002) and Chelsea (2008). He netted Germany's 2002 FIFA World Cup™ semi-final winner against South Korea but collected a yellow card which kept him out of their 2-0 defeat by Brazil in the Final. He then skippered the teams which lost to Italy in the 2006 FIFA World Cup™ semi-finals and to Spain at Euro 2008. He says he will make a decision about retirement after the 2010 tournament.

GERMANY AT THE FIFA WORLD CUP™

1930	did not enter
1934	3rd place
1938	1st round
1950	did not enter
1954	champions
1958	4th place
1962	quarter-finals
1966	runners-up
1970	3rd place
1974	champions
1978	2nd round
1982	runners-up
1986	runners-up
1990	champions
1994	quarter-finals
1998	quarter-finals
2002	runners-up
2006	3rd place

ONES TO WATCH

MIROSLAV KLOSE
Born: June 9, 1978
Club: Bayern Munich (Germany)

The Polish-born striker chose in 2001 to play for his father's country and has become one of Germany's most prolific scorers. He shot to fame by netting five goals as Germany reached the 2002 FIFA World Cup™ Final. He finished top scorer, again with five goals, at the 2006 finals. He is particularly strong in the air and has won more than 90 caps.

BASTIAN SCHWEINSTEIGER
Born: August 1, 1984
Club: Bayern Munich (Germany)

Schweinsteiger was a talented skier as well as a promising footballer. He opted for football after joining Bayern's youth section as a 14-year-old. The versatile midfielder has gained more than 70 caps. He played in Germany's run to third place in 2006 and in the Euro 2008 Final. He began as a combative defensive midfielder but has recently played a more attacking role to support.

back. Midfield star Ballack has scored more than 40 goals for his country, including four in the qualifiers. Bastian Schweinsteiger has begun to contribute important goals. Meanwhile, the skipper tips Mesut Ozil as a rising star, claiming the 21-year-old has "all the qualities to be a genuine No. 10." The Germans have plenty of midfield cover too – the experienced Piotr Trochowski and Thomas Hitzlsperger, plus young hopeful Thomas Muller.

Up front, Klose has been prolific since he made headlines at the 2002 finals. His partnership with Lukas Podolski is one of Germany's great strengths. Klose netted seven goals in the qualifiers, Podolski six.

Low rushed to their defence after criticism from Gerd Muller, the great striker whose goal won the 1974 Final. The coach says: "The game has developed so much in the art of defending. It's incredibly difficult for strikers now – but these two score regularly." He will pray that neither suffers injury or suspension, with Mario Gomez the only proven back-up.

Germany conceded only five goals in their 10 qualifying ties – four of them in two draws against Finland. Goalkeeper Rene Adler, another hero in Moscow, has established himself as the successor to Oliver Kahn and Jens Lehmann. Midfield anchor Simon Rolfes shields the back-line, which is built around experienced centre-back Per Mertesacker. But Metzelder, his 2006 partner, has been sidelined by persistent injuries and may not make the squad. Veteran full-back Arne Friedrich adds more experience, though Heiko Westermann will probably start ahead of him.

However far Low's men progress they will surely dedicate it to the memory of goalkeeper Robert Enke whose tragic suicide last autumn shocked both the German and the world game.

AUSTRALIA

SOCCEROOS

Australia's smooth passage into the 2010 FIFA World Cup™ finals contrasts vividly with their qualification four years earlier.

This time, they qualified from Asian Group One with two games to spare. An upright denied Tim Cahill a spectacular winner against Qatar in Doha, but the 0-0 draw was enough to see the Australians through to South Africa.

Australia climbed to 14th in the FIFA world rankings in September, their highest-ever position. That has boosted their belief that they can better their second-round finish in Germany in 2006.

Pim Verbeek's side topped their group thanks to a 2-0 home win over Bahrain and a 2-1 victory over Japan. Cahill scored twice as the Socceroos came from behind in front of 70,000 fans in Melbourne.

Goalkeeper Mark Schwarzer was the hero of the penalty shoot-out win over Uruguay which took Australia to Germany 2006. He says: "Qualifying this time was still an emotional moment. We worked hard for it over a long campaign and we deserved it."

Australia had previously dominated the qualifiers in FIFA's far-flung Oceania region. They, often, found themselves in a play off against a South American side for a place in the finals. Australia "escaped" to the Asian Confederation after the 2006 FIFA World Cup™ and they duly qualified direct for the first time.

Australia's Galatasaray midfielder Harry Kewell (once of Leeds and Liverpool) says: "This format worked to our advantage. The games were intense. That scenario suited us much better than several comfortable games followed by a two-leg play-off."

The Australians pre-qualified from a group including Qatar, China and Asian champions Iraq, then topped their final group unbeaten, with six wins and two draws.

COACH

PIM VERBEEK

Verbeek has emulated his mentor Guus Hiddink by steering Australia to the FIFA World Cup™ finals. This will be his third tournament. He was Hiddink's assistant when South Korea reached the last four in 2002 and No. 2 to Dick Advocaat at Germany 2006. He says steering Australia to South Africa 2010 is his greatest achievement, justifying a no-nonsense approach by saying: "I'm not here to please. I'm here to win games." He has remained focused on the task at hand without worrying about his off-pitch popularity. He hoped to use local A-League players for Australia's current Asian Cup qualifying campaign, to protect his overseas stars. But he had to call up his regulars after poor early results. He sparked a fierce debate when he questioned the A-League's quality, saying: "I'd prefer our players to go to Europe to develop, because the leagues there are better."

Australia's football team poses for a picture prior to their FIFA World Cup™ qualifier against Qatar.

STAR MAN

TIM CAHILL
Born: December 6, 1979
Club: Everton (England)

Cahill was described by former national coach Rale Rasic as "the best Australian player in my lifetime."

He was the first Australian to score in the FIFA World Cup™ finals when he shot an 84th-minute equaliser against Japan at Germany 2006. He added a second five minutes later, then set up John Aloisi to make it 3-1. His double against Japan also ensured that Australia finished top of their 2010 qualifying group.

Cahill is famous for scoring spectacular headers after breaking clear of defenders, hence his nickname, "the invisible man." At 5'10" (1.78m) he is smaller than most of his markers but possesses remarkable spring and power. He is also expert at timing late runs.

AUSTRALIA AT THE FIFA WORLD CUP™

1930–62	did not enter
1966	did not qualify
1970	did not qualify
1974	1st round
1978	did not qualify
1982	did not qualify
1986	did not qualify
1990	did not qualify
1994	did not qualify
1998	did not qualify
2002	did not qualify
2006	2nd round

Their Dutch coach Pim Verbeek was criticised early on in the campaign for cautious tactics which often featured two holding midfielders. But he was able to retort that Australia achieved their goal, adding: "We always attack with a minimum of five players."

Defence was their undoubted strength. The Socceroos conceded only one goal in those eight games. Skipper Lucas Neill marshalled the back line; Blackburn's Vince Grella and ex-PSV Eindhoven star Jason Culina stood with him.

Neill says: "Pim set the benchmark, which was to qualify and do it a certain way. He's made us very focused and hard to beat."

The Everton full back adds: "We started with a win in Uzbekistan which was a massive three points. Then we won in Bahrain, which we probably didn't deserve. That set us up and we were delighted with the way our campaign went."

Yet Palermo midfielder Mark Bresciano's 93rd-minute winner in Bahrain was one of only 12 goals the Aussies scored. They have lacked a prolific striker since 2006 captain

ONES TO WATCH

MARK SCHWARZER
Born: October 6, 1972
Club: Fulham (England)

Schwarzer became a national hero with two penalty saves against Uruguay which sent Australia to the 2006 finals. He commands his penalty area, has a fine understanding with his defenders and can make match-turning saves – as he has proved through his consistent form in the Premier League. Schwarzer also has a particular superstition: he has worn the same shinpads since his professional debut.

BRETT EMERTON
Born: February 22, 1979
Club: Blackburn Rovers (England)

Emerton's return to the squad – for the friendly against Holland in October – delighted manager Pim Verbeek. The Blackburn star suffered a cruciate ligament injury in January 2009 and needed surgery. He is fast, direct and can double up at right midfield or wing back. He has scored a number of valuable goals, including two against Qatar in Australia's 4-0 home qualifying win.

Mark Viduka quit the international scene. Viduka, who has struggled with injury, pulled out of the qualifiers against Bahrain, Qatar and Japan to "consider his future".

The giant Josh Kennedy, of Japanese club Grampus Eight, could step up as Australia's spearhead after scoring in home wins over Qatar and Uzbekistan. Verbeek will expect Cahill, Kewell

and Blackburn's Brett Emerton to add goals from midfield.

Australia have optimistically targeted a quarter-final place. Neill says: "We won't be the surprise package this time. But we still have the core of the team from 2006 and we have a lot more experience. Anything is possible if we can get through the group stage."

SERBIA

WHITE EAGLES

South Africa 2010 offers Raddy Antic and his Serbia squad the chance to re-establish themselves as the leading football nation reborn out of the old Yugoslavia, ahead of bitter rivals Croatia.

They also have the chance to burnish their country's image – and erase the memory of their appearance at Germany 2006. Then – competing as Serbia & Montenegro – they were eliminated at the group stage after defeats by Holland and Ivory Coast and a 6-0 hammering by Argentina.

The split between Serbia and Montenegro was confirmed on June 28, 2006. So this will be the first time

Serbia has entered the finals as an independent state. They were still known as Yugoslavia when they lost 2-1 to Holland in the last 16 at France 98 (while the Croats reached the semi-finals). Antic is setting no targets, but he says: "Even in the group, I was thinking about a lot more than qualification."

Serbian morale was sinking when Antic ended a four-year retirement to take over the squad in 2008. They had failed to qualify for Euro 2008 (Croatia reached the quarter-finals) and their under-23 squad had flopped at the Beijing Olympics.

Yet Serbia eased past favourites France to top European qualifying Group Seven, while Croatia were knocked out, finishing behind England and Ukraine in Group Six.

Serbia lost in Paris and drew 1-1 with

the French in Belgrade but their away wins in Austria and Romania proved crucial. France lost in Vienna and drew both games against Romania.

Milos Krasic, Milan Jovanovic and Ivan Obradovic scored in the first 24 minutes as Serbia beat Austria 3-1. Jovanovic, an own goal and a strike by Chelsea defender Branislav Ivanovic clinched a 3-2 win over Romania.

Serbia qualified with a game to spare, after routing the Romanians 5-0. Skipper Dejan Stankovic said: "We've raised the bar for ourselves now. After the second goal, we were really flying."

Antic was a respected club coach in Spain for 16 years. He says: "I cannot compare the jobs. But I took on the challenge with relish and I think I have arrived now that we are going to the FIFA World Cup™ finals."

COACH

RADOMIR "RADDY" ANTIC

Serbia's impressive qualification was a triumph for Antic, who ended a four-year exile from the game to take charge. The one-time midfielder took over after Miroslav Dukic was sacked following Serbia's poor performance at the 2008 Olympics. His first move was to bring in his long-time assistant Resad Kunovac.

This was Antic's first national team job after years in the club game. But the circumstances suited him. He was able to do the job for a while continuing to live at his main home in Spain.

The former Zaragoza defender is something of a legend there. He is the only man who has coached Real Madrid and their two greatest rivals, Barcelona and Atletico Madrid.

Although making their finals debut as an independent state, Serbia are a team to be respected.

STAR MAN

DEJAN STANKOVIC
Born: September 11, 1978
Club: Internazionale (Italy)

Stankovic is Serbia's captain and leader on the pitch. The defensive central midfielder is a battle-hardened veteran of 12 seasons so far at the top of Serie A, and more than 80 appearances with the national team.

A tough tackler and a clever strategist, Stankovic is capable of splitting opponents with a single through ball. He is also Serbia's dead ball expert, with a powerful shot.

He made his international debut in 1998 and knows Serbia have yet to fulfil their potential in international tournaments. He says: "We've had an impressive run to the finals and we've raised expectations so we don't want to let the fans down."

SERBIA AT THE FIFA WORLD CUP™

(as Yugoslavia)	
1930	semi-finals
1934	did not qualify
1938	did not qualify
1950	1st round
1954	quarter-finals
1958	quarter-finals
1962	4th place
1966	did not qualify
1970	did not qualify
1974	2nd round
1978	did not qualify
1982	1st round
1986	did not qualify
1990	did not qualify
1994	did not qualify
1998	2nd round
2002	did not qualify
(as Serbia & Montenegro)	
2006	1st round

ONES TO WATCH

NEMANJA VIDIC
Born: October 21, 1981
Club: Manchester United (England)

Centre back Vidic is a key figure for club and country. He is another grizzled veteran after winning the Champions League and three Premiership titles with United. He is a tough, mobile stopper whose style is to attack the ball. Vidic is strong in the air and poses a serious threat at dead ball moves.

MILAN JOVANOVIC
Born: April 18, 1981
Club: Standard Liege (Belgium)

Jovanovic led Serbia's scorers with five goals in qualifying. He was barely known to many Serb fans when coach Javier Clemente gave him an international debut in 2007. But he has been a prolific scorer since he arrived at Liege in 2006 and was voted Belgium's Player of the Year in 2008. He likes to operate as a second striker and arrive late in the box.

Yet his method was to create almost a club spirit within the Serbian group. He says: "We achieved a really positive atmosphere with confidence high. We've genuinely turned into a big family."

He adds: "We've also tried to build a team with a winning mentality, able to impose their authority on the pitch."

Serbia lost only two qualifiers, including a meaningless last game in Lithuania. Centre back Nemanja Vidic is

excited by their prospects. He says: "This group can play together for another four or five years. We have the qualities to play attractive, attacking football."

Antic was able to name virtually the same squad for several qualifiers. He persuaded goalkeeper Vladimir Stojkovic to join Spanish club Getafe, on loan from Sporting Lisbon, to gain regular football. He wishes Ivanovic played more often for Chelsea. Yet Ivanovic netted three

times in the group and has built a fine understanding with Vidic. Young Borussia Dortmund defender Neven Subotic provides cover. He was born in Banja Luka (now Bosnia) and grew up in the United States but chose Serbia because of his Serb parents. Internazionale star Stankovic organises the midfield while the tall Nenad Milijas breaks forward. CSKA Moscow winger Krasic offers trickery on the right. Giant 2.03m (6ft 8in) Racing Santander forward Nikola Zigic spearheads the attack. He scored three times in qualification. Standard Liege's Jovanovic darts in behind him. If Serbia need fresh legs, they can call on Vidic's young United colleague Zoran Tosic.

But the Serbs are trying to do more than win matches in South Africa. Vidic is aware of his country's image after the 1990s Balkan conflicts. He says: "As sportsmen, I believe we are changing perceptions of our country. That's something I take very seriously."

GHANA

BLACK STARS

Ghana defender John Mensah is convinced that an African team will make a big impact on the first FIFA World Cup™ finals held in Africa. He hopes it will be the Black Stars.

The Lyon defender, who has been on loan at Sunderland, says: "I think an African side could be sensational. People are talking about Ivory Coast – but maybe it could be us."

Ghana made a big impression in their first finals appearance in 2006. After losing to eventual champions Italy in their opening game, they shocked the Czech Republic 2-0, then beat the United States 2-1 to reach the last 16 – where they were eliminated by Brazil.

Ghana were African champions in 1963, 1965, 1978 and 1982. But they wanted to show that they were more than just a regional power. So reaching South Africa 2010 became a crusade for the squad and coach Milovan Rajevac.

They became the first African nation to qualify, with a 2-0 home win over Sudan in Accra on September 6.

Rajevac said: "We had to be there, to show that our appearance in 2006 was not just an accident. To reach the finals for a second time is very significant. The squad was very hungry for this. We have a lot of talent and they all want to play for the jersey."

Midfield star Michael Essien adds: "This means so much to us and to the people of Ghana. Now we have to go on."

Mensah, Fulham full back John Pantsil, plus the formidable midfield trio of Michael Essien, Sulley Muntari and skipper Stephen Appiah all played in Germany. So did strikers Matthew Amoah, Eric Addo and Gyan Asamoah. So the Ghanaians will not lack experience.

Midfield is Ghana's strength. Essien plays with more freedom for his country than he does for Chelsea. That is because Ghana have their own midfield anchor in Anthony Annan.

COACH

MILOVAN RAJEVAC

Rajevac made a brave move when he took charge of Ghana in August 2008. It was his first overseas job. He had spent all his career in the former Yugoslavia and the new Serbia. He was a defender for Borac Cacak and Red Star Belgrade, then coached Red Star, Vojvodina and Borac. He was quickly subjected to criticism in his new role. Early losses – including FIFA World Cup™ qualifying defeats in Gabon and Libya – left him vulnerable. Simultaneously, the local media pointed up his failure to speak English.

But he won over the players, kept a settled side and achieved results when it mattered, in the second qualifying phase. He also waived a signing-on fee when he took over as Ghana coach. But he made sure he had a FIFA World Cup™ qualifying bonus in his contract which has earned him around $500,000.

With a number of their players lining up for top European sides, Ghana will be a team to fear.

STAR MAN

MICHAEL ESSIEN
Born: December 3, 1982
Club: Chelsea (England)

Michael Essien has become the poster boy of Ghanaian football. Local fans take huge pride in his achievements – for the national team, and for Chelsea as they chase Premiership and Champions League glory. Chelsea paid Lyon £24.5million to sign him, a record for an African player. He has given them vibrant energy, dynamism, versatility and the ability to score from outside the box.

Those are the qualities he brings to the Ghana team. His presence lifts the players around him. As Rajevac's assistant Kwesi Appiah said: "He's like a gift from God."

If Essien can control his impulse to make rash challenges – and collect yellow cards – he could be a major influence at the 2010 finals.

GHANA AT THE FIFA WORLD CUP™

1930–54	did not exist
1958	not eligible
1962	did not qualify
1966	did not enter
1970	did not enter
1974	did not qualify
1978	did not qualify
1982	did not enter
1986	did not qualify
1990	did not qualify
1994	did not qualify
1998	did not qualify
2002	did not qualify
2006	2nd round

Former national coach Claude Le Roy has already compared Annan to Claude Makelele. Annan says: "Michael is a unique player, powerful, strong and elegant. I stay behind and cover him. I let him do his things because he's an amazing player."

Chelsea's Essien is the driving force. He combines power with speed, skill and the ability to net vital goals – like the second against Sudan which saw Ghana through to the finals.

Inter's Muntari adds poise as well as a combative presence. Appiah has continued to shine for the national team despite a series of knee injuries which led to his controversial departure from Turkish side Fenerbahce of Istanbul.

Ghana's 2-0 win over Sudan was the culmination of a hard slog. They struggled through an opening group to reach the final stages, losing to Libya and Gabon. Only a 3-2 win in Lesotho saw them through.

Essien was hampered by injury in that competition. He was restored for the final group stage, when away wins in Mali and Sudan put Ghana in command.

ONES TO WATCH

SULLEY MUNTARI
Born: August 27, 1984
Club: Internazionale (Italy)

Muntari combines strength with craft. He has an eye for goal too, as he showed with the opener in Ghana's decisive 2-0 win over Sudan. He can pick a pass and he can run from box to box. The question mark remains over his disciplinary record. He was sent off three times for Udinese in 2006-7. He is one of Ghana's most important players so they want him to stay on the pitch.

MATTHEW AMOAH
Born: October 24, 1980
Club: NAC Breda (Holland)

Matthew Amoah has a happy habit of scoring vital goals for his country. Three in consecutive matches propelled Ghana to the 2006 finals. His double against Sudan in Omdurman virtually clinched their place this time. Amoah has proved his consistency at the top of the Dutch league too, netting more than 100 goals since joining Vitesse Arnhem in 1998.

Their key victory was the 2-0 success in Sudan. Amoah, who also scored in the win in Mali, netted both goals.

Rajevac, with typical thoroughness, had prepared for the trip to Omdurman by taking the team to a training camp in Naivasha, Kenya, which replicated the hot and sticky conditions the Ghanaians would face.

But, three days after qualification,

Ghana received a warning. They led 3-1 against Japan in a friendly in Utrecht (with two goals from Asamoah, the other scored by Amoah) – then conceded three in 13 minutes to lose 4-3. Rajevac made a series of substitutions which weakened his team's cohesion. He will not make the same mistake at the FIFA World Cup™ finals.

NETHERLANDS

ORANJE

Will it be different this time? That is the question the Dutch always ask before the finals of a major championship.

The Netherlands footballing history since 1974 is littered with instances of unfulfilled potential. The greatest Holland team of all, led by their greatest player, Johan Cruyff, lost the 1974 FIFA World Cup™ Final to West Germany. Four years later, the Dutch lost the Final in extra time to hosts Argentina. Cruyff had refused to join the squad, preferring to spend time at home with his wife and young family.

In 1998, they lost their semi-final against Brazil in a penalty shoot-out. They failed even to qualify for the 2002 finals after losing 1-0 to a 10-man Republic of Ireland side in Dublin.

They lost European Championship semi-finals on penalties to Denmark in 1992 and to 10-man Italy, in Rotterdam, at Euro 2000. Arguments in the dressing room are also almost obligatory with Holland squads. As 1974 midfield general Wim van Hanegem says: "We think there's a problem if we don't have a problem!"

Only at Euro 88 – when coach Rinus Michels imposed discipline on a team featuring Ruud Gullit, Frank Rijkaard, Ronald Koeman and Marco Van Basten – have the Dutch fulfilled their huge potential.

That is the task facing coach Bert Van Marwijk in South Africa. Holland's 2-1 win in Iceland on June 6, 2009 made them the first European side to qualify. They won all eight group games – against Iceland, Norway, Macedonia and Scotland – with a goal difference of 17-2.

Van Marwijk believes he has instilled organisation and a ruthless mentality. Holland's defensive record has been impressive. His decision to recall his son-in-law, Mark Van Bommel, as midfield anchor has been vindicated by results. Nigel De Jong can supplement Van Bommel if the

COACH

BERT VAN MARWIJK

Bert Van Marwijk's squad have raised expectations throughout Holland with their 100 per cent qualification record. Now the former Feyenoord coach has to deliver in South Africa. The Dutch federation (KNVB) is hoping for a place in the last four at least.

Van Marwijk, who steered Feyenoord to the UEFA Cup in 2002, has subtly changed the Dutch approach since succeeding Marco van Basten. He has emphasised defensive discipline and the importance of a compact unit, to complement Holland's traditional flair.

He is not afraid to make controversial decisions and Holland's early qualification has given him plenty of time to experiment.

Impressive in qualifying – could 2010 see the Netherlands go one better than in 1974 and 1978?

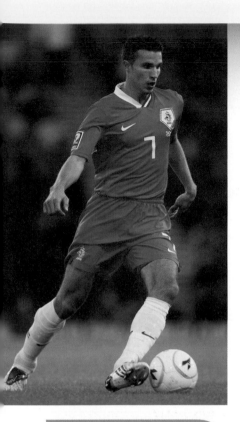

STAR MAN

ROBIN VAN PERSIE

Born: August 6, 1983
Club: Arsenal (England)

Van Persie's strained relationship with coach Van Marwijk seems to have reached a truce. He left Feyenoord for Arsenal after a series of clashes with Van Marwijk, who once demoted him to reserve status. Van Persie's talent is undoubted. His left foot is one of the most potent weapons in international football. He has immense skill on the ball and a fizzing finish to match. He brings versatility too. He can play as a lead striker – as he has recently for Arsenal and Holland – he can operate behind a front man, or attack from the flanks. Once, Van Persie's temperament was a problem. Now, though, it is his injury record. He faces a race against time to beat an ankle injury and recover in time to shine at the finals.

NETHERLANDS AT THE FIFA WORLD CUP™

1930	did not enter
1934	1st round
1938	1st round
1950	did not enter
1954	did not enter
1958	did not qualify
1962	did not qualify
1966	did not qualify
1970	did not qualify
1974	runners-up
1978	runners-up
1982	did not qualify
1986	did not qualify
1990	2nd round
1994	quarter-finals
1998	4th place
2002	did not qualify
2006	2nd round

ONES TO WATCH

WESLEY SNEIJDER
Born: June 9, 1984
Club: Internazionale (Italy)

The two-footed Sneijder is Holland's creative force in midfield. He is quick, strong, sees passes early and can deliver them over any distance. He is the team's dead ball expert. He also has a point to prove after being displaced from Real Madrid by Kaka's summer arrival. What better stage than the FIFA World Cup™ finals?

ARJEN ROBBEN
Born: January 23, 1984
Club: Bayern Munich (Germany)

Robben has a point to prove after Real Madrid sold him to Bayern Munich in August 2009 to make way for Cristiano Ronaldo. The left-footed winger can dribble defenders to distraction and boasts a healthy scoring record. But Van Marwijk will have to stop him indulging in over-elaboration.

Holland coach goes for containment. Rafael Van der Vaart and Wesley Sneijder offer creativity. Dirk Kuyt and the mercurial Arjen Robben work the flanks with Robin Van Persie or Klaas-Jan Huntelaar as a lone striker.

Meanwhile, Ruud Van Nistelrooy has come out of international retirement and hopes to add to his 33 Holland goals at the finals.

No wonder Van Marwijk is confident, with such talent available. But he knows the Dutch had an easy ride in qualifying. They always had something in reserve – as shown by Eljerio Elia's seemingly inevitable winner in Glasgow after Kenny Miller and Craig Brown had threatened for Scotland.

Skipper Gio van Bronckhorst knows the challenge. The ex-Arsenal left back says: "At the biggest tournament, you have to be on top form all the time. We learned that at Euro 2008. We played really well, then had one bad spell against Russia and were knocked out."

Andre Oijer and Frank de Boer were both on the losing side in the 1998 semi-final. Both detect a mental toughness in Van Marwijk's squad.

Veteran defender Oijer says: "Winning becomes a habit. Expecting to win is a big factor for us. It was important for us to keep that going in the last qualifier, against Scotland."

De Boer, now Van Marwijk's assistant, says: "We have a mission and that is to be world champions. If we can maintain the form and attitude we've shown so far, then we can beat anybody. We have a strong team, and, if you look at our bench, it's very encouraging."

Oijer adds: "Is there more to come from us? We'll see that at the finals. That's the real test. We've set a standard by our performances in qualifying. Can we win? If we play to our maximum – and have a bit of luck this time – I think that's possible."

DENMARK

DANISH DYNAMITE

In 1986 Morten Olsen captained the Danish side which shone so brilliantly. Now the long-serving coach leads his squad into the 2010 FIFA World Cup™ full of confidence after beating favourites Portugal to the top spot in qualifying.

They did so despite the enforced retirement of their star centre back, Aston Villa's Martin Laursen, because of persistent knee injuries.

Olsen says: "I played for Denmark for 19 years and now I've been coach for 10. So I've devoted almost half my life to the national team and I feel we have a point to prove after failing to qualify for Germany 2006 and Euro 2008."

An incredible victory in Portugal and two wins over old rivals Sweden gave the unfancied Danes the edge. They entered the campaign nicknamed "Landshold X" ("National team X") because they supposedly lacked stars. Yet they qualified with a game to spare by beating the Swedes 1-0 in Copenhagen.

Denmark's 3-2 win in Lisbon showed their resilience. Arsenal forward Nicklas Bendtner equalised Nani's opening goal with seven minutes left. Deco restored Portugal's lead from the penalty spot, but Christian Poulsen levelled in the 88th minute and Daniel Jensen grabbed the winner in the second minute of stoppage time.

That gave Denmark an early advantage over the favourites, which they reinforced with a 1-1 home draw.

Thomas Kahlenberg's goal clinched victory in Sweden. Jakob Poulsen's strike saw off the Swedes in Copenhagen, when the visitors had two goals disallowed. Veteran forward Jon Dahl Tomasson says: "Over the past 25 years, our fans have become used to us competing at the major tournaments. So qualifying this time was so important."

Tomasson says his best memories were of the 2002 finals when Olsen's Denmark topped their group and beat 1998 champions France. They lost 3-0 to England in the last 16. Four years earlier they had reached the quarter-finals, losing 3-2 to Brazil.

The Danes' greatest moment came when they shocked favourites Germany 2-0 to win the 1992 European Championship final.

But Tomasson reckons Denmark's first-ever FIFA World Cup™ finals appearance, in 1986, marked a turning point in their

COACH

MORTEN OLSEN

Defender Olsen was the first Danish player to reach 100 caps. He was Denmark's Player of the Year in 1983 and 1986, though he played virtually all his career in Belgium (Cercle Brugge, RWD Molenbeek and Anderlecht) and West Germany (FC Koln). He was appointed Denmark coach in 2000.

Only Olsen's 1986 FIFA World Cup™ coach Sepp Piontek has served longer in the modern era. After leaving FC Koln, he was out of football for two years before Ajax hired him in 1997. Olsen steered them to a Dutch league and cup double. He had previously led Brondby to two Danish titles and the 1991 UEFA Cup semi-finals.

The Denmark team has an excellent spine, and includes several promising young players.

STAR MAN

CHRISTIAN POULSEN
Born: February 28, 1980
Club: Juventus (Italy)

The combative Poulsen is a key man in Denmark's set-up. He is their midfield organiser, defensive protector and, at times, a tenacious man marker. He occasionally darts forward to score too, as he showed in the 3-2 away win over Portugal. He has proved himself at the highest levels of European football and was the first man to be voted Denmark's Player of the Year in successive seasons (2005 and 2006). But lack of self-discipline has often been his blind spot. He collected two yellow cards in three appearances at the 2002 FIFA World Cup™ finals, thus earning a ban. He was also red-carded for punching Sweden's Markus Rosenberg in the Euro 2008 qualifier and received a three-match suspension.

DENMARK AT THE FIFA WORLD CUP™

1930	did not enter
1934	did not enter
1938	did not enter
1950	did not enter
1954	did not enter
1958	did not qualify
1962	did not enter
1966	did not qualify
1970	did not qualify
1974	did not qualify
1978	did not qualify
1982	did not qualify
1986	2nd round
1990	did not qualify
1994	did not qualify
1998	quarter-finals
2002	2nd round
2006	did not qualify

ONES TO WATCH

THOMAS SORENSEN
Born: June 12, 1976
Club: Stoke City (England)

Goalkeeper Sorensen has impressively filled the almost impossible role of succeeding Denmark's most capped player, Peter Schmeichel. He has been a Premiership regular for more than a decade and has won more than 80 caps. He is a brilliant shot stopper, but occasionally liable to a high profile blunder, such as his own goal against England in 2002.

NICKLAS BENDTNER
Born: January 16, 1988
Club: Arsenal (England)

Bendtner established himself as Denmark's leading striker during the qualifiers. He is tall (6ft 4in), strong in the air and surprisingly mobile for his size. He can spearhead the Danish attack, or operate from the right where Arsenal use him. He has grown in confidence through starting regularly since Emmanuel Adebayor's departure, and Denmark have reaped the benefit.

He adds: "We have a good group of players right now and several promising younger guys, like Bendtner and Simon Kjaer."

Palermo's Kjaer and Daniel Agger of Liverpool have since formed a formidable centre back partnership, ahead of battle-hardened goalkeeper Thomas Sorensen. Blackburn full back Lars Jacobsen is another familiar figure.

Denmark boast a core of huge experience. Fiorentina midfielder Martin Jorgensen is a veteran of 1998 and 2002. Feyenoord's Tomasson netted four of Denmark's five goals in 2002; Ajax winger Dennis Rommedahl got the other. Tough-tackling Christian Poulsen was suspended when the Danes lost to England in 2002. The Juventus star will shield the back four in South Africa.

The Danes will look to Bendtner and Duisburg's Soren Larsen for goals. Larsen led their qualifying scorers with five, all against Malta and Albania. Bendtner contributed three – but netted in both games against Portugal.

history. A squad featuring Jesper Olsen, Michael Laudrup, Preben Elkjaer, Soren Lerby and Frank Arnesen sailed through their group. They beat Scotland 1-0, Uruguay 6-1 and West Germany 2-0. But midfield general Arnesen was sent off against the Germans and missed the last-16 game against Spain. The Danes charged forward after Emiliano Butragueno gave Spain a second-half lead. They were picked off by counter attacks and Butragueno scored four as Spain won 5-1.

Yet Tomasson says: "That tournament has gone down in our history. It showed we could compete against the world and play some great football."

Coach Olsen agrees. He says: "That was a special generation of players – and so many of us were playing for some of Europe's best clubs. With a bit of luck, we could have gone a lot further."

JAPAN

BLUE SAMURAI

Japan will enter the FIFA World Cup™ finals for the fourth time in a row in 2010 – with a burden on their shoulders because of coach Takeshi Okada's ambition.

He has targeted a semi-final spot as Japan's objective. After they clinched qualification in Uzbekistan, the players chanted: "We'll surprise the world," before spraying Okada with champagne.

The coach then outlined his vision for South Africa 2010. Skipper Yuji Nakamura says Okada's aim is "a huge flag for one person to carry." He adds: "We all have to be together to support it."

Japan were Asian champions in 2000 and 2004. But they found the step up to the FIFA World Cup™ finals hard to make, even on home ground in 2002 when they fell in the second round. Only one Asian team has ever reached the semi-finals – South Korea, when they co-hosted the tournament with Japan in 2002.

Okada's ambition was quickly questioned when Japan crashed 3-0 to Holland in Enschede. They recovered from a 3-1 deficit to beat Ghana 4-3 in Utrecht a few days later. But critics considered the coach's dream unrealistic.

Okada believes that meeting 2010 contenders is vital if his side are to improve before the finals. He says: "We have to do this to raise our level." Midfield star Shunsuke Nakamura agrees. He says: "We'll only find more quality by playing stronger countries."

So Okada is pleased that Nakamura joined Spanish club Espanyol. "Playing in such a strong competition as La Liga will offer many positives for him."

Yet the size of Japan's task is illustrated by a simple statistic. They have never won a finals match outside their own country. Okada was in charge when they lost to Argentina, Croatia and Jamaica in the group stage at France 1998. Eight years later, Zico's side lost 3-1 to Australia, drew 0-0 with Croatia, then crashed 4-1 to

COACH

TAKESHI OKADA

Okada is back at the FIFA World Cup™ finals 12 years after he steered Japan to their first-ever finals appearance at France 98. He salvaged their qualifying campaign after replacing Shu Kamo the previous year. But Japan were eliminated at the group stage after losing all three matches and Okada was succeeded by Philippe Troussier.

Okada returned to take over the national team in December 2007. He stepped in after previous coach Ivica Osim suffered a stroke and guided them comfortably to their fourth consecutive finals.

In between his spells with the national team, the former Japan defender coached Yokohama F Marinos to championships in 2003 and 2004 and was named Manager of the Year in successive seasons. Okada put pressure on himself when he said Japan's 2010 target was a semi-final place.

This is the fourth time in succession that Japan have qualified. Can they go beyond the second round?

STAR MAN

SHUNSUKE NAKAMURA
Born: June 24, 1978
Club: Espanyol (Spain)

Nakamura is the creative hub of Japan's midfield. He has been the most successful Japanese footballing export since Hidetoshi Nakata, the midfield general he succeeded in the national team.

He has an eye for an opening, an accurate left foot and the ability to score with dipping free kicks.

Nakamura helped Japan win the Asian Cup in 2000 and again in 2004 when he was voted Player of the Tournament. But his style did not fit in with coach Philippe Troussier's tactics so he missed out on the 2002 FIFA World Cup™ finals on home soil.

New coach Zico quickly restored him to the side. Nakamura gave Japan the lead against Australia at Germany 2006, before they succumbed 3-1. He has won more than 90 caps.

JAPAN AT THE FIFA WORLD CUP™

1930–50	did not enter
1954	did not qualify
1958	did not enter
1962	did not qualify
1966	did not enter
1970–94	did not qualify
1998	1st round
2002	2nd round
2006	1st round

Brazil in the group games in Germany.

Japan scored their only wins – 1-0 against Russia and 2-0 over Tunisia – when they were co-hosts in 2002. They went out 1-0 to Turkey in the last 16.

On the road to South Africa, Okada's side reached the final group phase with ease, then qualified comfortably, behind Australia. Their 1-0 win in Uzbekistan carried them through with two games to spare. But they scored only 11 goals in their eight qualifiers. Shinjo Okazaki hit the winner in Tashkent but that was his only strike. Partner Keiji Tamada netted twice; Yoshito Okubo did not score at all. The Catania striker Takayuki Morimoto offers Okada another option, but injuries and club commitments have limited his chances.

The coach's experiments will be confined to friendlies. Japan must qualify for the 2011 Asian Cup finals. Okada had intended to use only J.League players for that competition but a 1-0 defeat in Bahrain forced him to call up his Europe-based stars.

Wolfsburg's Makoto Hasebe, Venlo's Keisuke Honda and Saint-Etienne winger Daisuke Matsui offer

ONES TO WATCH

JUNICHI INAMOTO
Born: September 18, 1979
Club: Rennes (France)

Inamoto is a tough-tackling midfielder, expected to play a holding role in South Africa. He made his debut against Mexico in February 2000 and has won more than 70 caps. He was a rising star of the Japan side who won the Asian Cup in 2000 and scored twice in the 2002 FIFA World Cup™ finals. He also played in the 2006 finals.

YUJI NAKAZAWA
Born: February 25, 1978
Club: Yokohama F Marinos (Japan)

Centre back and skipper Nakazawa trained with the Brazilian club America Mineiro for a year before returning to Japan with Verdy Kawasaki. He played in Japan's Asian Cup-winning sides of 2000 and 2004, but was left out of the 2002 FIFA World Cup™ squad. He retired from international football after the 2006 finals. Former coach Ivan Osim persuaded him to rejoin the squad in March 2007.

experience in midfield, to complement Nakamura and his sidekick, Yasuhito Endo, from Gamba Osaka. Midfield is Japan's strongest area.

Okada is looking at FC Tokyo's Naohiro Ishikawa as cover for injury-prone Matsui. Tough-tackling Junichi Inamoto will play in front of the back four.

Captain Yuji Nakazawa and Marcus Tulio Tanaka anchor the defence.

Nakazawa is a reliable stopper, while Tanaka offers other options. He was born in Sao Paulo to a Brazilian-Japanese father and moved to Japan when he was 15. He can operate as a conventional centre back, a sweeper behind Nakazawa, or as a defensive midfielder. He also has a knack of chipping in with goals from dead ball moves, including two in the qualifiers.

CAMEROON

INDOMITABLE LIONS

Cameroon have been ground-breakers for African football. At Italy 1990, legendary striker Roger Milla's team upset holders Argentina 1-0 and became the first African side to reach the FIFA World Cup™ quarter-finals.

Former coach Otto Pfister, who took Cameroon to the 2008 African Nations Cup final, believes an African side can seriously challenge for the 2010 FIFA World Cup™. He says: "African football has come on in leaps and bounds. The top sides have definitely caught up with the rest of the world.

"I think an African team has a realistic chance of reaching the semi-finals in 2010. Cameroon, Nigeria and Ivory Coast are probably the strongest African sides and the familiar surroundings and atmosphere will favour them."

But Pfister will not lead Cameroon's challenge. He quit – and was succeeded by Paul Le Guen – after a shock defeat by Togo and a home draw against Morocco left the "Indomitable Lions" in deep trouble early in the final qualifiers. He says: "If you're Cameroon coach, you expect to be under constant pressure."

Le Guen had a history of bringing through African talent in his first coaching job at French side Rennes. He seems revitalised with Cameroon after bad experiences at Rangers in Scotland and again in France with Paris Saint-Germain.

He led Cameroon to qualification with four straight wins, starting with a 2-0 victory away to their toughest group rivals, Gabon. Achille Emana and Samuel Eto'o scored in the space of two minutes.

Eto'o, a Champions League-winner with Barcelona, netted decisive goals against Gabon and against Morocco in the final qualifier in Fes, where Achille Webo gave Cameroon an early lead and Eto'o's strike made sure they topped the group.

Eto'o also set up a spectacular second goal in the 3-0 home win over Togo, dribbling past four defenders before sliding a pass for Jean Makoun to tuck away.

Former Cameroon forward Patrick Mboma, Le Guen's colleague at PS-G in the 1990s, says: "Paul is ambitious and he has the talent to succeed. The ingredients are there. Cameroon has a core of very good players. Paul doesn't talk much to the media but he's a strong personality

COACH

PAUL LE GUEN

Le Guen has resurrected his coaching career with Cameroon, transforming their qualifying campaign after a poor start. He made his name at Rennes, developing young stars from Africa such as Shabani Nonda and El-Hadji Diouf. He later steered Lyon to three successive French titles and the Champions League quarter-finals. He has never been afraid to make controversial decisions – which led him to a speedy exit after seven months at Rangers. He later rescued his old club PS-G from relegation – but was sacked because of inconsistent league form, despite their cup successes. He took over the Cameroon team in July 2009, initially on a short-term contract, and restored a work ethic to a jaded squad.

In reaching the quarter-finals in 1990, Cameroon are Africa's highest achievers at the FIFA World Cup™.

STAR MAN

SAMUEL ETO'O
Born: March 10, 1981
Club: Internazionale (Italy)

Skipper Eto'o is one of the greats of African football. The powerful striker has been voted African Player of the Year three times and is the leading scorer in African Nations Cup history. This will be his third appearance at the FIFA World Cup™ finals. He was 17 when he made his debut during France 98. He shot to fame when Cameroon won gold at the Sydney 2000 Olympic football tournament. He has since helped Barcelona win the European Cup twice and netted more than 100 league goals during his time with them. He joined Internazionale in the summer of 2009, in a part-exchange for Zlatan Ibrahimovic. He has scored more than 40 goals for Cameroon.

CAMEROON AT THE FIFA WORLD CUP™

1930–58	did not exist
1962	did not enter
1966	withdrew
1970	did not qualify
1974	did not qualify
1978	did not qualify
1982	1st round
1986	did not qualify
1990	quarter-finals
1994	1st round
1998	1st round
2002	1st round
2006	did not qualify

ONES TO WATCH

IDRISS KAMENI
Born: February 18, 1984
Club: Espanyol (Spain)

The acrobatic goalkeeper became the youngest footballer to win an Olympic gold medal when, at just 16, he starred in Cameroon's victory at Sydney 2000. He joined Le Havre soon after but started only three times for them. He moved to Espanyol in 2004 and quickly became their first-choice keeper. He has won more than 50 Cameroon caps.

ALEX SONG
Born: September 9, 1987
Club: Arsenal (England)

Song established himself in the Bastia side as a 17-year-old. He was spotted by Arsene Wenger and is now a trusted defensive midfielder for Arsenal and his country. He made his international debut as a sub against Egypt in the 2008 African Nations Cup finals, joining his uncle Rigobert in the Cameroon line-up. He acknowledges Rigobert as a big influence on his development, after Alex's father died when he was three.

and will not take any nonsense."

Le Guen quickly made two important decisions. The first was to transfer the captaincy from veteran defender Rigobert Song to Eto'o. The second was to recall Mallorca striker Webo. Both delivered for him.

He also put his trust in Alex Song to patrol the space in front of the back four. The Arsenal anchor has become a crucial figure in Le Guen's formation.

Webo says: "At the beginning of the group, we'd become lackadaisical. We needed to work harder. We couldn't just turn up and win because we were Cameroon. We learned that lesson. The win over Gabon was a turning point."

This will be Cameroon's sixth appearance in the finals – a record for an African country. They have missed out only once since 1990 – Pierre Wome's penalty miss against Egypt costing them a place at Germany 2006.

Cameroon were eliminated at the group stage in 1994, 1998 and 2002. But they won the Olympic football gold in 2000 and remain a major power in Africa. Cameroon have also produced such stars as Rigobert Song, midfielder Marc-Vivien Foe, goalkeeper Jacques Songo'o and Eto'o.

Rigobert Song, who will be 34 during the finals, remains a commanding figure at the back. Former Real Madrid and Chelsea midfielder Geremi adds more experience.

Goalkeeper Idriss Kameni is another battle-hardened veteran and one of Africa's best, while defenders Sebastien Bassong and Benoit Assou-Ekotto are both Premiership regulars and Eto'o, Makoun and Webo provide the attacking threat, supported by Betis midfielder Emana. Alex Song, defender Nicolas Nkoulou and midfielder Joel Nguemo add youth to the side. But they know their country's traditions. Nguemo says: "He [Roger Milla] is a hero to all the young footballers in our country. He and his team-mates set the standard for us."

ITALY

AZZURRI

FIFA World Cup™ holders Italy qualified comfortably for South Africa but jaded performances, coupled with a disastrous FIFA Confederations Cup campaign, raised questions along the way about Marcello Lippi's ageing squad.

Lippi himself has remained relaxed. He says: "We've never shone in qualifying. We're a team for the finals. In those five or six weeks, everything will be different."

Lippi resisted the temptation to add "just like in 2006" when he masterminded Italy's fourth FIFA World Cup™ triumph. He "retired" after victory over France in the Final. But he bowed to popular pressure to return for the qualifiers. He replaced Roberto Donadoni whose side were eliminated by Spain in the Euro 2008 quarter-finals.

He has retained the core of the 2006 team. FIFA World Cup™ winners Gianluigi Buffon, Gianluca Zambrotta, Fabio Grosso, Daniele De Rossi, Andrea Pirlo, Mauro Camoranesi and Vincenzo Iaquinta all started against the Republic of Ireland when Italy sealed qualification. Midfield hardman Rino Gattuso came on as a substitute, while Fabio Cannavaro was suspended. Alberto Gilardino, who scored Italy's late equaliser, was another survivor from 2006, though he did not play in the final.

Four days later, Lippi fielded his back-up squad against Cyprus in Italy's final game. The fans' frustration boiled over as Cyprus took a 2-0 lead. Gilardino replied with a hat-trick, including a stoppage-time winner. But the coach was furious with the supporters. He claimed that they "lacked respect" and should be "ashamed." He noted that Italy had qualified unbeaten, with seven wins and three draws, six points ahead of the Irish.

Critics pointed to stuttering displays along the way. Italy needed Antonio De Natale's stoppage-time strike to win their opening game in Cyprus. They were lethargic in a 2-1 home win over Montenegro and won 2-0 in Georgia only thanks to two own-goals by Milan defender Kakha Kaladze.

In between, Italy's Confederations Cup trip to South Africa ended in embarrassment. They began with a 3-1

COACH

MARCELLO LIPPI

Lippi is one of the most successful coaches of the modern era. He is the only man to have led European Champions Cup winners (Juventus 1996) and FIFA World Cup™ winners (Italy 2006), though he says the FIFA World Cup™ victory was "my most satisfying moment as a coach." He made his name with Napoli, after working his way through the lower divisions. He took charge at Juventus in 1994 and led them to the title in his first season. He steered them to two more championships and European Cup finals in 1997 and 1998 before an abortive spell at Inter. On his return, he guided Juve to two further titles and the 2003 European Cup final. He was appointed Italy coach in July 2004.

Italy will be looking to add to their European record of four FIFA World Cup™ victories.

STAR MAN

GIANLUIGI BUFFON
Born: January 28, 1978
Club: Juventus (Italy)

The brave and acrobatic Buffon has been Italy's number one since 1997. He is firmly established among the world's top goalkeepers, despite a series of injury problems: he needed knee surgery after Italy qualified for South Africa. He cost £32m, a record for a goalkeeper, when Juventus signed him from Parma in 2001. He won two titles with them and played in the 2003 European Cup final. Juventus were relegated to Serie B in 2006 after a betting scandal. Buffon could have taken his pick of new clubs after starring in Italy's FIFA World Cup™ victory. But he chose to stay with Juve and helped them regain their Serie A status.

ITALY AT THE FIFA WORLD CUP™

1930	did not enter
1934	champions
1938	champions
1950	1st round
1954	1st round
1958	did not qualify
1962	1st round
1966	1st round
1970	runners-up
1974	1st round
1978	4th place
1982	champions
1986	2nd round
1990	3rd place
1994	runners-up
1998	quarter-finals
2002	2nd round
2006	champions

ONES TO WATCH

FABIO CANNAVARO
Born: September 13, 1973
Club: Juventus (Italy)

Centre-back Cannavaro skippered Italy to FIFA World Cup™ victory in 2006 after which he was voted FIFA World Player of the Year. At 32, he was the oldest player to win the award. He holds Italy's all-time caps record, having surpassed Paolo Maldini's total of 126 in a friendly against Switzerland in August 2009. He has promised to retire if he lifts the FIFA World Cup™ again in 2010.

DANIELE DE ROSSI
Born: July 24, 1983
Club: Roma (Italy)

De Rossi, a substitute in the 2006 Final, is now one of Lippi's key players. The Roma midfielder is a tough tackler and an energetic box-to-box runner. He plays a defensive role for his club, but, with Gattuso behind him, he goes forward more often for Italy. He has a powerful shot and can score spectacular goals, like his 30-yarder against Georgia.

win over 10-man United States then slumped 1-0 to African champions Egypt. Lippi was relaxed, despite the headlines. He called it "one of those games" and praised Egypt goalkeeper Essam Al-Hadary.

Italy's 3-0 defeat by Brazil, which sent them home early, provoked even more angry headlines. Lippi admitted it was "the toughest time I've had as Italy coach."

Lippi's problem is that the flow of young talent in a country which boasts a European record four FIFA World Cup™ wins has slowed to a trickle. He says: "I can't just bring in 20 new faces." Ten of the squad for their final qualifiers were over 30. Only two – teenage defender Davide Santon and US-born striker Giuseppe Rossi – were under 25.

Lippi may experiment with under-21 stars such as midfielder Sebastian Giovinco and Claudio Marchisio plus strikers Roberto Acquafresca and Mario Balotelli in the warm-up games, but it seems his veterans will make one last stand in South Africa.

Italy will be solid as always. Buffon is one of the world's great keepers. The defence, organised around the Azzurri's record international Cannavaro, remains formidable. Andrea Pirlo can still dictate the tempo – if he is given the time which the Brazilians denied him. So Lippi needs the dynamic Daniele De Rossi to drive his midfield. He will anxiously check the fitness of Liverpool's Alberto Acquilani too.

Lippi also needs to settle on his strike force. Iaquinta, Gilardino, Fabio Quagliarella, Giampaolo Pazzini, De Natale and Rossi all played during the qualifiers. Iaquinta looked the most established – but needs a regular partner.

Lippi, however, remains optimistic. He says: "The most important thing is to win. If we play well, all the better, but winning is what matters."

PARAGUAY

WHITE AND REDS

Paraguay hope a trio of gifted forwards will guide them towards a FIFA World Cup™ quarter-finals place for the first time.

The Paraguayans lost in the last 16 in 1986, 1998 and 2002. They have traditionally been solid and aggressive. But now they have Roque Santa Cruz, Nelson Haedo Valdez and ex-South American Player of the Year Salvador Cabanas in attack.

Defender Paulo Da Silva, currently with Sunderland, says: "For years, people spoke about our defensive strength. Now we've showed that we're an all-round team with some great players up front."

Valdez's winner against Argentina took Paraguay to their fourth successive FIFA World Cup™ finals with two games to spare. Cabanas controlled under pressure, twisted clear of two defenders, played a one-two with midfielder Edgar Barreto, then slid through a pass which Valdez finished with a left-foot shot.

Paraguay qualified despite the frequent absence of Santa Cruz too. He started only five matches because of knee trouble.

Coach Gerardo Martino says: "We even had the luxury of playing without Roque. Can you imagine Argentina playing for that time without Messi? Or Brazil without Kaka? That makes what we've done even more special."

Santa Cruz has been the team's talisman since he made his debut as a 17-year-old. Martino will be desperate for Santa Cruz, Valdez and Cabanas to combine at South Africa 2010.

The trio tormented the Brazilian defence in Paraguay's 2-0 win in Asuncion. Santa Cruz gave them the lead, and Cabanas added a second four minutes into the second half.

Paraguay made a flying start to their campaign. They won seven and drew

COACH

GERARDO MARTINO

Paraguay's Argentine coach is an intriguing mixture of the pragmatic and romantic. The pragmatist says: "Football is about the here and now, and we shouldn't get ahead of ourselves."

The romantic offers a different view: "We'll have to see what road we take. There are two things you can aim for as a coach – to get results, or go down in history. I'm after the latter."

Martino has had a huge influence on Paraguayan football for nearly a decade. His success with Cerro Porteno and Club Libertad made him an obvious successor to Anibal Ruiz as national coach in February 2007. He has nurtured probably the most gifted Paraguay squad for years through the rigours of qualifying, and calmed them when they were most under pressure. He commands a group of experienced players whose stars are at their peak. He will never have a better chance of achieving his ambition.

Paraguay have a stronger squad than in 2006 and could prove to be a surprise package.

STAR MAN

NELSON HAEDO VALDEZ
Born: November 28, 1983
Club: Borussia Dortmund (Germany)

Valdez has come a long way since he was a homeless teenager who slept under the terraces at Tembetary's stadium. Now he is one of Paraguay's biggest stars, with more than 50 caps. He is quick, technically gifted and has an eye for goal. He netted five times in the qualifying campaign. He was called into Paraguay's squad for the 2003 Under-20 FIFA World Cup™ finals – even though the coaches had hardly seen him play. He quickly advanced to the senior team. He waited and learned while understudying Germany's Miroslav Klose and Croatia forward Ivan Klasnic at Bremen and has become a national team regular since joining Borussia Dortmund in the summer of 2006.

PARAGUAY AT THE FIFA WORLD CUP™

1930	1st round
1934	did not enter
1938	did not enter
1950	1st round
1954	did not enter
1958	1st round
1962	did not qualify
1966	did not qualify
1970	did not qualify
1974	did not qualify
1978	did not qualify
1982	did not qualify
1986	2nd round
1990	did not qualify
1994	did not qualify
1998	2nd round
2002	2nd round
2006	1st round

ONES TO WATCH

SALVADOR CABANAS
Born: August 5, 1980
Club: Club America (Mexico)

Cabanas is the most versatile of Paraguay's attackers. He can play up front, out wide or drop deep to create, as he did for Valdez's winner against Argentina. Cabanas is a prolific scorer in Mexican football, with more than 100 goals. He led Paraguay's scorers with six goals in qualifying. He was South American Player of the Year in 2007.

ROQUE SANTA CRUZ
Born: August 16, 1981
Club: Manchester City (England)

Santa Cruz is the focal point of Paraguay's attack. The big striker holds the ball up and brings colleagues into play. He is outstanding in the air and has a poacher's instinct in the box. So Martino will pray that Santa Cruz stays free of the knee problems which have dogged his recent career.

two of their opening 10 games. They suffered their only early defeat, 4-2 against Bolivia, at altitude in La Paz.

Then they began to falter. They lost 2-0 in Uruguay and needed Edgar Benitez to rescue a point with a 92nd-minute equaliser in Ecuador. They slumped 2-0 at home to Chile and lost 2-1 in Brazil.

Those defeats coincided with the absence of Santa Cruz, sidelined for five months by a knee tendon injury which needed surgery.

Cabanas then scored the decisive penalty against Bolivia and, four days later, the celebrations began after victory over Argentina.

Maybe this side lacks an extrovert – such as Jose Luis Chilavert, the penalty-taking goalkeeper of 1998 and 2002. But Valdez says: "We play as a team now."

Paraguay are also determined to atone for their under-achievement at Germany 2006. They were eliminated at the group stage after

losing to England and Sweden. Several of the present squad – including Valdez – played in those games. He says: "It's an honour to be back for a second time and it's a chance to do better."

The Paraguayans have plenty of experience to support their stars. Goalkeeper Justo Villar, veteran of more than 70 matches, plays in Spain with Valldolid. Defenders Caceres and Claudio Morel are with top Argentine club Boca Juniors. Barreto turns out in Serie A for Atalanta. Back-up striker Oscar Cardozo joined Benfica in the summer of 2009. Midfielder Cristian Riveros plays for wealthy Mexican side Cruz Azul. Defender Dario Veron represents their rivals Universidad Nacional.

Paraguay have rarely entered a FIFA World Cup™ finals with such a strong squad. They will not be among the favourites. But they are dangerous outsiders, capable of springing a shock – if their stars stay fit.

NEW ZEALAND

ALL-WHITES

New Zealand are on a high. Their 1-0 victory over Bahrain, which clinched their place at South Africa 2010, was described as "NZ sport's biggest night of 2009". A record crowd of 35,000 packed the Westpac Stadium in Wellington to cheer the team home.

Suddenly the All-Whites captured the country's imagination – after years of playing second fiddle to the famous All-Blacks rugby union team – and competing with cricket and rugby league for public attention.

New Zealand have reached the FIFA World Cup™ finals only once before, in 1982. They were eliminated at the group stage in Spain, after losing to Scotland, the Soviet Union and Brazil.

But those games launched the career of New Zealand's most famous player, striker Wynton Rufer, who starred with Werder Bremen in the German Bundesliga. Coach Ricki Herbert and assistant Brian Turner both played in that campaign. Now their aim is to gain New Zealand's first point in the FIFA World Cup™ finals. It will not be an easy task.

New Zealand have bad memories of South Africa. The Oceania champions crashed there in the 2009 Confederations Cup. They lost 5-0 to Spain, 2-0 to South Africa and drew 0-0 with Iraq.

Yet skipper Ryan Nelsen believes that the experience aided them in their final qualifiers. He says: "We learned some harsh lessons from the defeats against Spain and South Africa. But the draw

against Iraq gave us belief that we could compete with the top teams."

Home critics reckoned the 2010 finals offered New Zealand's best opportunity for a generation. Their old rivals Australia had joined the Asian Confederation to try and gain automatic FIFA World Cup™ qualification (and succeeded in doing so). New Zealand were excused Oceania pre-qualifying. So they reached South Africa via six group games and the play-offs against fifth-placed Asian side Bahrain.

New Zealand easily topped the group with five wins out of six. They drew 0-0 in Bahrain, thanks to goalkeeper Mark Paston's heroics. Rory Fallon headed the winning goal in the return in Wellington – and Paston saved a penalty – to send the All-Whites through.

COACH

RICKI HERBERT

Herbert is one of a select band who have reached the FIFA World Cup™ finals as player and coach. He was a 21-year-old defender when New Zealand appeared in the 1982 finals, starting against the Soviet Union and Brazil. He later played in Australia and had a spell in England with Wolverhampton Wanderers. He combines the role of national coach with managing Wellington Phoenix, the only New Zealand side in Australia's A-League. Herbert has been associated with the national side since 1999, when he took charge of New Zealand's Olympic hopefuls. He has also been under-17 coach, national technical director and assistant to previous All-Whites boss Mick Waitt. He took over from Waitt in February 2005 and steered New Zealand to victory in the Oceania Nations Cup three years later.

In the reaching the 2010 Finals, the All-Whites can already regard their campaign as a success.

STAR MAN

RYAN NELSEN
Born: October 18, 1977
Club: Blackburn Rovers (England)

Centre-back Nelsen is New Zealand's most successful footballing export since Rufer. He is the leader and organiser of the side, as he showed in the closing stages against Bahrain. Nelsen left his home country in 1997 to play college soccer in the United States. He gained a degree in political science at Stanford University before making his name with Washington club D.C. United. He was twice named in Major League Soccer's "Team of the Season". He joined Blackburn in January 2005, becoming a Premiership regular and club captain. Injuries and club commitments restricted his international appearances between 2004 and 2008, but he returned to become a key figure in New Zealand's qualifying campaign.

NEW ZEALAND AT THE FIFA WORLD CUP™

1930-66	did not enter
1970	did not qualify
1974	did not qualify
1978	did not qualify
1982	1st round
1986	did not qualify
1990	did not qualify
1994	did not qualify
1998	did not qualify
2002	did not qualify
2006	did not qualify

ONES TO WATCH

RORY FALLON
Born: March 20, 1982
Club: Plymouth Argyle (England)

Fallon's decisive goal against Bahrain was his second in just his third New Zealand appearance. He chose to play for England at youth level and only became eligible for the country of his birth after a FIFA rule change in June 2009. He is the son of Kevin Fallon, assistant New Zealand coach at the 1982 FIFA World Cup™ finals.

MARK PASTON
Born: December 13, 1976
Club: Wellington Phoenix (New Zealand)

Paston was the hero of New Zealand's play-off success against Bahrain. He stepped in because regular keeper Glen Moss was suspended, and laid claim to a regular spot. He made a succession of saves in the 0-0 draw in the away leg, then pulled off the crucial penalty stop against Bahrain in Wellington. Herbert famously kissed him after the final whistle.

Herbert believes the players have achieved "iconic" status by reaching the finals. He says: "This group of players gave everything to achieve the dream. They believed and they never stopped believing. We've resurrected something that's incredibly important to us – going to the FIFA World Cup™."

Nelsen says: "It's a massive achievement in terms of the growth of football in our country."

Fallon adds: "Football in New Zealand had been in the dark days for a long time. But things are picking up now – and a place in the FIFA World Cup™ finals will take us to a new level."

Herbert named the same 18-man squad for both games against Bahrain. They will form the core of his FIFA World Cup™ party.

The New Zealanders of 1982 were all part-timers. The country still lacks a professional league. Herbert's Wellington Phoenix, who compete in Australia's A-League, are the country's only full-time professional club.

So New Zealand's best – such as goalkeeper Paston, defenders Ben Sigmund, Tony Lochhead and David Mulligan and midfielder Leo Bertos – play for Phoenix or go abroad. Only their most-capped player, defender Ivan Vicelich, defies the trend. He still plays for part-time Auckland City.

But midfielder Simon Elliott is with San Jose Earthquakes in the United States and Fallon plays for English Championship side Plymouth Argyle. Teenage striker Chris Woods is rising through the ranks at English Championship club West Bromwich. Experienced forward Chris Killen is with Celtic. Shane Smeltz, who led the Oceania scorers with eight goals, turns out for A-League team Gold Coast United. Ex-Celtic midfielder Michael McGlinchey plays for their rivals Central Coast Mariners.

Herbert has some tactics to work out too. He favoured a 3-4-3 formation in the play-offs, so that he could include Fallon, Killen and Smeltz up front. But he may want to reinforce his defence when New Zealand face stronger opposition.

SLOVAKIA

REPRE

Slovak fans eagerly await their team's FIFA World Cup™ finals debut after years of being overshadowed by their Czech neighbours.

Slovakia's 1-0 away win over Poland in a blizzard in Chorzow took them to their first-ever major finals since Czechoslovakia split in two in 1993. The Czechs, meanwhile, had been runners-up at Euro 96 and semi-finalists at Euro 2004.

Thus Slovak fans were delighted when their side won the "derby"

qualifier 2-1 in Prague then held on for a 2-2 draw in Bratislava despite playing the closing stages with 10 men.

Coach Vladimir Weiss's side were the surprise package of European qualifying Group Three. The Czech Republic and Poland had been the fancied teams. Slovakia seemed even wider outsiders when attacking midfielder Marek Mintal announced his international retirement to concentrate on his Bundesliga career with Nurnberg – even though Mintal noted at the time: "We do have a young team of talented players."

Slovakia captain Robert Vittek says: "No one expected us to do what we did, when we were drawn in what looked to be one of the toughest groups. But we were all hungry and

now we're hungry to play to our potential in the finals."

Still, Slovakia stumbled towards South Africa. A surprise 2-0 home defeat by Slovenia meant they had to win their final game, in Poland.

Vittek says: "Maybe we allowed the emotion of the occasion to bring down our performance." Others pointed to the absence of suspended top scorer Stanislav Sestak.

Goalkeeper Jan Mucha – who plays in Poland – called the decider "a game of life or death". Slovakia were weakened by four suspensions.

But luck favoured them when Poland's Severyn Gancarczyk turned a third-minute cross into his own net. Mucha produced a series of saves to preserve the points to spark Slovak celebrations.

COACH

VLADIMIR WEISS

It is fitting that Weiss was the first coach to guide Slovakia to a major finals since international football runs in his family's blood. He leads his squad into the FIFA World Cup™ finals 20 years after he played for the old Czechoslovakia at Italy 1990. The ex-Inter Bratislava midfielder won 19 caps for Czechoslovakia and 12 for Slovakia. His father, Vladimir, a centre back, gained three caps for Czechoslovakia. His son, also Vladimir, is a regular in the Slovakia squad. Weiss's success with Artmedia, the club he steered into the Champions League in 2005, made him the obvious candidate to succeed Jan Kocian in the summer of 2008. Weiss has emphasised organisation and team spirit and skilfully used the tag of 'underdogs' to draw the best from his players. Weiss has also encouraged young talent, such as his son Vladimir, midfielder Miroslav Stoch and forward Erik Jindrisek.

Slovakia topped a tough qualifying group, which saw them overcome their Czech neighbours.

STAR MAN

STANISLAV SESTAK
Born: December 16, 1982
Club: Bochum (Germany)

Sestak's reputation has grown steadily since his move to the Bundesliga in 2007. He led Slovakia's scorers in qualifying with six goals in six appearances, some of them match-winners. He was never on the losing side. He scored twice in three minutes (on 83 and 86 minutes) to overturn Poland's 1-0 lead and kick-start his team's campaign. Then he turned a tricky fixture in Northern Ireland with a 15th-minute goal which silenced the home crowd. He also netted in each derby against the Czech Republic. Weiss will look to Sestak for goals and hope he avoids suspension. Sestak collected a yellow card in that win over Northern Ireland, his second of the qualifers. That ruled him out of the home game against Slovenia when the Slovaks slumped to defeat.

SLOVAKIA AT THE FIFA WORLD CUP™

1930-1990	did not exist
1994	did not enter
1998	did not qualify
2002	did not qualify
2006	did not qualify

in Germany. Hamsik is with Napoli, striker Filip Holosko with Besiktas of Istanbul and Vittek with Lille after an impressive spell at Nurnberg.

Slovakia showed their resilience in the qualifiers. They came from a goal down with seven minutes left to beat Poland 2-1 in Bratislava, won the "derby" with the Czechs and they beat off Northern Ireland's tough challenge in Belfast.

Questions remain, especially after the evidence of a 2-1 home defeat by fellow qualifiers Chile in a warm-up friendly. Sestak scored Slovakia's goal but received little support. The visitors marked Hamsik tight which diluted the Slovaks' threat. Weiss praised the Chileans, saying "they were strong tactically and didn't let us get near the ball." But he has many points to ponder before his squad leave for South Africa. How will young defender Peter Pekarik, and midfielders Weiss junior and Stoch, cope with the pressure? Can veteran Zdenko Strba hold the midfield together at the highest level? Who can best support Stesak — Holosko or Vittek, who did not score in qualifying?

Slovakia's disciplinary record presents another problem. Roman Kratochvil was sent off in San Marino, Hasik was dismissed for a second yellow against the Czechs in Bratislava while Skrtel, Zabavnik, Stoch and Jan Durica were banned for the trip to Poland. Weiss needs those first choice players on the pitch in South Africa.

ONES TO WATCH

MARTIN SKRTEL
Born: December 15, 1984
Club: Liverpool (England)

Skrtel was a striker until he filled in at centre back for the Slovak youth team when he was 16. That has been his role ever since. The tough, mobile Liverpool defender is the cornerstone of Slovakia's back line. He is strong in the air and poses a threat at corners and free kicks. Also, he is the only Slovak with regular Champions League experience.

JAN MUCHA
Born: December 5, 1982
Club: Legia Warsaw (Poland)

Weiss promoted Mucha for the qualifier in Prague, a reward for the goalkeeper's form with Legia. Mucha repaid the coach with an "excellent" display in Slovakia's win. His confidence has grown rapidly since. The agile shot-stopper was outstanding in the away wins over Northern Ireland and Poland which saw his team through to the finals.

Sestak believes Slovakia had been steadily building for that success. The Bochum forward says: "We've been on the right track for a while. Our youth programmes have developed, our national league has grown stronger and more of our players are moving to bigger leagues."

Former Trencin centre back Martin Skrtel made the biggest move of all, from Zenit St Petersburg to Premier League and Champions League contenders Liverpool. Full back Marek Cech has played for West Bromwich Albion in the Premier League. Young midfielder Vladimir Weiss (the coach's son) is with Manchester City. Chelsea's Miroslav Stoch has been on loan at Twente Enschede.

Defensive midfielder Miroslav Karhan, the most capped of all Slovak players, has spent the last nine years

BRAZIL

LITTLE CANARIES

Brazil are the kings of the FIFA World Cup™. They are the only nation to have competed in every finals tournament and have samba-danced off with the trophy on a breathtaking record five occasions – thanks to a host of the game's most legendary players.

What a difference 15 months makes. On June 18, 2008, Brazil were booed off the pitch in Belo Horizonte after drawing 0-0 with Argentina in a FIFA World Cup™ qualifier. Three days earlier, they had lost 2-0 in Paraguay.

The players were derided as "donkeys." One magazine cover depicted national coach Dunga with his head inside a noose and the caption: "Hanged." One national newspaper said: "The future looks bleak."

On September 5, 2009, Brazil became the first team to qualify from the South American group – with three games to spare – after beating Argentina 3-1 in Rosario.

Skipper Lucio said: "It was special to qualify for the finals in Argentina. We showed we could handle the pressure – and I'm sure this squad will get even better."

The five-times FIFA World Cup™ winners had been expected to qualify comfortably, after a weakened team beat favourites Argentina 3-0 in the 2007 Copa America final. But they struggled after losing ex-World Player of the Year Kaka for 11 months to a string of injuries. Meanwhile, Dunga was searching for both a pattern and the players to make it work.

Kaka's return, in a 0-0 draw against Colombia, revitalised the squad. Sevilla striker Luis Fabiano netted nine goals on the road to qualification, including two at Rosario.

Dunga discovered a new centre back in Luisao (who also scored at Rosario) to partner Lucio. He added a left back, Andre Santos, to cement the defence.

In the end, Brazil qualified in style. They beat Peru 3-0, scored their first FIFA World Cup™ group win in Uruguay, 4-0, came from behind to pip Paraguay 2-1, then beat Argentina. Dunga warned Brazil not to relax. Four days

COACH

DUNGA (Carlos Caetano Bledorn Verri) Dunga was a controversial appointment when he succeeded Carlos Alberto Parreira in July 2006. The 1994 FIFA World Cup-winning captain had never coached a professional team before.

Dunga's single-minded approach quickly irritated critics who slammed his emphasis on power and physical preparation. But, after the home draw against Argentina, he said: "We have obligations. First, to win; second, to score lots of goals; and, third, to put on a show."

Brazil managed all three as they qualified early. They did so without three of their most famous players – Ronaldo, Ronaldinho and Adriano. Their reputations did not impress Dunga. He said: "I'll only pick players who are doing well at club level."

Coached by Dunga, Brazil showed impressive resilience to win the 2009 Confederations Cup.

STAR MAN

KAKA (Ricardo Izecson dos Santos Leite)
Born: April 22, 1982
Club: Real Madrid (Spain)

Kaka survived a spinal fracture at the age of 18 – in a swimming pool accident – to become one of the greats of modern football. The 2007 World Player of the Year was transferred from Milan to Real Madrid for what was briefly a world record £68.5million in the summer of 2009.

His return to the Brazil team, after months of nagging injuries, gave them the boost they needed to clinch early qualification. Brazil won just one of five matches in his absence. He was at his best against Argentina in Rosario. He set up the second goal with a deft pass to Gilberto, then split the home defence for Luis Fabiano to hit the third. Kaka is not just a playmaker either, being able to glide past opponents and score from long range as easily as from close in.

BRAZIL AT THE FIFA WORLD CUP™

1930	1st round
1934	1st round
1938	3rd place
1950	runners-up
1954	quarter-finals
1958	champions
1962	champions
1966	1st round
1970	champions
1974	4th place
1978	2nd round
1982	2nd round
1986	quarter-finals
1990	2nd round
1994	champions
1998	runners-up
2002	champions
2006	quarter-finals

ONES TO WATCH

LUCIO (Lucimar Ferreira da Silva)
Born: May 8, 1978
Club: Internazionale (Italy)

Lucio has established himself as Brazil's captain, leader, and Dunga's lieutenant on the pitch. The vastly experienced 2002 FIFA World Cup™ winner is a vigilant marker who organises the back line. He has a remarkable ability to tackle without collecting yellow cards. He is outstanding in the air which means he is also a perpetual danger at attacking free kicks and corners.

ROBINHO (Robson de Souza)
Born: January 25, 1984
Club: Manchester City (England)

Robinho has often proved a frustrating figure in the Premiership's physical turmoil, but the mobile winger has always been a threat for Brazil. He has netted consistently in more than 70 appearances. The man who cost Manchester City a British record £32m works best playing off a lead striker, which is why his Brazilian partnership with Luis Fabiano has proved so profitable.

after that win in Rosario, Nilmar – in for the injured Luis Fabiano – scored a hat-trick as they beat Chile 4-2.

But this is not a Brazil team of popular myth. The coach has stressed defence and discipline. Before the triumph in Rosario, he ordered his players: "Keep 11 men on the pitch and we'll win."

Brazil conceded only seven goals in their first 15 qualifiers. Internazionale goalkeeper Julio Cesar is probably their best keeper since Gilmar 50 years ago. He was outstanding when Brazil drew 1-1 against Ecuador at altitude in Quito and again against Uruguay in Montevideo. Lucio and his Inter colleague Maicon are a formidable presence.

Dunga has placed two defensive midfielders in front of them. The vastly experienced ex-Arsenal man Gilberto was a 2002 FIFA World Cup™ winner, like Lucio. Felipe Melo, now of Juventus, was a surprise choice. But, on his debut, he subdued Italy playmaker Andrea Pirlo and Brazil won that friendly 2-0. He has been a fixture since.

That solidity allows Brazil's attackers free rein. Kaka "floats" in a free role. Elano is his accomplice.

Robinho twists and turns in front of his old Manchester City colleague Elano. He enjoys international football much more than the physical rigours of the Premiership. Luis Fabiano has eased memories of Ronaldo and Adriano. His two goals turned the 2009 Confederations Cup final after the United States led 2-0 inside 30 minutes. Lucio headed the winner as Brazil recovered to win 3-2.

That showed both the flair and the resilience in Dunga's squad. Those qualities make them one of the favourites in South Africa.

NORTH KOREA

WINGED HORSES

North Korea's gritty goalless draw in Saudi Arabia clinched their place in the FIFA World Cup™ finals for the first time since 1966. They pipped the Saudis on goal difference to qualify as group runners-up behind their neighbours and arch rivals South Korea.

It had been a long road for coach Kim Jong-Hun and his squad, whose qualifying campaign began with a 4-1 win over Mongolia in Ulan Bator on October 21, 2007.

It is impossible to consider the North Koreans' achievement without looking at the story behind it. The country has been virtually sealed to the outside world for decades. It is the planet's only remaining Stalinist state. It was run by a "Great Leader" in Kim Il-Sung. Now it is dominated by another "Great Leader" in his son Kim Jong-Il.

Politics runs right through North

Korean football. When the team qualified, FA secretary Kim Jong-Su was quoted thus: "The Great Leader gave in-depth guidance on the development of Korean football. He proposed the tactics most relevant for the physiological characteristics of the Korean players."

Kim Jong-Hun allegedly said: "Perhaps there's no other team in the world who would be fighting with such dedication to please the leader and bring fame to the fatherland."

The decision that North Korea should play their qualifiers against South Korea in Shanghai was all about politics too. The North said the South could come to Pyongyang but that their anthem would not be played before the match. The South objected. The North threatened to boycott the game. A compromise was reached, and North Korea's "home" games against the South – in pre-

qualifying and the final group – were switched to the Chinese city.

The North Koreans' 0-0 draw with French club Nantes on October 9, 2009 was their first appearance in Europe since the 1966 FIFA World Cup™ quarter-final against Portugal, more evidence of their isolation.

Yet North Korea's heroics in 1966 have become the stuff of legend. They needed to beat fancied Italy in their last group match to reach the quarter-finals. Pak Do-Ik hit the only goal in the 42nd minute. The North Koreans then led 3-0 against the Portuguese, before the great Eusebio netted four to steer his team to a 5-3 victory.

North Korea did not qualify again, and – after their defeat by South Korea in the 1994 qualifiers – they refused to enter the qualifying competition for 1998 and 2002.

COACH

KIM JONG-HUN

Kim is known as a meticulous planner who does not believe in taking chances. He had monitored the Saudi performances throughout the qualifiers – and his team for the crucial game in Riyadh was expertly designed to frustrate them.

Kim favours a highly defensive 5-4-1 formation, with a sweeper and two centre backs. The full backs rarely attack. He seeks more defensive insurance with two midfield anchors, while Hong Yong-jo and Mun In-Guk support lead striker Jong Tae-Se. He says: "This is the best way to play for us. We want to maximise our organisation."

North Korea are relishing the prospect of returning to football's greatest stage.

STAR MAN

JONG TAE-SE
Born: March 2, 1984
Club: Kawasaki Frontale (Japan)

Jong was born in Japan to a Korean family. He was entitled to South Korean citizenship, but opted for the North. He attended a school which was partially funded by North Korea, hence his support for them. He says: "I'd like to do my best for other young North Koreans growing up in Japan." He adds that if he were asked to move to the South's K-League: "Honestly, I wouldn't want to go."

Jong is known as The Bulldozer because of his physical style. He scored only once in North Korea's final qualifying group. But South Korea coach Huh Jung-moo believes he can make an impact at the FIFA World Cup™ finals. Huh says: "Jong is the total package. He has pace, skill and finishing ability."

NORTH KOREA AT THE FIFA WORLD CUP™

1930–38	did not exist
1950–54	outside FIFA
1958	did not enter
1962	did not enter
1966	quarter-finals
1970	withdrew
1974	did not qualify
1978	withdrew
1982-94	did not qualify
1998	did not enter
2002	did not enter
2006	did not qualify

This time around, North and South both comfortably emerged from their pre-qualifying group, which also included Jordan and Turkmenistan.

They soon met again, in Shanghai. The North had much the better of a 1-1 draw, but Ki Sung-Yeung levelled five minutes after Hong Yong-Jo's penalty had put the northerners ahead.

Lack of firepower was a theme throughout the qualifying campaign. North Korea managed only seven goals in eight games. They could have qualified earlier had they beaten Iran in Pyongyang.

They play on the counter, trying to support star striker Jong Tae-Se with quick breaks. Hong Yong-Jo is their most cultured midfielder, while Mun In-Guk was their most deadly in the group games. The veteran midfielder's winner against Saudi Arabia – from Hong Yong-Jo's backheel – set up their qualifying chance. His 93rd-minute effort in the 2-0 win over UAE gave their goal difference a useful boost too.

But defence was North Korea's strength. They conceded only five goals. Goalkeeper Ri Myong-Guk was outstanding against the Saudis and Iran. He was nominated as a candidate

ONES TO WATCH

AN YOUNG-HAK
Born: October 25, 1978
Club: Suwon Bluewings (South Korea)

An is another "Korean" who was born in Japan. The experienced defensive midfielder began his career in the J.League, then switched to South Korea's K-League, first with Busan, then with Bluewings. He is the only North Korean star in the competition. An is a determined, disciplined marker who is also recognised as the "motivator" of the side.

HONG YONG-JO
Born: May 22, 1982
Club: FC Rostov (Russia)

Hong captained North Korea through most of the qualifying campaign. The clever Rostov attacking midfielder has won more than 40 caps, and is the only North Korean with significant European experience. He is the team's dead ball expert and was one of 15 candidates nominated for the Asian Footballer of the Year prize in 2009.

for Asian Player of the Year 2009. Cha Jong-Hyok, Ri Jun-Il, Ri Kwang-Chon and Ji Yun-Nam are formidable defenders; An Young-Hak offers protection in front of them.

North Korea held out for a 0-0 draw in Riyadh, in stifling heat, despite having defender Kim Yong-Jun sent off. Kim Jung-Hun says: "We noticed that the Saudis had a lack of prolific strikers and we focused on defending. So we were well prepared and that showed up."

He adds: "We're not going to the FIFA World Cup™ to make up the numbers. We choose to deploy a defensive strategy. But Hong Yong-Jo and Jong Tae-Se can catch out opponents with speed in attack."

The 1966 hero Pak Do-Ik is not convinced. He says: "We're still far from becoming a world-class team. We need to be strong in defence against good teams. Then we must create more chances, and put them away."

CÔTE D'IVOIRE

LES ÉLÉPHANTS

Côte d'Ivoire's star striker Didier Drogba reckons his side can do more than just challenge at the 2010 FIFA World Cup™. He believes that Ivorian success would make a statement, for their country – and for the whole of Africa.

The Chelsea top scorer says: "We want to leave our mark on the history of Ivorian football. It's a special project for us. We'll face great teams like Brazil, Italy and Germany who have won the FIFA World Cup™ many times.

"We're really motivated. We want to make our country proud. We hope we can make the Final and win the tournament. We also want to change the way that people in the rest of the world think about Africa and African football.

"This is a chance for the African continent to show another side of itself to the one people usually see – by which I mean war or poverty. We hope these finals will change a lot of stereotypes."

The Germany 2006 group draw handed the Ivorians the short straw in their first appearance. They lost 2-1 to Argentina – when Drogba scored their first-ever finals goal – lost 2-1 to Holland, then beat Serbia & Montenegro 3-2 after trailing 2-0. Midfielder Yaya Toure says: "We played well but we were unlucky to be in such a tough group. With that experience though, we can do much better in South Africa."

Ivory Coast's Bosnian coach Vahid Halilhodzic says: "We're proud to be competing for a second consecutive time – and this time it's going to be better."

Not everyone supports that optimistic view. Former Cannes coach Jean-Marc Guillou set up the ASEC Mimosas academy which has produced a succession of stars for European clubs, such as the Kone brothers, Didier Zokora and Kolo and Yaya Toure.

He claims Halilhodzic has yet to develop a style of play and relies too much on individual flair. Guillou says: "Under Halilhodzic, Ivory Coast no longer play so much as a team. Yes, they have qualified again, but that was essentially because of the individual brilliance of the players." Guillou predicts that the Ivorians will fail to reach the last 16 in South Africa.

COACH

VAHID HALILHODZIC

The Bosnian coach has made a success of his first international job, but he must live up to big expectations in the finals.

Halilhodzic made his name with French side Lille, steering them from the second division to a Champions League place between 1998 and 2002. He also guided Paris Saint-Germain to league runners-up spot and the French cup in 2004 then led Al-Ittihad to the Saudi title in 2007. He took over the Ivory Coast squad in May 2008, succeeding German coach Uli Stielike.

Former Yugoslavia forward Halilhodzic is still remembered at Nantes for his scoring feats between 1981 and 1986.

Ivory Coast will be making their second consecutive appearance at the FIFA World Cup™.

STAR MAN

DIDIER DROGBA
Born: March 11, 1978
Club: Chelsea (England)

Drogba on form is one of the most fearsome strikers in world football. He can terrorise defenders with his physical strength. He is excellent in the air, a clinical converter of half chances and a free-kick expert too.

Doubts have been raised about his temperament. He was sent off in the 2008 Champions League final and seemed strangely uninterested during Luiz Felipe Scolari's reign at Chelsea. But the national team is a cause close to his heart, as his record of more than 40 goals shows. He made his breakthrough at French side Guingamp in 2003. His impressive record for Marseille the following season earned him a £24m move to Jose Mourinho's Chelsea. He was African Footballer of the Year in 2006.

IVORY COAST AT THE FIFA WORLD CUP™

1930–58	did not exist
1962–70	did not enter
1974	did not qualify
1978	did not qualify
1982	did not qualify
1986	did not qualify
1990	did not qualify
1994	did not qualify
1998	did not qualify
2002	did not qualify
2006	1st round

Skipper Drogba defends Halilhodzic. He says: "The coach has been quick to adapt to the particular demands of Ivorian football – and he's met a group of players who want to listen."

He adds: "We learned a lot from playing against tough opponents in Germany. We spent too long watching them and not enough time competing with them. We were a bit naïve then. Now we've much more experience and we hope that the win over Serbia will lead to many more."

The Ivorians eased unbeaten through a preliminary group that included Botswana, Mozambique and Madagascar. They did so without Drogba, injured and suspended, and his experienced striking partner Arouna Kone, sidelined by a long-term cruciate ligament injury.

Sevilla midfielder Romaric gave them a great start in the qualifiers proper, netting in the first minute in a 5-0 home win against Malawi. They won 2-1 in Guinea and 3-2 in Burkina Faso. A 5-0 home romp over the Burkinabe virtually guaranteed their finals place.

Halilhodzic fielded an experimental side in Malawi. But Drogba and Yaya

ONES TO WATCH

YAYA TOURE
Born: May 13, 1983
Club: Barcelona (Spain)

Yaya is a product of the ASEC Mimosas youth academy, like older brother Kolo. He joined Barcelona from Monaco in a £6m deal in the summer of 2007 and helped win the European Champions League, Spanish title and Spanish cup "treble" in 2009. He is tall, deceptively quick and a strong tackler – ideal to play the defensive anchor role for club and country.

BAKARY KONE
Born: September 17, 1981
Club: Marseille (France)

Kone, younger brother of Arouna, is another product of the ASEC Mimosas youth academy. He is one of the smallest international strikers around at 1.63m (5ft 4in). But he is quick, clever and a predator in the box. His form for Nice – 19 goals in 30 games in 2007–8 – earned him a move to Marseille that summer. He was voted Ivorian Player of the Year in 2009, ahead of Yaya Toure.

Toure stepped off the bench after the home side took the lead. Drogba, who led the Ivorian scorers with six goals, netted the equaliser two minutes after his entry.

The Ivorian players are used to the big occasion. Yaya Toure is a Champions League winner with Barcelona, Drogba and Kolo Toure have both played for big European clubs while Chelsea's Salomon

Kalou and Arsenal's Emmanuel Eboue compete at the top of the Premiership. Romaric starts most weeks for Sevilla in Spain, Guy Demel plays for Bundesliga giants Hamburg and goalkeeper Boubacar Barry is with Lokeren in Belgium. Kader Keita joined Turkey's Galatasaray in the summer of 2009.

So it seems the Ivorians are well set to back Drogba's stirring words.

PORTUGAL

SELECÇÃO DAS QUINAS

Portugal, the 2006 FIFA World Cup™ semi-finalists, are upbeat about their chances in South Africa despite their struggle to qualify. They led Sweden by just one point to secure a play-off place and reached the finals after home and away wins against Bosnia.

Yet coach Carlos Queiroz says: "We'll be firm contenders to win, or at least finish on the podium." Striker Liedson adds: "We have the players, the pedigree and the determination and we made a statement in the play-off games."

Portugal have talent throughout their squad, led by the great Cristiano Ronaldo. He was not at his best in the qualifiers. But the Real Madrid forward can attack from any position: he has pace and power, can score with either foot or his head and strikes thunderous free-kicks. There is a mutual respect between him and Queiroz, after three years together at Manchester United, and the coach will pray that Ronaldo is free of the ankle trouble which plagued him earlier in the season. Queiroz seems to bring the best out of Nani too. The 23-year-old winger has been inconsistent for United since Queiroz left but he was one of Portugal's most dynamic performers in qualification.

Chelsea full-back Jose Bosingwa, his club colleague Ricardo Carvalho, Real Madrid's Pepe and Porto defender Bruno Alves are battle-hardened veterans. Alves is always likely to nick a goal too. He scored Portugal's first-leg winner against Bosnia.

Veteran Chelsea midfielder Deco is a Champions League winner, like Carvalho. Atletico Madrid winger Simao combines experience with goals. Raul Meireles, who scored the winner in Bosnia, is a determined midfield anchor. Queiroz hopes Liedson – Brazilian-born, like Deco and Pepe – will follow in the prolific tradition of Nuno Gomes and Pauleta.

The coach is likely to employ three centre-backs, with wing-backs Bosingwa and Malaga's Duda pressing into midfield. Deco, Simao and Nani will support Liedson.

Queiroz has younger talents such as Hugo Almeida, Fabio Coentrao, Miguel Veloso and Joao Moutinho in reserve.

Goalkeeper remains a problem position, though the coach settled on Braga's Eduardo in the qualifiers ahead of the more experienced Quim Benfica.

COACH

CARLOS QUEIROZ

Queiroz will make his first FIFA World Cup™ finals appearance in South Africa. Ironically, he coached South Africa to Japan/South Korea 2002, but left before the finals after a row with the South African association. He is in his second spell as Portugal coach. He was in charge between 1991 and 1993 but quit after they failed to qualify for Euro 1992 or the 1994 FIFA World Cup™ finals. He had made his name with the Under-20s, developing stars such as Luis Figo, Rui Costa and Joao Pinto. His brief spell at Real Madrid ended after constant pressure from president Florentino Perez. But his influence was widely acknowledged in his spells as Sir Alex Ferguson's assistant at Manchester United.

With stars such as Cristiano Ronaldo and Simao, Portugal will always be seen as trophy contenders.

STAR MAN

CRISTIANO RONALDO
Born: February 5, 1985
Club: Real Madrid (Spain)

Ronaldo is arguably the world's greatest player. He certainly became the most expensive when he moved from Manchester United to Real Madrid for £85m on July 1, 2009. He had starred as United won the UEFA Champions League in 2008 and three Premier League titles. He was Europe's top scorer in 2008, when he was voted World and European Player of the Year. Having made his international debut at 18, in August 2003, Ronaldo has since played around 70 games for his country. He was named in UEFA's Team of the Tournament when Portugal reached the Euro 2004 final and has since helped Portugal to the 2006 FIFA World Cup™ semi-finals and the quarter-finals of Euro 2008.

PORTUGAL AT THE FIFA WORLD CUP™

1930	did not enter
1934	did not qualify
1938	did not qualify
1950	did not qualify
1954	did not qualify
1958	did not qualify
1962	did not qualify
1966	third place
1970	did not qualify
1974	did not qualify
1978	did not qualify
1982	did not qualify
1986	1st round
1990	did not qualify
1994	did not qualify
1998	did not qualify
2002	1st round
2006	4th place

ONES TO WATCH

RAUL MEIRELES
Born: March 17, 1983
Club: Porto (Portugal)

Meireles may lack the explosive qualities of Ronaldo, Deco, Simao and Nani, but he plays a crucial role in Portugal's plans. He was the only player to start all 12 of their qualifiers. His job is to protect the defence, win the ball, then set his more creative colleagues free. He boasts a powerful long-range shot and occasionally breaks to score important goals, such as the winner in Bosnia.

LIEDSON
Born: December 17, 1977
Club: Sporting Clube (Portugal)

The Brazil-born striker scored a match-saving equaliser in Denmark on his debut then added another in the 3-0 win over Hungary. He was granted Portuguese nationality in August 2009 after six years of residence and Queiroz immediately fast-tracked him into the squad. He is nicknamed Levezinho – "slender one" – because of his light build but he has scored a heavyweight 150-plus goals for Sporting since joining them in 2003.

He believes Portugal's qualifying struggles have bonded the squad. He says: "It's been a long journey, with some hiccups along the way. But we're moving in the right direction. We have great solidarity and fighting spirit."

Qualification was a triumph for Queiroz. He had a hard act to follow when he succeeded Luiz Felipe Scolari in 2008. Scolari had won the FIFA World Cup™ with Brazil. He steered Portugal to the 2006 semi-finals and the Euro 2004 final. Queiroz's problems began when Portugal suffered a shock 3-2 home defeat by Denmark after leading 2-1 with two minutes left. They followed up with three 0-0 draws, two against Sweden, the other at home to Albania. Critics began to doubt the coach.

Bruno Alves's stoppage-time winner in Albania thus proved a significant landmark on the road to South Africa. So did Liedson's 86th-minute leveller against Denmark in Copenhagen. That meant Portugal had to win their last three games to qualify. Pepe headed the decider in Hungary. Simao netted twice and Liedson added another as Portugal beat Hungary 3-0 at home, while Sweden lost 1-0 in Denmark. That was the break Portugal needed, and a 4-0 home win over Malta clinched their play-off place.

Portugal's recent history has been a tale of just falling short. They lost 1-0 to France – and Zinedine Zidane's penalty – in 2006 (shades of Euro 2000, when Zidane's spot-kick had settled a bad-tempered semi-final). They lost the Euro 2004 final to unfancied Greece, and were eliminated by Germany in the Euro 2008 quarter-finals. Queiroz and company are confident that will change in South Africa.

SPAIN

RED FURY

Spain won the 2008 European Championship in style. They qualified for the 2010 FIFA World Cup™ finals as the only European team to win all their 10 qualifying group ties. Thus they will head to South Africa among the favourites.

But Vicente Del Bosque's squad have bad memories of their last trip there, when they met unfancied United States at Bloemfontein in the 2009 Confederations Cup semi-finals. Spain had just equalled Brazil's world record

COACH

VICENTE DEL BOSQUE
Del Bosque fell victim to one of the strangest sackings of recent years when he was fired by Real Madrid in 2003, having steered Madrid to Champions League victories in 2000 and 2002 and Spanish titles in 2001 and 2003. He was dismissed a day after the 2003 title success because Madrid had lost in the European Cup semi-finals. Del Bosque reportedly turned down an approach to coach Spain after Euro 2004. Since taking the role in 2008, he has maintained continuity, following his predecessor Luis Aragones' tactics and using virtually the same players. But Del Bosque is one of the game's great man-managers. He coaxed and cajoled huge egos at Madrid and his measured reaction helped spur the players' quick recovery at last year's Confederation Cup.

of 35 games unbeaten and had won their previous 15. But that was the end of both sequences as the European champions suffered a shock 2-0 defeat.

US manager Bob Bradley had targeted playmaker Xavi Hernandez and the Spanish midfield. He says: "We never let them feel comfortable. We defended as a group and we were aggressive when we had the ball."

Had Bradley laid down a template to beat Spain? Or had the Spanish simply suffered an off-night?

Skipper and goalkeeper Iker Casillas thought they had lost concentration. He says: "Something like this had to happen. It was one of those games you play 10 times and win nine. This time we lost. "

A little pride was restored when Spain hit back from a goal down to beat South Africa in extra time in the

third-place play-off. They followed up in style in the FIFA World Cup™ qualifiers in which they became the only one of the European finalists to win all their 10 group ties. They began by by thrashing Belgium 5-0 and wrapped things up with a 3-0 win over Estonia.

On the way, they came from behind to win 2-1 in both Belgium and Turkey. David Villa grabbed an 88th-minute decider against the Belgians. Albert Riera scored even later against the Turks.

Both opponents adopted a physical approach. Spain beat them with technique and quick movement, just as they overcame Italy and Germany at Euro 2008.

Luis Aragones, coach at that tournament, laid down the pattern. Successor Del Bosque has followed it. He says: "Basically we've continued with what the squad have been doing."

If Spain can recreate their impressive form of Euro 2008, very few teams will be able to compete with them.

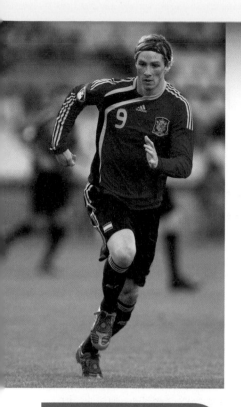

STAR MAN

FERNANDO TORRES
Born: March 20, 1984
Club: Liverpool (England)

Torres's greatest moment for Spain – so far – was the right-foot chip which settled the Euro 2008 final against Germany. He had the strength to hold off Philip Lahm, the pace to run clear and the composure to finish coolly.

Torres scores with both feet and his head. He can threaten as a lone striker, as he does for Liverpool, or in partnership with a quicksilver colleague like David Villa. Their link-up is one of the most potent in international football.

Torres has already won more than 70 caps since his debut as a 19-year-old. He recorded Spain's fastest-ever hat-trick when he scored three inside 17 minutes against New Zealand in a 5-0 Confederations Cup victory.

SPAIN AT THE FIFA WORLD CUP™

1930	did not enter
1934	quarter-finals
1938	did not enter
1950	4th place
1954	did not qualify
1958	did not qualify
1962	1st round
1966	1st round
1970	did not qualify
1974	did not qualify
1978	1st round
1982	2nd round
1986	quarter-finals
1990	2nd round
1994	quarter-finals
1998	1st round
2002	quarter-finals
2006	2nd round

ONES TO WATCH

XAVI HERNANDEZ
Born: January 25, 1980
Club: Barcelona (Spain)

The compact midfielder is Spain's attacking fulcrum. He drops deep to start moves, then drives forward to keep them flowing and exploit gaps with telling passes. He was so influential at Euro 2008 that he was named Player of the Tournament. One year later he was a European champion at club level with Barcelona. Spain's opponents always target him as a priority.

IKER CASILLAS
Born: May 20, 1981
Club: Real Madrid (Spain)

The teenage Casillas made his name in Vicente Del Bosque's Real Madrid team and is now regarded as one of the world's top keepers. He made his international debut at 19 and is closing in on Andoni Zubizareta's record of 126 Spanish caps. He has already beaten Zubizareta's tally of clean sheets. As captain, he leads by example with match-turning saves.

Spain's intricate game revolves around their midfield. Marcos Senna plays the anchor role in front of the back four. Xavi pulls the strings while Andres Iniesta probes, passes and dribbles. If Del Bosque wants variation, he can send on Xabi Alonso or Cesc Fabregas. Both would feature in most of their rivals' starting teams.

David Silva is a tricky, goal-scoring winger who drops deep when Spain lose possession. Fernando Torres and David Villa pose a lethal attacking threat. Torres has pace, strength and composure. Villa is already closing in on Raul's record of 44 goals for Spain. They can score from all over the pitch, even when they're stuttering, as centre back Gerard Pique demonstrated with his winning goal against Turkey in Madrid. Defence is supposed to be Spain's problem area, though Casillas is one of the world's top keepers. Opponents frequently try to exploit the space left by Sergio Ramos when he attacks, or pressure occasionally erratic centre backs Carles Puyol and David Marchena. Yet the Spanish conceded only five goals in the qualifying competition – and none against Italy, Russia and Germany in the knock-out stages of Euro 2008.

The quarter-final win over Italy in the European Championship was crucial to Spain's evolution. It was Spain's first-ever competitive victory over the Italians – and showed that they could win a penalty shoot-out. Casillas was the hero with two saves, before Fabregas tucked away the winning spot kick. It was as if a historic weight had been lifted from their shoulders. Spain had not won a major championship since lifting the fledgling European Championship – then known as the Nations Cup – in front of their own fans in 1964.

Spain's best FIFA World Cup™ finish was fourth, in 1950. Left back Joan Capadevila says: "We've shown what we can do. Now let's see if we can finally do well at the FIFA World Cup™."

SWITZERLAND

SCHWEIZER NATI

Ottmar Hitzfeld's Switzerland recovered from disappointment and humiliation to top Group Two in the European qualifiers and reach the FIFA World Cup™ finals for the second time in succession.

Hitzfeld – known as "the General" for his strategic thinking – has steered both Borussia Dortmund and Bayern Munich to Champions League triumph. But reviving Switzerland's faltering FIFA World Cup™ campaign must rank as one of his most impressive achievements.

Their chance seemed gone by the end of their second qualifier. First, they let a 2-0 lead slip in Israel after Ben Sahar snatched an equaliser in the second minute of stoppage time. Then they crashed to an embarrassing 2-1 home defeat by Luxembourg.

Fons Leweck netted the 87th-minute decider. It was Luxembourg's first FIFA World Cup™ qualifying win for 36 years and on the coach's home competitive debut too.

Hitzfeld's one-time Bayern goalkeeper Oliver Kahn says: "I learned from him, never to give up. All you can do is keep going. That's the situation in which he found himself."

Hitzfeld remained calm, treated the defeat as an unfortunate "blip" and concentrated on the future. He described the next four games as "four cup finals". Blaise N'Kufo's winner beat Latvia 2-1. He was on target again when the Swiss scored the win which turned the group their way, 2-1 over Greece in Piraeus. Two victories over Moldova gave Switzerland momentum for the return against Greece.

Switzerland beat Greece 2-0.

Stephane Grichting and Marco Padalino netted in the last six minutes, after Greece's Loukas Vintra was sent off for a second yellow card.

A draw in Latvia and a 3-0 win in Luxembourg left Switzerland needing only a point in their final game, against Israel, to qualify. A 0-0 home draw was enough to see them through, a point ahead of Greece.

Derdiyok, who headed the equaliser in Latvia, says: "Hitzfeld is a fantastic coach. He's so organised, so calm and he gets the best out of the players. He invests a lot of time in talking to them, especially the younger players."

Hitzfeld had previously turned down offers to coach his native Germany. But his Swiss associations run long and deep. He played for Basel, Lugano and Luzern, before guiding Aarau to a Swiss Cup victory and Grasshoppers to

COACH

OTTMAR HITZFELD

Hitzfeld is one of the world's great coaches. He guided Borussia Dortmund to two Bundesliga titles and to Champions League triumph in 1997. He steered Bayern Munich to victory in the 2001 Champions League final after an unlucky defeat against Manchester United two years earlier. He also steered them to four Bundesliga championships. Coaching Switzerland is probably Hitzfeld's last job. He says: "I don't think I'd want to move back to the hectic world of club management again. I'm very happy with my current role."

Switzerland's best FIFA World Cup™ performance to date was reaching the quarter-finals in 1954.

STAR MAN

ALEXANDER FREI
Born: July 15, 1979
Club: FC Basel (Switzerland)

This is probably Frei's last chance to shine in a major tournament. Switzerland's all-time top scorer suffered a torn knee ligament in the first half of their opening Euro 2008 game against the Czech Republic, which sidelined him for the rest of the competition. So he feels he has a point to prove. He has won more than 70 caps and is the only Swiss player to reach 40 international goals. He is also one of Switzerland's most successful footballing exports. He scored 48 goals in 100 league games for Rennes and 31 in 69 Bundesliga appearances for Borussia Dortmund.

SWITZERLAND AT THE FIFA WORLD CUP™

1930	did not qualify
1934	quarter-finals
1938	quarter-finals
1950	1st round
1954	quarter-finals
1958	did not qualify
1962	1st round
1966	1st round
1970	did not qualify
1974	did not qualify
1978	did not qualify
1982	did not qualify
1986	did not qualify
1990	did not qualify
1994	1st round
1998	did not qualify
2002	did not qualify
2006	2nd round

ONES TO WATCH

GOKHAN INLER
Born: June 27, 1984
Club: Udinese (Italy)

Inler is the energetic heart of the Swiss midfield. He usually plays the deepest of Hitzfeld's quartet. He is a determined tackler with a huge work ethic – and a shrewd eye for a quick pass to keep play moving. He also possesses a powerful shot, though often he plays too far back to prove it.

PHILIPPE SENDEROS
Born: February 14, 1985
Club: Arsenal (England)

The powerful Senderos has become a key figure for his country, although his club career has stalled after a promising start. He has the physique and ability to be a dominant centre back, but questions remain about his attitude. He is strong in the air at both ends of the pitch – and his two headed goals in Luxembourg took Switzerland to the brink of qualification.

two Swiss titles and two cup successes.

Swiss expectations of their national team are far less intense than those of their German neighbours too. German fans regard anything less than a last-four finish as failure. For the Swiss, reaching the finals is an achievement in itself – and if Hitzfeld could steer them to the last eight, he would be a national hero. Hitzfeld says: "This is already a huge achievement for Switzerland. We shouldn't forget

that Switzerland's population is about a tenth of Germany's. The effects of that are obvious when we suffer from injuries or suspensions."

Switzerland have reached the last 16 twice in the last 16 years. In 1994, they lost 3-0 to Spain. At Germany 2006, they went out to Ukraine on a penalty shoot-out after a 0-0 draw.

Skipper Alexander Frei heads the list of Germany 2006 campaigners who want to do better in South Africa.

He is Switzerland's all-time international top scorer and should again spearhead the attack. N'Kufo began with a blaze of goals in qualifying but has struggled over the last year. So Hitzfeld may gamble on gangling Derdiyok to support Frei.

Diego Benaglio has established himself as Switzerland's top keeper while veterans Grichting and Ludovic Magnin are constants in the back line. Centre back Philippe Senderos is an important figure for his country. But the possible loss of Johan Djourou, after surgery to his left knee, would leave a gap in their defensive cover.

Tranquillo Barnetta and Gokhan Inler run the midfield. Both are neat and tidy, and Barnetta occasionally breaks forward, while Inler can snap at opponents too. But the Swiss lack a goalscoring midfielder – unless the much-travelled Johan Vonlanthen can re-discover the form that made him Switzerland's teenage star at Euro 2004.

HONDURAS

LOS CATRACHOS

Honduras reached the FIFA World Cup™ finals for only the second time, thanks to a 1-0 win in El Salvador – and a goal almost two thousand miles away in Washington.

They went into their final qualifier two points behind Costa Rica in the race for the third automatic qualifying place. Top scorer Carlos Pavon scored the winner in San Salvador, but he and his team-mates left the pitch thinking they were out because Costa Rica were leading group winners the United States 2-1 heading into stoppage time.

COACH

REINALDO RUEDA

The Colombian coach is a Honduran hero after guiding his adopted country to its first FIFA World Cup™ finals appearance for 28 years.

He took over the Honduras squad in 2007 and quickly earned the players' respect. They have nicknamed him "the Professor." Valladares says: "He's patient, dedicated and he's given us confidence and a determined mindset." Pavon adds: "He's been a positive influence, right through the qualifiers."

Rueda coached Colombia in the 2006 qualifiers when they lost out to Uruguay for fifth place. He had previously steered Colombia's youngsters to victory in the 2000 Toulon Under-21 tournament and runners-up spot the following year. He also holds a degree in physical education.

Midfielder Julio De Leon says: "Suddenly I heard an almighty roar from our travelling supporters. I realised instinctively what had happened and dropped to the turf with emotion."

US defender Jonathan Bornstein had headed an equaliser, in the fourth minute of stoppage time, to lift Honduras into the third place which guaranteed qualification for the finals on goal difference and relegate the Costa Ricans to a play-off against Uruguay.

Pavon says: "We could hardly find the words to describe how we felt. We were dejected. Then we saw our fans celebrating in the stands and found out the Americans had equalised!"

Coach Reinaldo Rueda did not even see the drama unfold. He had been banished from the bench after a row with the referee. He says: "I went into the dressing room, got down on my knees and prayed for a miracle in the United States."

With three games left, the Hondurans looked favourites to join the US and Mexico as automatic qualifiers. Then they went down 1-0 to a late penalty in Mexico City and lost 3-2 at home to the US. De Leon scored both goals but Pavon squandered several chances, including a penalty.

But Costa Rica failed to take advantage, losing 1-0 in San Salvador. Pavon says: "El Salvador did us a big favour. We weren't expecting that and it gave us a chance."

The Honduran government declared a public holiday to mark the team's progress to the finals for the first time

Honduras will make only their second FIFA World Cup™ appearance in South Africa.

STAR MAN

CARLOS PAVON
Born: October 9, 1973
Club: Real Espana (Spain)

Pavon has travelled far and wide in a chequered club career. But the veteran striker has long been a match-winner for Honduras. He is their all-time top scorer, netting more than 50 goals as he approaches the 100-cap mark. He led their scorers in qualifying with seven goals, including the winner in El Salvador. He is the current Honduran Footballer of the Year and previously won the award in 2000. He finished top scorer in Mexico in 1997 and second-division top scorer with Celaya. He netted a famous hat-trick in Honduras's 3-1 win over Mexico in 2001. He says of his country's qualification: "We've waited so long for this. I've been through so many qualifying cycles. So have the fans. This one was unforgettable. It was tough going but we deserved it."

HONDURAS AT THE FIFA WORLD CUP™

1930	no federation
1934	no federation
1938–58	did not enter
1962–74	did not qualify
1978	did not enter
1982	1st round
1986	did not qualify
1990	did not qualify
1994	did not qualify
1998	did not qualify
2002	did not qualify
2006	did not qualify

ONES TO WATCH

DAVID SUAZO
Born: November 5, 1979
Club: Internazionale (Italy)

Suazo was the first Honduran to shine in Europe. Coach Oscar Tabarez brought him to Cagliari in 1999. His form in Serie B earned him the nickname "the panther." He helped them gain promotion in 2004 and netted 22 Serie A goals in 2006, when he was voted joint "Best Foreign Player" (with Milan's Kaka). He added 18 the following season, which brought him to Inter's attention.

WILSON PALACIOS
Born: July 29, 1984
Club: Tottenham Hotspur (England)

Palacios is probably Honduras's most successful footballing export. He began on the right of midfield for Honduran team Olimpia and scored regularly. But Steve Bruce, the manager who took him to England, thought his discipline, energy and tackling made him an ideal midfield anchor. Palacios has made the role his own – for Wigan, Tottenham, and his country.

since 1982. Honduras were eliminated at the group stage in that appearance. They started with a 1-1 draw against hosts Spain, drew 1-1 with Northern Ireland but went home after a 1-0 defeat by Yugoslavia.

That squad was composed of players from the Honduran league. Now Honduran stars play all over the world. Forward David Suazo leads the way. He netted 95 league goals in 255 games for Italian club Cagliari between 1999 and 2007. He subsequently joined Internazionale in a £9.5m deal and had a loan spell with Portuguese giants Benfica. De Leon has played in Italy since 2001. He is currently on loan at Torino after spells with Reggina, Genoa and Parma. Pacy right wing-back Edgar Alvarez is with Bari.

Pavon has appeared in Mexico, Spain and Italy – and for Los Angeles Galaxy in Major League Soccer. Skipper Amado Guevara – the team's midfield "motor" – plays in MLS for Toronto.

Defensive midfielder Wilson Palacios has become a Premiership star, first with Wigan, then Tottenham. Spurs

paid £15m to sign him in January 2009, a record fee for a player from Central America.

His old colleague, left-back Maynor Figueroa, is a Wigan regular. Striker Carlos Costly – two-goal hero of the 4-0 home win over Costa Rica – plays for Polish club GKS Belchatow.

Coach Rueda has combined the "foreign legion" with the pick of the

domestic league. Noel Valladares is one of Central America's top keepers and hopes for a move to Europe after the finals, as does left wing-back Emilio Izaguirre.

For most Hondurans, their side's run to the finals is a triumph itself. Pavon, 36, knows how they feel. He says: "This is what I've dreamt about for so long – the icing on the cake."

CHILE

THE RED

Chile's Argentine coach Marcelo Bielsa has delivered the revolution he envisaged when he took over for the 2010 FIFA World Cup™ qualifiers.

Chile's 4-2 win in Colombia saw them through to their first finals since 1998, with a game to spare. They finished second, a point behind group winners Brazil and ahead of Paraguay on goal difference.

Bielsa had a brief, undistinguished playing career with Newell's Old Boys, before retiring at 25 to qualify as a physical education teacher. He has since become one of South America's most respected coaches – though his unconventional approach has earned him the nickname El Loco ("The Crazy One").

He spent four years in charge of Argentina. Former defender Roberto Ayala says: "Some days we wouldn't see any of the strikers because he'd have them training at a different time. It was the same with the midfielders too. He is an innovator and one of the people from whom I've learned most during my career."

He has long followed his own path. He was born into an influential family: his brother Rafael and his sister Maria Eugenia are both senior politicians. Marcelo chose football instead. He says: "I come from a family of professionals, but they never objected to my choice."

Bielsa has changed Chile's mentality and their personnel. He says: "I feel good when my team spends more time attacking than defending." His positive approach in away games was crucial to Chile's success. They won early games in Bolivia and Venezuela, before away victories over Peru, Paraguay and Colombia clinched their Finals place.

Bielsa also guided Chile to their first-ever competitive victory over Argentina, 1-0 which prompted the resignation of Argentine coach Alfio Basile.

Bielsa briefly brought back veteran striker Marcelo Salas early in the group games when Chile were hit by injuries. He held his nerve after they crashed 3-0 at home to Paraguay, their second defeat in the first four games. But Salas talked up the squad's potential and urged the fans to stay hopeful. After victory in Colombia,

COACH

MARCELO BIELSA
Bielsa is in his second spell as an international boss. He succeeded Daniel Passarella as Argentina coach in 1998 and led them to the 2002 FIFA World Cup™ finals. He kept his job although they were eliminated at the group stage. He steered Argentina to the final of the 2004 Copa America and to the gold medal in the Olympic football tournament the same year. He quit at the end of 2004, saying he had 'insufficient energy' to carry on. He was out of the game for nearly three years before taking the Chile job. He led Newell's Old Boys (his former club) to the Copa Libertadores final in 1992. They lost to Sao Paulo on penalties.

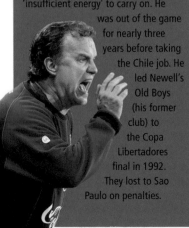

Chile's coach Bielsa will have a talented and determined crop of players at his disposal in 2010.

STAR MAN

HUMBERTO SUAZO
Born: May 10, 1981
Club: Monterrey (Mexico)

Suazo follows in the line of prolific Chilean strikers such as Salas and Zamorano. He topped the qualifying scorers with 10 goals, including a stoppage-time winner in Venezuela. Suazo is relatively short but quick and strong with a poacher's instinct in the box. He came to the big clubs' attention by scoring 40 goals in 40 games for third-division side San Luis in 2003–4. He continued to score freely for top-division Audax, then averaged nearly a goal a game for Chilean giants Colo-Colo. Monterrey paid $8m to take him to Mexico in 2007. Suazo made a slow start but has since become their top striker. He has netted more than 20 goals for Chile.

CHILE AT THE FIFA WORLD CUP™

1930	1st round
1934	withdrew
1938	did not enter
1950	1st round
1954	did not qualify
1958	did not qualify
1962	3rd place
1966	did not qualify
1970	did not qualify
1974	1st round
1978	did not qualify
1982	1st round
1986	did not qualify
1990	did not qualify
1994	suspended
1998	1st round
2002	did not qualify
2006	did not qualify

ONES TO WATCH

CLAUDIO BRAVO
Born: April 13, 1983
Club: Real Sociedad (Spain)

Bravo is Chile's undisputed No. 1 goalkeeper and played every minute of his country's 18 qualifiers. He made his international debut in 2004 and is now approaching 50 caps. He joined Real Sociedad in a €1.2m deal in 2006 and has been a regular starter for the past two seasons. He is not the biggest goalkeeper, at 1.83m (6ft), but is a noted shot-stopper.

ALEXIS SANCHEZ
Born: December 19, 1988
Club: Udinese (Italy)

Sanchez is Chile's bright young hope, a tricky dribbler with an eye for goal. He made his league debut at 16 and won his first cap as a 17-year-old. Udinese signed him for £2m in the summer of 2006, then loaned him to Colo-Colo and River Plate in Argentina in successive seasons. He is now established in Serie A and has won more than 30 international caps.

Bielsa praised their "resilience."

In the meantime, the coach had gone for youth, fast-tracking several of the side which finished third in the 2007 Under-20 FIFA World Cup™. Defender Arturo Vidal, midfielders Gary Medel, Mauricio Isla and Carlos Carmona and attacker Alexis Sanchez all became regulars.

Udinese's Sanchez was the star of that group. Vidal says: "He can weave past three or four defenders and win games on his own." Ivan Zamorano, skipper of the France 98 side, says: "He's a class player with some spectacular attributes."

Sanchez scored three goals in qualifying, despite missing the first four games through injury. The Sporting Lisbon midfielder Matias Fernandez hit four. They will support Bielsa's most lethal weapon, prolific striker Humberto Suazo.

Suazo led the South American qualifying scorers with 10 goals. He was a late developer who admits to "wasting" his early footballing years. He has hit form at Mexican club Monterrey after initially struggling to settle. He will be 29 when the finals start, so South Africa 2010 offers him the opportunity of a lifetime.

Suazo may be Chile's most famous player but goalkeeper Claudio Bravo is Bielsa's leader – on the pitch and off it. Most coaches prefer an outfield skipper, but Bielsa was relaxed when Bravo's team-mates chose him to succeed Salas as captain. The keeper is a shrewd defensive organiser with a keen sense of responsibility.

He insists: "I don't have exclusive rights on leadership." But he says: "There are a lot of young players in the squad, so I try and look out for them and offer advice."

Bielsa has built an eager, hungry squad. and experienced midfielder Jorge Valdivia says: "Bielsa says the credit should go to the players. But he has changed everything: the discipline of the group, the state of the training camp – and the way that other teams look at us."

PLAYERS OF THE FIFA WORLD CUP™

Great players build their reputations on the great stages and there is none greater than the FIFA World Cup™ finals. Italy's Giuseppe Meazza in the 1930s, Brazil's Pele in the 1950s and 1960s, England's Bobby Charlton, Germany's Franz Beckenbauer, Holland's Johan Cruyff and on via the likes of Diego Maradona and Ronaldo and Zinedine Zidane – who will follow in those illustrious footsteps?

Diego Maradona dribbles his way to scoring one of the greatest goals in FIFA World Cup™ history against England in Mexico 1986.

Fernando Torres

Born: March 20, 1984
Club(s): Atletico de Madrid (2001–2007),
Liverpool (England: 2007–)
Position: Centre-forward

FIFA World Cup™ contenders Spain will hope Fernando Torres, their star striker, continues his happy knack of scoring the only goal of important cup finals.

The most significant, of course, was his deft finish against Germany in the final of the 2008 European Championship, which ended his country's 44-year wait for a trophy. But as one of the most promising young talents in Europe, he had done the same against France in the final of the Under-16 European Championship in 2001 and versus Germany in their Under-19 European Championship showdown the following year.

Torres was 17 when he made his league debut for boyhood favourites Atletico de Madrid in May 2001, and was just 19 when made club captain.

Atletico fans adored him, both for his loyalty to the cause – in a city dominated by rivals Real Madrid – but also for his devastating blend of control, pace and killer goalscoring instincts.

After making his international debut as a 19-year-old in September 2003, his reputation flourished further after three handsome goals during Spain's four matches at the 2006 FIFA World Cup™ finals.

Finally, Torres and Atletico were tempted into accepting a £25m transfer to Liverpool in summer 2007 and he proved an instant hit in the English Premier League.

His 24 league goals in 2007–08 – including two hat-tricks in a row at home ground Anfield – was the best first-season haul of any foreign arrival in England's top division, beating the record set by Manchester United's Dutch striker Ruud Van Nistelrooy.

Torres's Euro 2008-winning exploits provided the perfect climax to that season. He and Spanish strike partner David Villa were named in the official team of the tournament and Torres later finished third in the 2008 World Footballer of the Year rankings.

But, with time on his side, plenty more is expected of the man nicknamed "El Niño", or "The Kid", who will be 26 when the 2010 FIFA World Cup™ kicks off.

The last time Torres was in South Africa, he scored the fastest international hat-trick in Spain's history – taking just 17 minutes to put three past New Zealand in the first round of the 2009 FIFA Confederations Cup.

A nation must be breathing a sigh of relief that he never saw through his early childhood ambition of playing in goal instead.

Wayne Rooney

Born: October 24, 1985
Club(s): Everton (2002–2004),
Manchester United (2004–)
Position: Forward

England's hopes of finally winning a second FIFA World Cup™ depend largely on Wayne Rooney retaining both his fitness and his temper.

The Manchester United striker has a habit of making a dramatic impression, only for a big tournament to end unhappily and, indeed, painfully.

He first shot to fame aged 16 in October 2002, when rocketing a spectacular last-minute winner for boyhood favourites Everton against Arsenal.

Blessed with the physique and battling spirit of a boxer to go with his skilful feet, Rooney's dazzling early performances for Everton won him an England debut at Wembley in February 2003.

At the time, he was England's youngest international. Although that record has since been broken, he remains his country's youngest goalscorer, thanks to a neat finish against Macedonia in September 2003.

But it was at the 2004 European Championship that Rooney captured both fans' imagination and global admiration. His four goals against Switzerland and Croatia were struck with maturity and panache but a broken bone in his foot forced Rooney to limp off early in England's quarter-final defeat to Portugal.

They were also the opponents when England crashed out of the FIFA World Cup™ at the same stage two years later after Rooney had again left the pitch prematurely. But this time he was sent off in disgrace for stamping on opponent Ricardo Carvalho. Rooney's petulance was blamed partly by some on the fact he lacked full fitness after rushing back from a pre-finals foot injury.

This was not the only time Rooney's fiery temper had landed him in trouble but that did not stop Manchester United manager Sir Alex Ferguson paying £25.6m to sign him from Everton in 2004.

Again, Rooney made a dramatic entrance – scoring a UEFA Champions League hat-trick against Fenerbahce on his United debut in September 2004.

Since moving to Old Trafford, he has won Premier League titles, the Carling Cup, the World Club Cup – at which he was winning goalscorer and player of the Tournament in 2008 – and, most impressively, that same year's Champions League.

Rooney himself has conceded that he should score more goals, even though Ferguson has often defied his wish to play at centre-forward by making the most of his tireless work-rate on the wings.

England coach Fabio Capello seems to have brought out the prolific best in Rooney, however. In the European group stage of 2010 FIFA World Cup™ qualifiers, only Greece's Theofanis Gekas scored more than Rooney's nine goals in nine matches.

Perhaps England might even have reached the 2008 European Championship had an ankle injury not ruled Rooney out of the decisive qualifier against Croatia in November 2007.

The South Africa showpiece gives Rooney the perfect chance to make up for lost time – and to make it third time lucky at a major international tournament.

Gianluigi Buffon

Born: January 28, 1978
Club(s): Parma (1995–2001), Juventus (2001–)
Position: Goalkeeper

Gianluigi Buffon remains the world's most expensive goalkeeper, almost a decade after switching clubs for £30m, and Italy fans would argue he has been worth every penny.

Juventus paid that record price to take him from Serie A rivals Parma in 2000 and have been rewarded not only with title-winning saves, agility and charismatic penalty-box presence.

They have also benefited from the loyalty which kept Buffon at the club when they were punished for corruption offences by being relegated in 2006.

Italy's national team, of course, put

domestic scandal behind them that summer to lift a fourth FIFA World Cup™ with Buffon one of the most important elements.

He conceded only two goals during that tournament. One was an own goal by Christian Zaccardo, the other a penalty in the final by France's Zinedine Zidane.

Buffon commands respect and inspires

assurance among his defenders, and fear in strikers faced by his towering frame.

Sporting ability and strength clearly run in the family, since his father was a weightlifter and his mother a discus thrower. His grandfather's cousin Lorenzo Buffon was also an international goalkeeper who won championship medals and 16 Italian caps in the late 1950s and early 1960s.

But the younger Buffon has deservedly become a more permanent fixture in the national team, having made his Italy debut at 17 in 1997.

A year earlier he had been a member of Italy's triumphant team at the Under-21 European Championship and further prizes came when Parma lifted the treble of UEFA Cup, Italian Cup and Italian Supercup in 1999.

When he moved to Juventus, his performances contributed greatly to their four Serie A title triumphs, even though two were later rescinded. He was also the outstanding goalkeeper of the 2003 UEFA Champions League season, though he was unfortunate to finish with only a runners-up medal as Juventus lost the final on penalties to AC Milan.

A shoot-out also ended Italy's challenge at Euro 2008, in a quarter-final against Spain, though Buffon still made the judges' team of the tournament. As well as his trademark neckscarf, he also wore the captain's armband throughout that tournament in the absence through injury of Fabio Cannavaro.

Even if the veteran Cannavaro leads Italy again in 2010, he and his fellow defenders will feel a lot more confident of defending their crown as long as Buffon is behind them.

Michael Ballack

Born: September 26, 1976
Club(s): Chemnitzer FC (1995–1997), 1. FC Kaiserslautern (1997–1999), Bayer Leverkusen (1999-2002), Bayern Munich (2002–2006), Chelsea (England: 2006–)
Position: Midfielder

Eight years after suffering FIFA World Cup™ agony, Michael Ballack may find in South Africa a final opportunity to atone.

Even more so than goalkeeper Oliver Kahn, driving midfielder Ballack dragged a workmanlike German side to the 2002 FIFA World Cup™ final against Brazil.

But he was forced to miss the match through suspension, having earned a second yellow card in the semi-final for a cynical foul that prevented a likely South Korean goal.

That capped a miserable end to the 2001–02 season for Ballack, whose Bayer Leverkusen team finished runners-up in the UEFA Champions League, Bundesliga and German Cup.

More successful, league title-winning spells at Bayern Munich and current club Chelsea have helped shake Ballack's unenviable reputation for invariably finishing second.

But he had to be satisfied with a losing medal again when captaining Germany to the final of the 2008 European Championship against Spain.

At least Ballack has no real rival to the claim of being the outstanding German footballer of his generation, combining pin-sharp passing with clever movement and bustling work-rate. In recent years he has settled into a more deep-lying role for both club and country but his darting runs into the box and nose for goal make him an attacking threat still.

East German-born Ballack made his German top-flight breakthrough with Kaiserslautern where his first season also brought a Bundesliga title in 1997–98. After three impressive years at Leverkusen, his almost inevitable sale to Bayern in 2002 was followed by two league and cup doubles and his appointment as German captain after Kahn's retirement.

Ballack led the host nation into the 2006 FIFA World Cup™ at which Jurgen Klinsmann's side delighted home fans and surprised neutrals with their free-flowing football.

Although Italy denied them a second successive final, Ballack could claim great credit for Germany's admirable third-place finish – and was soon earning more money than any other footballer in England, after an end-of-contract free transfer to Chelsea.

His time at Stamford Bridge has been hampered by injuries, as well as occasional barbs about his commitment. But his determined return from injury in the second half of the 2007–08 season was key to Chelsea running Manchester United achingly close in the Premier League title run-in and Champions League Final.

He was also his country's star performer during their run to the Euro 2008 Final, his stunning free-kick against hosts Austria one of the goals of the tournament.

Kaka

Full name: Ricardo Izecson dos Santos Leite
Born: April 22, 1982
Club(s): Sao Paulo (2001–03), AC Milan (Italy: 2003–09), Real Madrid (Spain: 2009–)
Position: Forward

Kaka has already experienced the joy of winning the FIFA World Cup™ once but would love to make a more lasting contribution this time around.

He was a member of Brazil's triumphant squad in South Korea and Japan in 2002 but played only 25 minutes of the tournament, against Costa Rica in the first round. To achieve even that much was astounding enough.

After all, Ricardo Izecson dos Santos Leite was almost paralysed as an 18-year-old after fracturing his spine when he toppled from a swimming pool diving board. He recovered not only to play professional football again but blossom into one of the finest players of his era.

His FIFA World Footballer of the Year prize in 2007 was clinched after setting up both AC Milan's goals in their UEFA Champions League Final win over Liverpool in Athens.

The previous year he had been one of Brazil's most effective players in a disappointingly vain defence of their FIFA World Cup™ crown. A line-up in which he was crammed uncomfortably between Ronaldinho and Ronaldo struggled to gel and fell to France in the quarter-finals.

Kaka's response, for both club and country, was impeccable, with his performances demonstrating why Milan had spent £5.5m to pluck him from Brazilian club Sao Paulo in 2003.

His vision, poise on the ball and prolific strike-rate from a support-striker role made him an icon among supporters both in Brazil and Italy.

AC Milan supporters staged outraged protests when the club came close to selling him to Manchester City in January 2009. But although City were ultimately foiled in their big-money bid, Real Madrid were more successful in June that year when they paid Milan a then world record £56m for his signing. Cristiano Ronaldo would soon prove even more expensive, joining Kaka as part of the Spanish club's new "Galacticos" project.

The Real Madrid move appeared to offer no distraction as Kaka inspired his country to success at the 2009 FIFA Confederations Cup in South Africa.

He was named man of the match after Brazil's thrilling comeback in the final against the United States, before picking up the Golden Ball as player of the tournament.

While Kaka famously wears a T-shirt vowing "I belong to Jesus" Seleção supporters will pray he ensures the FIFA World Cup™ again belongs to Brazil in July 2010.

Lionel Messi

Born: June 24, 1987
Club(s): Barcelona (Spain: 2004–)
Position: Forward

Qualification turned out to be a closer shave than anyone expected but Argentina's Lionel Messi goes into the 2010 FIFA World Cup™ as officially the world's best footballer.

He had to be satisfied with only a couple of brief cameo appearances as his country dazzled then disappointed with a quarter-final exit in Germany in 2006.

But despite his meagre height, Messi's career has gone from strength to strength since then, culminating in his majestic 2008–09 season.

His 38 goals helped Barcelona clinch, in elegant fashion, an unprecedented clean sweep of UEFA Champions League, Spanish league and cup titles.

Messi scored the second of Barcelona's two goals in their Champions League Final dismantling of Manchester United. His powerful header, leaping clear of Rio Ferdinand, was the perfect riposte to slights about his aerial ability and his previous failure to score against English opposition.

Despite being born in the Argentine city of Rosario, Messi has been at the Catalan club since the age of 13. His move to Europe, from Newell's Old Boys, was aided by Barcelona's agreement to pay for growth hormone treatment. (River Plate were also interested in Messi but could not afford to pay for the treatment.

Messi's prodigious dribbling skills helped land him with the "new Maradona" label – approved by El Diego himself. But, unlike previous pretenders such as Ariel Ortega and Andres D'Alessandro, the description seems to suit Messi just fine.

His Barcelona goal against Getafe in April 2007, a winding solo run from the halfway line, was uncannily similar to Diego Maradona's legendary second goal against England at the 1986 FIFA World Cup™. Less admirably, later that same season he punched the ball into the net – and saw it stand – echoing Maradona's infamous Hand of God goal against England.

Under Maradona's management of the national team, however, Messi struggled initially to mirror his Barcelona form. He scored only four goals in 18 games during their scrappy qualifying campaign for the 2010 finals, appearing uncomfortable in striking line-ups alongside the likes of Carlos Tevez and Sergio Agüero.

Messi was much more influential as Argentina took Olympic gold at the 2008 Beijing Olympics, setting up Angel Di Maria's winner in the final against Nigeria.

A trophy of the same colour awaits if the current European Footballer of the Year can once more emulate Maradona but this time on the biggest stage of them all.

Cristiano Ronaldo

Born: February 5, 1985
Club(s): Sporting Clube (2001–03), Manchester United (England: 2003–09), Real Madrid (Spain: 2009–)
Position: Forward

Irritated – or envious – critics often condemn Cristiano Ronaldo for his alleged arrogance but Portugal's captain is hardly alone in valuing himself extravagantly.

He is, after all, the most expensive footballer of all time, after an £80m transfer to Real Madrid which not merely broke but smashed all previous records.

And there could have been little disputing the decision to name him 2008 World Footballer of the Year, after an incredible goalscoring streak for Manchester United.

Eyebrows were raised when United paid Lisbon's Sporting Clube £12m for the little-known teenager in 2003. But it quickly became clear why Sir Alex Ferguson was so impressed by his early sightings of the Madeira-born youngster named after former United States President Ronald Reagan.

His play-acting and stepovers annoy some – including, at times, his own team-mates. But Ronaldo's mazy dribbling, mighty shooting, forceful heading and hefty strength form an often unstoppable package.

During United's Champions League-winning season of 2007–08, he scored 42 goals in all competitions – theoretically as a winger, though often playing a roaming forward role. He even got lucky when it mattered, fluffing his penalty in the final's shoot-out against Chelsea only to see the Londoners miss two of their own.

But his career success owes much, much more to not just natural flair, but his dedication to honing both physique and technique. His explosive free-kicks, for example, are the product of long hours on the training ground.

He also showed flinty strength of character to stay and thrive in England after being widely vilified by fans and media for his role in Wayne Rooney's red card at the 2006 FIFA World Cup™.

His prolonged and unsubtle flirtation with Real Madrid finally ended in July 2009, when United accepted that record bid. Ronaldo's last season at Old Trafford had been described as something of a disappointment – perhaps too harshly, considering he scored 26 times and won another league title. But that only demonstrates how high a benchmark Ronaldo has set and expectations soared equally high as he launched Madrid's new Galacticos era.

All of Portugal also looks to him for leadership and his goals and assists helped them to second place at the 2004 European Championship and fourth at the FIFA World Cup™ two years later. But he was below-par at Euro 2008 and in 2010 FIFA World Cup™ qualifiers – by Ronaldo's lofty standards anyway.

Long-suffering defenders know, however, that even a sub-standard Ronaldo can produce more magic than most.

Steven Pienaar

Born: March 17, 1982
Club(s): Ajax Cape Town (1999–01), Ajax Amsterdam (Holland: 2001–06), Borussia Dortmund (Germany: 2006–08), Everton (England: loan 2007–08, permanent 2008–)
Position: Midfielder/winger

The last time South Africa competed in a FIFA World Cup™ finals, Steven Pienaar was stuck on the bench throughout.

He seems in little danger of suffering a similar fate in summer 2010, as long as he remains fit, after emerging as his country's playmaker and most noted footballing export.

Back in 2002, Pienaar travelled with the squad to South Korea and Japan after having made his international debut only in the final warm-up match.He was left unused as South Africa were eliminated at the first-round stage but his international breakthrough was bound to happen eventually.

At that point the nimble midfielder was already tentatively establishing himself in Europe after signing for Ajax. Pienaar had begun his footballing life at the South African School of Excellence, before graduating to Ajax Cape Town – one of the Amsterdam club's satellites. A move to the Dutch club followed in 2001 and he stayed for five years to celebrate two league championship triumphs.

Pienaar then endured an unhappy season in Germany with Borussia Dortmund where he inherited Tomas Rosicky's No. 10 shirt but little of his success.

However, Pienaar has since thrived in England with Everton after initially agreeing a one-year loan in 2007 and completing a bargain £2m transfer 12 months later.

His insightful passing, combined with wispy, darting runs down either wing, have complemented the Goodison club's neat, well-drilled midfield.

His occasional goals have also contributed to two consecutive fifth-place finishes in the English Premier League and a run to the 2009 FA Cup final. Pienaar that day became only the fifth South African to appear in the climax of the world's oldest cup competition.

If, sometimes, he has proved unable to transfer his club form to international colours, then last summer's FIFA Confederations Cup on home turf may have marked a turning-point.

Pienaar was dogged by an ankle injury in the run-up to the tournament before illness restricted him to only a late substitute appearance in South Africa's opening game, against Iraq. But he was influential in the displays that followed, including a 2-0 win over New Zealand and teasingly narrow losses to Brazil and Spain – inspiring hopes of even better to come on the main stage itself.

FIFA WORLD CUP™ HISTORY

The FIFA World Cup™ is the tournament that matters – nothing else comes close. The most exciting teams, the brightest individual talents, the most outstanding coaches and the most dramatic incidents combine every four years to create a vivid spectacle that burns itself into the memories of fans across the world and adds a new name to the illustrious list of those who have won football's most prestigious trophy.

Brazil's Pele is hoisted on the shoulders of his team-mates after Brazil won their third FIFA World Cup™ in 1970.

The FIFA World Cup™ sets standards. Fans, coaches, directors and players watch every kick, every tackle and every goal hoping to learn something new to give them an edge in the seasons ahead. Above all there is the prospect, for just one nation, of being able to call themselves champions of the world.

World football's organizing body, FIFA, was formed in 1904 and Jules Rimet became its president in 1921.

In 1928, at a special conference in Amsterdam, Jules Rimet and Henri Delaunay, general secretary of the French Football Federation, proposed that FIFA hold a tournament every four years open to any country. The FIFA World Cup™ was born.

Thirteen nations took part in the first tournament in Uruguay in 1930, with only four countries making the long ocean crossing from Europe.

This FIFA World Cup™ was not the meticulously organised event of today.

Running on to treat a player in the semi-final against Argentina, the US trainer tripped and fell, breaking a bottle of chloroform. He was carried off unconscious. In an earlier game, with France fighting back at 1-0 against Argentina, the referee blew the final whistle six minutes early. A near riot forced play to start again but Argentina held on to win. Football's greatest competition was up and running ...

FIFA President Jules Rimet presents the FIFA World Cup™ to Dr Paul Jude, President of the Uruguayan Football Association, following his team's 4-2 win in the Final.

1930 URUGUAY

FIFA's French president Jules Rimet saw his dream come to fruition when Uruguay both hosted and won the inaugural FIFA World Cup™. Only four European nations dared the long sea crossing. Continental powers such as Italy, Austria, Hungary and Czechoslovakia stayed away and the British home nations had already quit FIFA in a row over amateurism. Uruguay had won hosting rights by promising to build a new stadium and pay all travel costs as part of their centenary celebrations. France opened the tournament with a 4-1 win over Mexico despite losing goalkeeper Alex Thepot through injury after only 10 minutes. Inside forward Lucien Laurent scored the historic first goal. However, the group was ultimately won by Argentina who then thrashed the United States 6-1 in the semi-finals. Hosts Uruguay, also the reigning Olympic champions, defeated Yugoslavia by the same score in the other semi. Tension ran so high ahead of the final that fans were searched for firearms before the Uruguayans hit back from 2-1 down to win the first final 4-2.

POOL 1

France	4	Mexico	1
Argentina	1	France	0
Chile	3	Mexico	0
Chile	1	France	0
Argentina	6	Mexico	3
Argentina	3	Chile	1

	P	W	D	L	F	A	Pts
Argentina	3	3	0	0	10	4	6
Chile	3	2	0	1	5	3	4
France	3	1	0	2	4	3	2
Mexico	3	0	0	3	4	13	0

POOL 2

Yugoslavia	2	Brazil	1
Yugoslavia	4	Bolivia	0
Brazil	4	Bolivia	0

	P	W	D	L	F	A	Pts
Yugoslavia	2	2	0	0	6	1	4
Brazil	2	1	0	1	5	2	2
Bolivia	2	0	0	2	0	8	0

POOL 3

Romania	3	Peru	1
Uruguay	1	Peru	0
Uruguay	4	Romania	0

	P	W	D	L	F	A	Pts
Uruguay	2	2	0	0	5	0	4
Romania	2	1	0	1	3	5	2
Peru	2	0	0	2	1	4	0

POOL 4

USA	3	Belgium	0
USA	3	Paraguay	0
Paraguay	1	Belgium	0

	P	W	D	L	F	A	Pts
USA	2	2	0	0	6	0	4
Paraguay	2	1	0	1	1	3	2
Belgium	2	0	0	2	0	4	0

SEMI-FINALS

Argentina	6	USA	1
Uruguay	6	Yugoslavia	1

FINAL – July 30: Centenario, Montevideo

Uruguay 4 (Dorado 12, Cea 57, Iriarte 68, Castro 90)   **Argentina 2** (Peucelle 20, Stabile 37)
HT: 1–2. **Att:** 93,000. **Ref:** Langenus (Belgium)
Uruguay: Ballestreros, Nasazzi, Mascheroni, Andrade, Fernandez, Gestido, Dorado, Scarone, Castro, Cea, Iriarte.
Argentina: Botasso, Della Torre, Paternoster, Evaristo, Monti, Suarez, Peucelle, Varallo, Stabile, Ferreira, Evaristo.
Top scorer: 8 Stabile (Argentina)

1934 ITALY

Italy emulated Uruguay by winning the second FIFA World Cup™ as hosts. Angry that Europe had snubbed their party in 1930, the Uruguayans stayed away. Dictator Benito Mussolini had demanded that his organising officials and players use the event to demonstrate the superiority of Italy's fascist system. That he got his way was due partly to the shrewd management of Vittorio Pozzo and partly to the intimidatory effect of the atmosphere on several referees – notably in the quarter-final victory over Spain. Austria's famed Wunderteam, led by the great Matthias Sindelar, proved too old and fragile for the challenge and lost to the Italians in the semi-finals. Czechoslovakia came through the other side of the draw, inspired by their left-wing partnership of Oldrich Nejedly and Antonin Puc. In the final Puc gave the Czechs the lead only for Italy to equalise nine minutes from time through Raimundo Orsi, who had been a final loser with Argentina four years earlier. Italy's flagging veteran centre forward Angelo Schiavio won it for the hosts in extra time.

FIRST ROUND

Italy	7	USA	1
Czechoslovakia	2	Romania	1
Germany	5	Belgium	2
Austria	3	France	2*
Spain	3	Brazil	1
Switzerland	3	Holland	2
Sweden	3	Argentina	2
Hungary	4	Egypt	2

After extra time

THIRD-PLACE MATCH

| Germany | 3 | Austria | 2 |

SECOND ROUND

Germany	2	Sweden	1
Austria	2	Hungary	1
Italy	1	Spain	1*
Italy	1	Spain	0r
Czechoslovakia	3	Switzerland	2

After extra time; r=Replay

SEMI-FINALS

| Czechoslovakia | 3 | Germany | 1 |
| Italy | 1 | Austria | 0 |

FINAL – June 10: Flaminio, Rome

Italy 2 (Orsi 81, Schiavio 95)   **Czechoslovakia 1** (Puc 71)*
HT: 0-0. 90min: 1-1. **Att:** 55,000. **Ref:** Eklind (Sweden).
Italy: Combi, Monzeglio, Allemandi, Ferraris IV, Monti, Bertolini, Guaita, Meazza, Schiavio, Ferrari, Orsi.
Czechoslovakia: Planicka, Zenisek, Ctyroky, Kostalek, Cambal, Kreil, Junek, Svoboda, Sobotka, Nejedly, Puc.
Top scorers: 5 Nejedly (Czechoslovakia), Schiavio (Italy), Conen (Germany).

After extra time

1938 FRANCE

The shadow of war hung over the 1938 finals in France. Argentina and Uruguay stayed away in anger at the event remaining in Europe, while Austria withdrew after the country was swallowed up into Hitler's Greater Germany. The football was equally tense. In the knock-out-style first round, Hungary and France were the only teams to progress without needing extra time or replays. The most dramatic game saw Brazil beat Poland 6-5 after extra time in Strasbourg with centre-forwards Leonidas and Ernst Willimowski each scoring hat-tricks. Brazil then needed a replay to beat Czechoslovakia and earn a semi-final joust with Italy, whose captain Giuseppe Meazza converted the winning penalty. Hungary beat Sweden 5-1 in the other semi-final to earn the right to face Italy in the final in the Stade Colombes in Paris. Ruthless manager Vittorio Pozzo had retained only two of his 1934 winners in the shape of inside forward Meazza and Gioanin Ferrari. But Italy had few problems retaining the cup. Gino Colaussi and Silvio Piola each scored twice in a 4-2 win.

FIRST ROUND

Switzerland	1	Germany	1*
Switzerland	4	Germany	2r
Cuba	3	Romania	3*
Cuba	2	Romania	1r
Hungary	6	Dutch East Indies	0
France	3	Belgium	1
Czechoslovakia	3	Holland	0*
Brazil	6	Poland	5*
Italy	2	Norway	1*

After extra time; r=Replay

THIRD-PLACE MATCH

| Brazil | 4 | Sweden | 2 |

SECOND ROUND

Sweden	8	Cuba	0
Hungary	2	Switzerland	0
Italy	3	France	1
Brazil	1	Czechoslovakia	1*
Brazil	2	Czechoslovakia	1r

After extra time; r=Replay

SEMI-FINALS

| Italy | 2 | Brazil | 1 |
| Hungary | 5 | Sweden | 1 |

FINAL – June 19: Colombes, Paris

Italy 4 (Colaussi 5, 35, Piola 16, 82)   **Hungary 2** (Titkos 7, Sarosi 70)
HT: 3-1. **Att:** 55,000. **Ref:** Capdeville (France).
Italy: Olivieri, Foni, Andreolo, Rava, Serantoni, Locatelli, Biavati, Meazza, Piola, Ferrari, Colaussi.
Hungary: Szabo, Polgar, Biro, Szalay, Szucs, Lazar, Sas, Vincze, Sarosi, Szengeller, Titkos.
Top scorer: 7 Leonidas (Brazil); 7 Szengeller (Hungary); 5 Piola (Italy).

1950 BRAZIL

The finals in Brazil were marked by two of the greatest shocks in the history of the FIFA World Cup™. Joint favourites before kick-off were the hosts and the old masters from England, competing for the first time. Brazil at least reached the final but England did not progress beyond the first-round group stage after a humiliating 1-0 defeat by a scratch team from the United States. Holders Italy also crashed out in the first round, having failed to recover from the effects of the Torino air disaster a year earlier in which 10 Italian internationals had been killed. There was no formal final for the one and only time. Brazil, Uruguay, Sweden and Spain qualified for a final group in which the hosts walked out to face Uruguay in the last match needing only a draw to win the FIFA World Cup™. Uruguay had to win. Almost 200,000 delirious fans jammed Rio's Maracana stadium but by the final whistle they had been plunged into despair after the visitors hit back from 1-0 down to win 2-1. After 20 years, and against all the odds, the Cup had returned to Uruguay.

FINAL POOL

Uruguay	2	Spain	2
Brazil	7	Sweden	1
Uruguay	3	Sweden	2
Brazil	6	Spain	1
Sweden	3	Spain	1
Uruguay	2	Brazil	1

	P	W	D	L	F	A	Pts
Uruguay	3	2	1	0	7	5	5
Brazil	3	2	0	1	14	4	4
Sweden	3	1	0	2	6	11	2
Spain	3	0	1	2	4	11	1

POOL 1

Brazil	4	Mexico	0
Yugoslavia	3	Switzerland	0
Yugoslavia	4	Mexico	1
Brazil	2	Switzerland	2
Brazil	2	Yugoslavia	0
Switzerland	2	Mexico	1

	P	W	D	L	F	A	Pts
Brazil	3	2	1	0	8	2	5
Yugoslavia	3	2	0	1	7	3	4
Switzerland	3	1	1	1	4	6	3
Mexico	3	0	0	3	2	10	0

POOL 2

Spain	3	USA	1
England	2	Chile	0
USA	1	England	0
Spain	2	Chile	0
Spain	1	England	0
Chile	5	USA	2

	P	W	D	L	F	A	Pts
Spain	3	3	0	0	6	1	6
England	3	1	0	2	2	2	2
Chile	3	1	0	2	5	6	2
USA	3	1	0	2	4	8	2

POOL 3

Sweden	3	Italy	2
Sweden	2	Paraguay	2
Italy	2	Paraguay	0

	P	W	D	L	F	A	Pts
Sweden	2	1	1	0	5	4	3
Italy	2	1	0	1	4	3	2
Paraguay	2	0	1	1	2	4	1

POOL 4

| Uruguay | 8 | Bolivia | 0 |

	P	W	D	L	F	A	Pts
Uruguay	1	1	0	0	8	0	2
Bolivia	1	0	0	1	0	8	0

FINAL – July 16: Maracana, Rio de Janeiro

Brazil 1 (Friaca 47)   **Uruguay 2** (Schiaffino 66, Ghiggia 79)
HT: 0–0. **Att:** 199,854. **Ref:** Reader (England).
Brazil: Barbosa, Da Costa, Juvenal, Bauer, Alvim, Bigode, Friaca, Zizinho, Ademir, Jair, Chico.
Uruguay: Maspoli, Gonzales, Tejera, Gambetta, Varela, Andrade, Ghiggia, Perez, Miguez, Schiaffino, Moran.
Top scorer: Top scorer: 7 Ademir (Brazil)

1954 SWITZERLAND

The magic of Ferenc Puskas and Sandor Kocsis meant Hungary were hottest-ever favourites on their arrival in FIFA's own back yard in Switzerland. They were Olympic champions, had inflicted England's first home defeat by continental opposition and fired 17 goals in their opening two group matches against South Korea and West Germany. But no one could know the significance of the ankle injury inflicted on Puskas by a heavy tackle from German defender Werner Liebrich. Without their captain, Hungary outfought Brazil 4-2 in a quarter-final dubbed the "Battle of Bern", then defeated holders Uruguay 4-2 in a wonderful semi-final. The Uruguayans had previously beaten an England side boasting 39-year-old Stanley Matthews. Hungary gambled on recalling Puskas for the final repeat against the Germans. He scored an early goal as Hungary raced to 2-0 ahead but his lack of fitness proved a crucial handicap in the closing stages when Germany battled back to win 3-2. Hungary, unbeaten in four years, had lost the one match which mattered most.

POOL 1

Yugoslavia	1	France	0			
Brazil	5	Mexico	0			
France	3	Mexico	2			
Brazil	1	Yugoslavia	1			

	P	W	D	L	F	A	Pts
Brazil	2	1	1	0	6	1	3
Yugoslavia	2	1	1	0	2	1	3
France	2	1	0	1	3	3	2
Mexico	2	0	0	2	2	8	0

POOL 2

Hungary	9	South Korea	0			
West Germany	4	Turkey	1			
Hungary	8	West Germany	3			
Turkey	7	South Korea	0			

	P	W	D	L	F	A	Pts
Hungary	2	2	0	0	17	3	4
West Germany	2	1	0	1	7	9	2
Turkey	2	1	0	1	8	4	2
South Korea	2	0	0	2	0	16	0

POOL 3

Austria	1	Scotland	0			
Uruguay	2	Czechoslovakia	0			
Austria	5	Czechoslovakia	0			
Uruguay	7	Scotland	0			

	P	W	D	L	F	A	Pts
Uruguay	2	2	0	0	9	0	4
Austria	2	2	0	0	6	0	4
Czechoslovakia	2	0	0	2	0	7	0
Scotland	2	0	0	2	0	8	0

POOL 4

England	4	Belgium	4			
England	2	Switzerland	0			
Switzerland	2	Italy	1			
Italy	4	Belgium	1			

	P	W	D	L	F	A	Pts
England	2	1	1	0	6	4	3
Italy	2	1	0	1	5	3	2
Switzerland	2	1	0	1	2	3	2
Belgium	2	0	1	1	5	8	1

PLAY-OFF

Switzerland	4	Italy	1
West Germany	7	Turkey	2

QUARTER-FINALS

West Germany	2	Yugoslavia	0
Hungary	4	Brazil	2
Austria	7	Switzerland	5
Uruguay	4	England	2

SEMI-FINALS

West Germany	6	Austria	1
Hungary	4	Uruguay	2

THIRD-PLACE MATCH

Austria	3	Uruguay	1

FINAL – July 4: Wankdorf, Bern

West Germany 3 (Morlock 10, Rahn 18, 82)   **Hungary 2** (Puskas 6, Czibor 8)
HT: 2-2. **Att:** 60,000. **Ref:** Ling (England)
West Germany: Turek, Posipal, Liebrich, Kohlmeyer, Eckel, Mai, Rahn, Morlock, O Walter, F Walter, Schafer.
Hungary: Grosics, Buzansky, Lorant, Lantos, Bozsik, Zakarias, Czibor, Kocsis, Hidegkuti, Puskas, Toth.
Top scorer: 11 Kocsis (Hungary)

1958 SWEDEN

Brazil became the first nation to win the FIFA World Cup™ on the "wrong" continent after introducing the world to the outstanding individual talents of Didi, Garrincha and Pele, as well as a revolutionary tactical formation known as 4-2-4. They thrashed hosts Sweden 5-2 in the final in Stockholm. France finished a best-yet third thanks to the record-breaking marksmanship of centre-forward Just Fontaine who scored 13 goals, including four in the third-place victory over deposed champions West Germany. For the only time, all four British home nations reached the finals. Wales and Northern Ireland reached the quarter-finals but England and Scotland fell in the group stage. England, weakened by the Munich air crash deaths of Manchester United players including Duncan Edwards, lost a first-round play-off to FIFA World Cup™ newcomers the Soviet Union. Pele, 17, was omitted for the Brazilians' opening two matches but ended with six goals including a semi-final hat-trick against France and two more in the final against the Swedes.

POOL 1

West Germany	3	Argentina	1			
Northern Ireland	1	Czechoslovakia	0			
West Germany	2	Czechoslovakia	2			
Argentina	3	Northern Ireland	1			
West Germany	2	Northern Ireland	2			
Czechoslovakia	6	Argentina	1			

	P	W	D	L	F	A	Pts
West Germany	3	1	2	0	7	5	4
Czechoslovakia	3	1	1	1	8	4	3
N. Ireland	3	1	1	1	4	5	3
Argentina	3	1	0	2	5	10	2

POOL 2

France	7	Paraguay	3			
Yugoslavia	1	Scotland	1			
Yugoslavia	3	France	2			
Paraguay	3	Scotland	2			
France	2	Scotland	1			
Yugoslavia	3	Paraguay	3			

	P	W	D	L	F	A	Pts
France	3	2	0	1	11	7	4
Yugoslavia	3	1	2	0	7	6	4
Paraguay	3	1	1	1	9	12	3
Scotland	3	0	1	2	4	6	1

POOL 3

Sweden	3	Mexico	0			
Hungary	1	Wales	1			
Wales	1	Mexico	1			
Sweden	2	Hungary	1			
Sweden	0	Wales	0			
Hungary	4	Mexico	0			

	P	W	D	L	F	A	Pts
Sweden	3	2	1	0	5	1	5
Hungary	3	1	1	1	6	3	3
Wales	3	0	3	0	2	2	3
Mexico	3	0	1	2	1	8	1

POOL 4

England	2	Soviet Union	2			
Brazil	3	Austria	0			
England	0	Brazil	0			
Soviet Union	2	Austria	0			
Brazil	2	Soviet Union	0			
England	2	Austria	2			

	P	W	D	L	F	A	Pts
Brazil	3	2	1	0	5	0	5
England	3	0	3	0	4	4	3
Soviet Union	3	1	1	1	4	4	3
Austria	3	0	1	2	2	7	1

PLAY-OFF

Northern Ireland	2	Czechoslovakia	1
Wales	2	Hungary	1
Soviet Union	1	England	0

QUARTER-FINALS

France	4	Northern Ireland	0
West Germany	1	Yugoslavia	0
Sweden	2	Soviet Union	0
Brazil	1	Wales	0

SEMI-FINALS

Brazil	5	France	2
Sweden	3	West Germany	1

THIRD-PLACE MATCH

France	6	West Germany	3

FINAL – June 29: Rasunda, Stockholm

Brazil 5 (Vava 9, 30, Pele 55, 90, Zagalo 68)   **Sweden 2** (Liedholm 4, Simonsson 80)
HT: 2-1. **Att:** 49,737. **Ref:** Guigue (France)
Brazil: Gilmar, D Santos, Bellini, Orlando, N Santos, Zito, Didi, Garrincha, Vava, Pele, Zagalo.
Sweden: Svensson, Bergmark, Gustavsson, Axbom, Borjesson, Parling, Hamrin, Gren, Simonsson, Liedholm, Skoglund.
Top scorer: 13 Fontaine (France)

1962 CHILE

Brazil retained their world crown despite losing Pele, now indisputably the world's finest player, to injury after only two matches. The holders amply compensated for both his loss and the ageing of their team by converting their 4-2-4 system into a more cautious 4-3-3. The bow-legged Garrincha took centre stage in Pele's absence, scoring twice in both the quarter-finals against England and the semi-final against hosts Chile. The "Little Bird" was also sent off against the Chileans but was cleared for the final in which Brazil beat Czechoslovakia 3-1. The Czechs succumbed after taking the lead through playmaker Josef Masopust whose consolation prize was to be hailed as European Footballer of the Year. The finals were marred, however, by violence – most infamously in the "Battle of Santiago" between Chile and Italy. Two Italians were sent off by English referee Ken Aston who somehow missed the flagrant, flailing left hook with which Chile's Leonel Sanchez broke the nose of Italy's Humberto Maschio.

GROUP 1

Uruguay	2	Colombia	1
Soviet Union	2	Yugoslavia	0
Yugoslavia	3	Uruguay	1
Soviet Union	4	Colombia	4
Soviet Union	2	Uruguay	1
Yugoslavia	5	Colombia	0

	P	W	D	L	F	A	Pts
Soviet Union	3	2	1	0	8	5	5
Yugoslavia	3	2	0	1	8	3	4
Uruguay	3	1	0	2	4	6	2
Colombia	3	0	1	2	5	11	1

GROUP 2

Chile	3	Switzerland	1
West Germany	0	Italy	0
Chile	2	Italy	0
West Germany	2	Switzerland	1
West Germany	2	Chile	0
Italy	3	Switzerland	0

	P	W	D	L	F	A	Pts
West Germany	3	2	1	0	4	1	5
Chile	3	2	0	1	5	3	4
Italy	3	1	1	1	3	2	3
Switzerland	3	0	0	3	2	8	0

GROUP 3

Brazil	2	Mexico	0
Czechoslovakia	1	Spain	0
Brazil	0	Czechoslovakia	0
Spain	1	Mexico	0
Brazil	2	Spain	1
Mexico	3	Czechoslovakia	1

	P	W	D	L	F	A	Pts
Brazil	3	2	1	0	4	1	5
Czechoslovakia	3	1	1	1	2	3	3
Mexico	3	1	0	2	3	4	2
Spain	3	1	0	2	2	3	2

GROUP 4

Argentina	1	Bulgaria	0
Hungary	2	England	1
England	3	Argentina	1
Hungary	6	Bulgaria	1
Argentina	0	Hungary	0
England	0	Bulgaria	0

	P	W	D	L	F	A	Pts
Hungary	3	2	1	0	8	2	5
England	3	1	1	1	4	3	3
Argentina	3	1	1	1	2	3	3
Bulgaria	3	0	1	2	1	7	1

QUARTER-FINALS

Yugoslavia	1	West Germany	0
Brazil	3	England	1
Chile	2	Soviet Union	1
Czechoslovakia	1	Hungary	0

SEMI-FINALS

Brazil	4	Chile	2
Czechoslovakia	3	Yugoslavia	1

THIRD-PLACE MATCH

Chile	1	Yugoslavia	0

Final – June 17: Nacional, Santiago

Brazil 3 (Amarildo 18, Zito 69, Vava 77)   **Czechoslovakia 1** (Masopust 16)
HT: 1-1. **Att:** 68,679. **Ref:** Latishev (Soviet Union)
Brazil: Gilmar, D Santos, Mauro, Zozimo, N Santos, Zito, Didi, Zagallo, Garrincha, Vava, Amarildo.
Czechoslovakia: Schroiff ,Tichy, Pluskal, Popluhar, Novak, Kvasniak, Kadraba, Masopust, Pospichal, Scherer, Jelinek.
Top scorer: 4 Garrincha (Brazil), Vava (Brazil), L Sanchez (Chile), Jerkovic (Yugoslavia), Albert (Hungary), V Ivanov (Sov).

1966 ENGLAND

England, home of the game, celebrated the nation's only FIFA World Cup™ triumph after a tournament rich in drama. The hosts provided some, though not all, through the contrasts of a bad-tempered quarter-final defeat of Argentina, a classic semi-final defeat of Portugal and a controversial 4-2 extra-time triumph over West Germany in the final. The Queen was in the crowd to see Geoff Hurst become the only player in FIFA World Cup™ history to score a final hat-trick including a controversial second which may, or may not, have crossed the goal-line. England's explosive Bobby Charlton, West Germany's graceful young Franz Beckenbauer and Portugal's thunderous Eusebio, the tournament's nine-goal top scorer, took the individual honours. The mystery men from North Korea provided the greatest upset, defeating mighty Italy in the first round with a goal from dentist-turned-inside forward Pak Do Ik. Brazil, too old for the challenge this time around, limped home in great disappointment after being kicked to first-round elimination.

GROUP 1

England	0	Uruguay	0
France	1	Mexico	1
Uruguay	2	France	1
England	2	Mexico	0
Uruguay	0	Mexico	0
England	2	France	0

	P	W	D	L	F	A	Pts
England	3	2	1	0	4	0	5
Uruguay	3	1	2	0	2	1	4
Mexico	3	0	2	1	1	3	2
France	3	0	1	2	2	5	1

GROUP 2

West Germany	5	Switzerland	0
Argentina	2	Spain	1
Spain	2	Switzerland	1
Argentina	0	West Germany	0
Argentina	2	Switzerland	0
West Germany	2	Spain	1

	P	W	D	L	F	A	Pts
West Germany	3	2	1	0	7	1	5
Argentina	3	2	1	0	4	1	5
Spain	3	1	0	2	4	5	2
Switzerland	3	0	0	3	1	9	0

GROUP 3

Brazil	2	Bulgaria	0
Portugal	3	Hungary	1
Hungary	3	Brazil	1
Portugal	3	Bulgaria	0
Portugal	3	Brazil	1
Hungary	3	Bulgaria	1

	P	W	D	L	F	A	Pts
Portugal	3	3	0	0	9	2	6
Hungary	3	2	0	1	7	5	4
Brazil	3	1	0	2	4	6	2
Bulgaria	3	0	0	3	1	8	0

GROUP 4

Soviet Union	3	North Korea	0
Italy	2	Chile	0
Chile	1	North Korea	1
Soviet Union	1	Italy	0
North Korea	1	Italy	0
Soviet Union	2	Chile	1

	P	W	D	L	F	A	Pts
Soviet Union	3	3	0	0	6	1	6
North Korea	3	1	1	1	2	4	3
Italy	3	1	0	2	2	2	2
Chile	3	0	1	2	2	5	1

QUARTER-FINALS

England	1	Argentina	0
West Germany	4	Uruguay	0
Portugal	5	North Korea	3
Soviet Union	2	Hungary	1

SEMI-FINALS

West Germany	2	Soviet Union	1
England	2	Portugal	1

THIRD-PLACE MATCH

Portugal	2	Soviet Union	1

FINAL – July 30: Wembley, London

*****England 4** (Hurst 19, 100, 120, Peters 77)   **West Germany 2** (Haller 13, Weber 89)
HT: 1-1. **90min:** 2-2. **Att:** 96,924. **Ref:** Dienst (Switzerland)
England: Banks, Cohen, J Charlton, Moore, Wilson, Ball, Stiles, R Charlton, Peters, Hurst, Hunt.
West Germany: Tilkowski, Hottges, Schulz, Weber, Schnellinger, Haller, Beckenbauer, Overath, Seeler, Held, Emmerich.
Top scorer: 9 Eusebio (Portugal)

* After extra time

Brazil's Pele celebrates after scoring the opening goal in the South American side's 4-1 defeat of Italy in the 1970 FIFA World Cup™ Final.

1970 MEXICO

The heat and altitude of Mexico enforced a slower rhythm on the finals which resulted in some of the most skilful football seen thus far in the FIFA World Cup™. Brazil, rebuilt around a revived Pele, revelled in the conditions. Jairzinho – the right-wing heir to Garrincha – made history by scoring in all seven matches up to and including the classic 4-1 final thrashing of Italy in Mexico City's Azteca stadium. Fatigue, as well as Brazilian verve, got the better of an Italian side who had barely recovered from a dramatic 4-3 extra-time victory over West Germany in the semi-finals. The Germans, inspired by a new goal machine in Gerd Müller, had hardly caught their breath themselves after a thrilling 3-2 comeback victory over outgoing champions England in the quarter-finals. England had badly missed FIFA World Cup-winning goalkeeping hero Gordon Banks, ruled out by illness. He had been one of the stars of the first round, courtesy of an amazing save from Pele in a group game against Brazil.

QUARTER-FINALS

West Germany	3	England	2*
Brazil	4	Peru	2
Italy	4	Mexico	1
Uruguay	1	Soviet Union	0
			* After extra time

SEMI-FINALS

Italy	4	West Germany	3*
Brazil	3	Uruguay	1
			* After extra time

THIRD-PLACE MATCH

West Germany	1	Uruguay	0

GROUP 1

Mexico	0	Soviet Union	0
Belgium	3	El Salvador	0
Soviet Union	4	Belgium	1
Mexico	4	El Salvador	0
Soviet Union	2	El Salvador	0
Mexico	1	Belgium	0

	P	W	D	L	F	A	Pts
Soviet Union	3	2	1	0	6	1	5
Mexico	3	2	1	0	5	0	5
Belgium	3	1	0	2	4	5	2
El Salvador	3	0	0	3	0	9	0

GROUP 3

England	1	Romania	0
Brazil	4	Czechoslovakia	1
Romania	2	Czechoslovakia	1
Brazil	1	England	0
Brazil	3	Romania	2
England	1	Czechoslovakia	0

	P	W	D	L	F	A	Pts
Brazil	3	3	0	0	8	3	6
England	3	2	0	1	2	1	4
Romania	3	1	0	2	4	5	2
Czechoslovakia	3	0	0	3	2	7	0

GROUP 2

Uruguay	2	Israel	0
Italy	1	Sweden	0
Uruguay	0	Italy	0
Sweden	1	Israel	1
Sweden	1	Uruguay	0
Italy	0	Israel	0

	P	W	D	L	F	A	Pts
Italy	3	1	2	0	1	0	4
Uruguay	3	1	1	1	2	1	3
Sweden	3	1	1	1	2	2	3
Israel	3	0	2	1	1	3	2

GROUP 4

Peru	3	Bulgaria	2
West Germany	2	Morocco	1
Peru	3	Morocco	0
West Germany	5	Bulgaria	2
West Germany	3	Peru	1
Morocco	1	Bulgaria	1

	P	W	D	L	F	A	Pts
West Germany	3	3	0	0	10	4	6
Peru	3	2	0	1	7	5	4
Bulgaria	3	0	1	2	5	9	1
Morocco	3	0	1	2	2	6	1

FINAL – June 21: Azteca, Mexico City

Brazil 4 (Pele 18, Gerson 66, Jairzinho 71, Carlos Alberto 86)   **Italy 1** (Boninsegna 37)
HT: 1-1. **Att:** 107,000. **Ref:** Glockner (East Germany)
Brazil: Felix, Carlos Alberto, Brito, Piazza, Everaldo, Clodoaldo, Gerson, Rivelino, Jairzinho, Tostao, Pele.
Italy: Albertosi, Facchetti, Cera, Burgnich, Rosato, Domenghini, Bertini (Juliano 75), De Sisti, Mazzola, Boninsegna (Rivera 84), Riva.
Top scorer: 9 Müller (West Germany)

1974 WEST GERMANY

West Germany's Bayern Munich had just taken over from Holland's Ajax Amsterdam as Europe's top club and that tilt in the balance of power was repeated at national-team level. The Dutch played the finest football of the finals as their "total football" swirled them to the final in Munich. But despite going ahead inside two minutes with the first-ever final penalty – converted by Johan Neeskens – they lost 2-1. Their captain and inspiration Johan Cruyff wasted too much of his energy arguing over decisions with English referee Jack Taylor. No fewer than six Bayern players, headed by skipper and attacking sweeper Franz Beckenbauer, laid their hands on the FIFA World Cup™ in their home stadium. Earlier the hosts had lost a group game to their cousins from communist East Germany, while Brazil had been dethroned by the Dutch. Olympic champions Poland, surprise victors over England in the qualifying competition, finished third. Striker Grzegorz Lato was the tournament's seven-goal top scorer.

FIRST ROUND – GROUP 1

West Germany	1	Chile	0
East Germany	2	Australia	0
West Germany	3	Australia	0
East Germany	1	Chile	1
East Germany	1	West Germany	0
Chile	0	Australia	0

	P	W	D	L	F	A	Pts
East Germany	3	2	1	0	4	1	5
West Germany	3	2	0	1	4	1	4
Chile	3	0	2	1	1	2	2
Australia	3	0	1	2	0	5	1

FIRST ROUND – GROUP 3

Holland	2	Uruguay	0
Sweden	0	Bulgaria	0
Holland	0	Sweden	0
Bulgaria	1	Uruguay	1
Holland	4	Bulgaria	1
Sweden	3	Uruguay	0

	P	W	D	L	F	A	Pts
Holland	3	2	1	0	6	1	5
Sweden	3	1	2	0	3	0	4
Bulgaria	3	0	2	1	2	5	2
Uruguay	3	0	1	2	1	6	1

FIRST ROUND – GROUP 2

Brazil	0	Yugoslavia	0
Scotland	2	Zaïre	0
Brazil	0	Scotland	0
Yugoslavia	9	Zaïre	0
Scotland	1	Yugoslavia	1
Brazil	3	Zaïre	0

	P	W	D	L	F	A	Pts
Yugoslavia	3	1	2	0	10	1	4
Brazil	3	1	2	0	3	0	4
Scotland	3	1	2	0	3	1	4
Zaïre	3	0	0	3	0	14	0

FIRST ROUND – GROUP 4

Italy	3	Haiti	1
Poland	3	Argentina	2
Italy	1	Argentina	1
Poland	7	Haiti	0
Argentina	4	Haiti	1
Poland	2	Italy	1

	P	W	D	L	F	A	Pts
Poland	3	3	0	0	12	3	6
Argentina	3	1	1	1	7	5	3
Italy	3	1	1	1	5	4	3
Haiti	3	0	0	3	2	14	0

SECOND ROUND – GROUP A

Brazil	1	East Germany	0
Holland	4	Argentina	0
Holland	2	East Germany	0
Brazil	2	Argentina	1
Holland	2	Brazil	0
Argentina	1	East Germany	1

	P	W	D	L	F	A	Pts
Holland	3	3	0	0	8	0	6
Brazil	3	2	0	1	3	3	4
East Germany	3	0	1	2	1	4	1
Argentina	3	0	1	2	2	7	1

SECOND ROUND – GROUP B

Poland	1	Sweden	0
West Germany	2	Yugoslavia	0
Poland	2	Yugoslavia	1
West Germany	4	Sweden	2
Sweden	2	Yugoslavia	1
West Germany	1	Poland	0

	P	W	D	L	F	A	Pts
West Germany	3	3	0	0	7	2	6
Poland	3	2	0	1	3	2	4
Sweden	3	1	0	2	4	6	2
Yugoslavia	3	0	0	3	2	6	0

THIRD-PLACE MATCH

Poland	1	Brazil	0

FINAL – July 7: Olympia, Munich

West Germany 2 (Breitner 25 pen, Müller 43)
Holland 1 (Neeskens 2 pen)
HT: 2-1. **Att:** 77,833. **Ref:** Taylor (England)
West Germany: Maier, Vogts, Schwarzenbeck, Beckenbauer, Breitner, Bonhof, Hoeness, Overath, Grabowski, Müller, Holzenbein.
Holland: Jongbloed, Suurbier, Rijsbergen (De Jong 69), Haan, Krol, Jansen, Neeskens, Van Hanegem, Cruyff, Rep, Rensenbrink (R Van de Kerkhof 46).
Top scorer: 7 Lato (Poland)

Argentina captain Daniel Passarella shows off the FIFA World Cup™ to the celebrating Argentina fans as they mob the players.

1978 ARGENTINA

Argentina very nearly did not host the FIFA World Cup™. It took enormous investment from the military junta to bring infrastructure and organisation up to speed amid worldwide controversy over the country's policy of political repression. Nonetheless, the Argentine nation thrilled to their team's first-ever FIFA World Cup™ win. Manager Cesar Menotti left out the precocious teenager Diego Maradona in favour of just one foreign-based player. But that player, the Valencia striker Mario Kempes, proved the tournament's outstanding individual. He top-scored with six goals including two in the extra-time defeat of Holland – runners-up again – in the final. Holders West Germany faded away in the second round, while Brazil finished third. Scotland were British football's sole representatives. They fell in the first round but there was delight over a "goal of the tournament" by Archie Gemmill against Holland.

FIRST ROUND – GROUP 1

Argentina	2	Hungary	1
Italy	2	France	1
Argentina	2	France	1
Italy	3	Hungary	1
Italy	1	Argentina	0
France	3	Hungary	1

	P	W	D	L	F	A	Pts
Italy	3	3	0	0	6	2	6
Argentina	3	2	0	1	4	3	4
France	3	1	0	2	5	5	2
Hungary	3	0	0	3	3	8	0

FIRST ROUND – GROUP 2

West Germany	0	Poland	0
Tunisia	3	Mexico	1
Poland	1	Tunisia	0
West Germany	6	Mexico	0
Poland	3	Mexico	1
West Germany	0	Tunisia	0

	P	W	D	L	F	A	Pts
Poland	3	2	1	0	4	1	5
West Germany	3	1	2	0	6	0	4
Tunisia	3	1	1	1	3	2	3
Mexico	3	0	0	3	2	12	0

FIRST ROUND – GROUP 3

Austria	2	Spain	1
Sweden	1	Brazil	1
Austria	1	Sweden	0
Brazil	0	Spain	0
Spain	1	Sweden	0
Brazil	1	Austria	0

	P	W	D	L	F	A	Pts
Austria	3	2	0	1	3	2	4
Brazil	3	1	2	0	2	1	4
Spain	3	1	1	1	2	2	3
Sweden	3	0	1	2	1	3	1

FIRST ROUND – GROUP 4

Peru	3	Scotland	1
Holland	3	Iran	0
Scotland	1	Iran	1
Holland	0	Peru	0
Peru	4	Iran	1
Scotland	3	Holland	2

	P	W	D	L	F	A	Pts
Peru	3	2	1	0	7	2	5
Holland	3	1	1	1	5	3	3
Scotland	3	1	1	1	5	6	3
Iran	3	0	1	2	2	8	1

SECOND ROUND – GROUP A

Italy	0	West Germany	0
Holland	5	Austria	1
Italy	1	Austria	0
Austria	3	West Germany	2
Holland	2	Italy	1
Holland	2	West Germany	2

	P	W	D	L	F	A	Pts
Holland	3	2	1	0	9	4	5
Italy	3	1	1	1	2	2	3
West Germany	3	0	2	1	4	5	2
Austria	3	1	0	2	4	8	2

SECOND ROUND – GROUP B

Argentina	2	Poland	0
Brazil	3	Peru	0
Argentina	0	Brazil	0
Poland	1	Peru	0
Brazil	3	Poland	1
Argentina	6	Peru	0

	P	W	D	L	F	A	Pts
Argentina	3	2	1	0	8	0	5
Brazil	3	2	1	0	6	1	5
Poland	3	1	0	2	2	5	2
Peru	3	0	0	3	0	10	0

THIRD-PLACE MATCH

Brazil	2	Italy	1

FINAL – June 25: Monumental, Buenos Aires

*Argentina 3 (Kempes 37, 104, Bertoni 114)
Holland 1 (Nanninga 81)
HT: 1-0. 90min: 1-1. Att: 77,260. Ref: Gonella (Italy)
Argentina: Fillol, Olguin, Galvan, Passarella, Tarantini, Ardiles (Larrosa 66), Gallego, Bertoni, Kempes, Ortiz (Houseman 75), Luque.
Holland: Jongbloed, Krol, Poortvliet, Brandts, Jansen (Suurbier 73), R Van de Kerkhof, Neeskens, W Van de Kerkhof, Haan, Rep (Nanninga 59), Rensenbrink.
Top scorer: 6 Kempes (Argentina)

* After extra time

1982 SPAIN

Italy emulated Brazil's FIFA World Cup™ hat-trick despite drawing all three of their first-round matches. Paolo Rossi was their unlikely hero. He top-scored with six goals, including a second-round hat-trick to beat Brazil, despite having only just returned after an 18-month ban following a betting-and-bribes scandal. Italy also saw off holders Argentina whose new prodigy, Diego Maradona, achieved only notoriety after being sent off in a defeat by Brazil. Hosts Spain were another disappointment, never recovering confidence or momentum after a surprise early defeat by Northern Ireland. The most memorable match was a semi-final in Seville in which West Germany beat France in a first finals shoot-out after a 3-3 extra-time draw. France's Michel Platini put in a man-of-the-match performance in vain. The Germans, undermined by the fragile fitness of skipper Karl-Heinz Rummenigge, progressed only to a 3-1 defeat in the final. Italy won a third cup despite seeing Antonio Cabrini commit a first-ever final failure from the penalty spot.

FIRST ROUND – GROUP 1

Italy	0	Poland	0	
Peru	0	Cameroon	0	
Italy	1	Peru	1	
Poland	0	Cameroon	0	
Poland	5	Peru	1	
Italy	1	Cameroon	1	

	P	W	D	L	F	A	Pts
Poland	3	1	2	0	5	1	4
Italy	3	0	3	0	2	2	3
Cameroon	3	0	3	0	1	1	3
Peru	3	0	2	1	2	6	2

FIRST ROUND – GROUP 2

Algeria	2	West Germany	1	
Austria	1	Chile	0	
West Germany	4	Chile	1	
Austria	2	Algeria	0	
Algeria	3	Chile	2	
West Germany	1	Austria	0	

	P	W	D	L	F	A	Pts
West Germany	3	2	0	1	6	3	4
Austria	3	2	0	1	3	1	4
Algeria	3	2	0	1	5	5	4
Chile	3	0	0	3	3	8	0

FIRST ROUND – GROUP 3

Belgium	1	Argentina	0	
Hungary	10	El Salvador	1	
Argentina	4	Hungary	1	
Belgium	1	El Salvador	0	
Belgium	1	Hungary	1	
Argentina	2	El Salvador	0	

	P	W	D	L	F	A	Pts
Belgium	3	2	1	0	3	1	5
Argentina	3	2	0	1	6	2	4
Hungary	3	1	1	1	12	6	3
El Salvador	3	0	0	3	1	13	3

FIRST ROUND – GROUP 4

England	3	France	1	
Czechoslovakia	1	Kuwait	1	
England	2	Czechoslovakia	0	
France	4	Kuwait	1	
France	1	Czechoslovakia	1	
England	1	Kuwait	0	

	P	W	D	L	F	A	Pts
England	3	3	0	0	6	1	6
France	3	1	1	1	6	5	3
Czechoslovakia	3	0	2	1	2	4	2
Kuwait	3	0	1	2	2	6	1

FIRST ROUND – GROUP 5

Spain	1	Honduras	1	
Northern Ireland	0	Yugoslavia	0	
Spain	2	Yugoslavia	1	
Northern Ireland	1	Honduras	1	
Yugoslavia	1	Honduras	0	
Northern Ireland	1	Spain	0	

	P	W	D	L	F	A	Pts
N. Ireland	3	1	2	0	2	1	4
Spain	3	1	1	1	3	3	3
Yugoslavia	3	1	1	1	2	2	3
Honduras	3	0	2	1	2	3	2

FIRST ROUND – GROUP 6

Brazil	2	Soviet Union	1	
Scotland	5	New Zealand	2	
Brazil	4	Scotland	1	
Soviet Union	3	New Zealand	0	
Scotland	2	Soviet Union	2	
Brazil	4	New Zealand	0	

	P	W	D	L	F	A	Pts
Brazil	3	3	0	0	10	2	6
Soviet Union	3	1	1	1	6	4	3
Scotland	3	1	1	1	8	8	3
New Zealand	3	0	0	3	12	0	0

SECOND ROUND – GROUP A

Poland	3	Belgium	0	
Soviet Union	1	Belgium	0	
Soviet Union	0	Poland	0	

	P	W	D	L	F	A	Pts
Poland	2	1	1	0	3	0	3
Soviet Union	2	1	1	0	1	0	3
Belgium	2	0	0	2	0	4	0

SECOND ROUND – GROUP B

West Germany	0	England	0	
West Germany	2	Spain	1	
England	0	Spain	0	

	P	W	D	L	F	A	Pts
West Germany	2	1	1	0	2	1	3
England	2	0	2	0	0	0	2
Spain	2	0	1	1	1	2	1

SECOND ROUND – GROUP C

Italy	2	Argentina	1	
Brazil	3	Argentina	1	
Italy	3	Brazil	2	

	P	W	D	L	F	A	Pts
Italy	2	2	0	0	5	3	4
Brazil	2	1	0	1	5	4	2
Argentina	2	0	0	2	2	5	0

SECOND ROUND – GROUP D

France	1	Austria	0	
Northern Ireland	2	Austria	2	
France	4	Northern Ireland	1	

	P	W	D	L	F	A	Pts
France	2	2	0	0	5	1	4
Austria	2	0	1	1	2	3	1
N.Ireland	2	0	1	1	3	6	1

SEMI FINALS

Italy	2	Poland	0
West Germany	3 (5)	France	3 (4)*

* After extra time (pens)

THIRD-PLACE MATCH

Poland	3	France	2

FINAL – July 11: Bernabeu, Madrid

Italy 3 (Rossi 5G, Tardelli 69, Altobelli 80) **West Germany 1** (Breitner 82)
HT: 0-0. **Att:** 90,000. **Ref:** Coelho (Brazil)
Italy: Zoff, Scirea, Bergomi, Gentile, Collovati, Cabrini, Oriale, Tardelli, Conti, Graziani (Altobelli 8; Causio 88), Rossi.
West Germany: Schumacher, Kaltz, K Forster, Stielike, B Forster, Breitner, Dremmler (Hrubesch 63), Briegel, Littbarski, Fischer, Rummenigge (H Muller 70).
Top scorer: 6 Rossi (Italy)

Italian captain Dino Zoff raises the trophy and celebrates with his team-mates in 1982.

Diego Maradona of Argentina celebrates at the end of the FIFA World Cup™ Final in the Atzeca Stadium, Mexico City.

1986 MEXICO

Diego Maradona, for both good and ill, dominated Argentina's second FIFA World Cup™ triumph in three attempts. Now captain, he produced a series of inspirational displays to rank alongside those of the likes of Pele. Even in the 3-2 final win over West Germany, when he had been largely marked out of the game by Lothar Matthaus, he found crucial time and space in the closing minutes to create the winner for Jorge Burruchaga. Maradona also scored two wonderful solo goals against England and Belgium but earned equal notoriety with his infamous "Hand of God" goal in the quarter-final defeat of the English. Brazil fell at the same stage on penalties against France for whom skipper Michel Platini marked his 31st birthday by scoring a goal in normal time but failing in the shoot-out. The French then subsided tamely in the semi-finals against a workmanlike West German side managed by their 1974 FIFA World Cup-winning captain, Franz Beckenbauer. Mexico, late substitute hosts after Colombia pulled out, lost on penalties to Germany in the second round.

SECOND ROUND

Mexico	2	Bulgaria	0
Belgium	4	Soviet Union	3*
Brazil	4	Poland	0
Argentina	1	Uruguay	0
France	2	Italy	0
West Germany	1	Morocco	0
England	3	Paraguay	0
Spain	5	Denmark	1

After extra time

QUARTER-FINALS

France	1 (4)	Brazil	1 (3)*
West Germany	0 (4)	Mexico	0 (1)*
Argentina	2	England	1
Spain	1 (5)	Belgium	1 (4)*

After extra time (pens)

SEMI FINALS

Argentina	2	Belgium	0
West Germany	2	France	0

THIRD-PLACE MATCH

France	4	Belgium	2

FIRST ROUND – GROUP A

Bulgaria	1	Italy	1
Argentina	3	South Korea	1
Italy	1	Argentina	1
Bulgaria	1	South Korea	1
Argentina	2	Bulgaria	0
Italy	3	South Korea	2

	P	W	D	L	F	A	Pts
Argentina	3	2	1	0	6	2	5
Italy	3	1	2	0	5	4	4
Bulgaria	3	0	2	1	2	4	2
South Korea	3	0	1	2	4	7	1

FIRST ROUND – GROUP C

Soviet Union	6	Hungary	0
France	1	Canada	0
Soviet Union	1	France	1
Hungary	2	Canada	0
France	3	Hungary	0
Soviet Union	2	Canada	0

	P	W	D	L	F	A	Pts
Soviet Union	3	2	1	0	9	1	5
France	3	2	1	0	5	1	5
Hungary	3	1	0	2	2	9	2
Canada	3	0	0	3	0	5	0

FIRST ROUND – GROUP E

West Germany	1	Uruguay	1
Denmark	1	Scotland	0
Denmark	6	Uruguay	1
West Germany	2	Scotland	1
Scotland	0	Uruguay	0
Denmark	2	West Germany	0

	P	W	D	L	F	A	Pts
Denmark	3	3	0	0	9	1	6
West Germany	3	1	1	1	3	4	3
Uruguay	3	0	2	1	2	7	2
Scotland	3	0	1	2	1	3	1

FIRST ROUND – GROUP B

Mexico	2	Belgium	1
Paraguay	1	Iraq	0
Mexico	1	Paraguay	1
Belgium	2	Iraq	1
Paraguay	2	Belgium	2
Mexico	1	Iraq	0

	P	W	D	L	F	A	Pts
Mexico	3	2	1	0	4	2	5
Paraguay	3	1	2	0	4	3	4
Belgium	3	1	1	1	5	5	3
Iraq	3	0	0	3	1	4	0

FIRST ROUND – GROUP D

Brazil	1	Spain	0
Northern Ireland	1	Algeria	1
Spain	2	Northern Ireland	1
Brazil	1	Algeria	0
Spain	3	Algeria	0
Brazil	3	Northern Ireland	0

	P	W	D	L	F	A	Pts
Brazil	3	3	0	0	5	0	6
Spain	3	2	0	1	5	2	4
N.Ireland	3	0	1	2	2	6	1
Algeria	3	0	1	2	1	5	1

FIRST ROUND – GROUP F

Morocco	0	Poland	0
Portugal	1	England	0
England	0	Morocco	0
Poland	1	Portugal	0
England	3	Poland	0
Morocco	3	Portugal	1

	P	W	D	L	F	A	Pts
Morocco	3	1	2	0	3	1	4
England	3	1	1	1	3	1	3
Poland	3	1	1	1	1	3	3
Portugal	3	1	0	2	2	4	2

FINAL – June 29: Azteca, Mexico City

Argentina 3 (Brown 22, Valdano 56, Burruchaga 84)   **West Germany 2** (Rummenigge 73, Völler 82)
HT: 1-0. **Att:** 114,590. **Ref:** Arppi Filho (Brazil)
Argentina: Pumpido, Cuciuffo, Brown, Ruggeri, Giusti, Burruchaga (Trobbiani 89), Batista, Enrique, Olarticoechea, Maradona, Valdano.
West Germany: Schumacher, Berthold, Jakobs, Forster, Eder, Brehme, Matthaus, Magath (D Hoeness 63), Briegel, Allofs (Völler 46), Rummenigge.
Top scorer: 6 Lineker (England).

The West Germany team celebrate with the FIFA World Cup™ in 1990.

1990 ITALY

West Germany joined Brazil and Italy as hat-trick winners though the standard of football never matched the passionate enthusiasm of host Italy's fans. The shocks started immediately with Cameroon defeating holders Argentina 1-0 in the opening match. Argentina recovered to reach the final but Diego Maradona was restricted by a knee injury and they needed the penalty-saving heroics of goalkeeper Sergio Goycochea to see off Yugoslavia and Italy along the way. England marked their first return since 1970 by reaching the semi-finals. Germany, as in 1982 against France, again had the edge in the penalty shoot-out after a 1-1 draw. The Germans also won the final with a penalty, albeit in normal play, to beat Argentina 1-0 in Rome. Argentina, blaming defeat on everyone from FIFA president Joao Havelange down, finished with nine men. Pedro Monzon and Gustavo Dezotti were the first players ever sent off in a FIFA World Cup™ final. Franz Beckenbauer became the first man to both captain and then manage FIFA World Cup™ winners.

SECOND ROUND

Cameroon	2	Colombia	1*
Czechoslovakia	4	Costa Rica	1
Argentina	1	Brazil	0
West Germany	2	Holland	1
Rep. of Ireland	0 (5)	Romania	0 (4)*
Italy	2	Uruguay	0
Yugoslavia	2	Spain	1*
England	1	Belgium	0*

After extra time (pens)

QUARTER-FINALS

Argentina	0 (3)	Yugoslavia	0 (2)*
Italy	1	Rep of Ireland	0
West Germany	1	Czechoslovakia	0
England	3	Cameroon	2*

After extra time (pens)

SEMI-FINALS

Argentina	1 (4)	Italy	1 (3)*
West Germany	1 (4)	England	1 (3)*

After extra time (pens)

THIRD-PLACE MATCH

Italy	2	England	1

GROUP A

Italy	1	Austria	0
Czechoslovakia	5	USA	1
Italy	1	USA	0
Czechoslovakia	1	Austria	0
Italy	2	Czechoslovakia	0
Austria	2	USA	1

	P	W	D	L	F	A	Pts
Italy	3	3	0	0	4	0	6
Czechoslovakia	3	2	0	1	6	3	4
Austria	3	1	0	2	2	3	2
USA	3	0	0	3	2	8	0

GROUP C

Brazil	2	Sweden	1
Costa Rica	1	Scotland	0
Brazil	1	Costa Rica	0
Scotland	2	Sweden	1
Brazil	1	Scotland	0
Costa Rica	2	Sweden	1

	P	W	D	L	F	A	Pts
Brazil	3	3	0	0	4	1	6
Costa Rica	3	2	0	1	3	2	4
Scotland	3	1	0	2	2	3	2
Sweden	3	0	0	3	3	6	0

GROUP E

Belgium	2	South Korea	0
Uruguay	0	Spain	0
Belgium	3	Uruguay	1
Spain	3	South Korea	1
Spain	2	Belgium	1
Uruguay	1	South Korea	0

	P	W	D	L	F	A	Pts
Spain	3	2	1	0	5	2	5
Belgium	3	2	0	1	6	3	4
Uruguay	3	1	1	1	2	3	3
South Korea	3	0	0	3	1	6	0

GROUP B

Cameroon	1	Argentina	0
Romania	2	Soviet Union	0
Argentina	2	Soviet Union	0
Cameroon	2	Romania	1
Argentina	1	Romania	1
Soviet Union	4	Cameroon	0

	P	W	D	L	F	A	Pts
Cameroon	3	2	0	1	3	5	4
Romania	3	1	1	1	4	3	3
Argentina	3	1	1	1	3	2	3
Soviet Union	3	1	0	2	4	4	2

GROUP D

Colombia	2	UAE	0
West Germany	4	Yugoslavia	1
Yugoslavia	1	Colombia	0
West Germany	5	UAE	1
West Germany	1	Colombia	1
Yugoslavia	4	UAE	1

	P	W	D	L	F	A	Pts
West Germany	3	2	1	0	10	3	5
Yugoslavia	3	2	0	1	6	5	4
Colombia	3	1	1	1	3	2	3
UAE	3	0	0	3	2	11	0

GROUP F

England	1	Rep. of Ireland	1
Holland	1	Egypt	1
England	0	Holland	0
Egypt	0	Rep. of Ireland	0
England	1	Egypt	0
Holland	1	Rep. of Ireland	1

	P	W	D	L	F	A	Pts
England	3	1	2	0	2	1	4
Rep. of Ireland	3	0	3	0	2	2	3
Holland	3	0	3	0	2	2	3
Egypt	3	0	2	1	1	2	2

FINAL – July 8: Olimpico, Rome

West Germany 1 (Brehme 84 pen)   **Argentina 0**

HT: 0-0. **Att:** 73,603. **Ref:** Codesal (Mexico)

West Germany: Illgner, Berthold (Reuter 74), Kohler, Augenthaler, Brehme, Hassler, Buchwald, Matthaus, Littbarski, Völler, Klinsmann.

Argentina: Goycochea, Lorenzo, Ruggeri (Monzon 46), Serrizuela, Sensini, Simon, Basualdo, Burruchaga (Calderon 53), Maradona, Troglio, Dezotti. **Sent off:** Monzon, Dezotti.

Top scorer: 6 Schillaci (Italy)

1994 USA

Awarding the finals to the United States upset football's purists but American fans responded with gusto. Record crowds thrilled to football vastly improved by a crackdown on cynical play. On the debit side, Argentina captain Diego Maradona was expelled after failing a dope test, Germany sent home their own Stefan Effenberg for a rude gesture to fans and Colombia's Andres Escobar was shot dead on returning home after scoring an own goal in a crucial first-round defeat by their American hosts. Brazil were deserved winners, inspired by Romario who scored five goals and claimed a hand in all their other six. However, Brazil owed victory to an unsatisfactory first-ever final penalty shoot-out in which they beat Italy after a goalless draw, with Italy's star performer Roberto Baggio missing the decisive last spot-kick.

GROUP A

USA	1	Switzerland	1
Colombia	1	Romania	3
USA	2	Colombia	1
Romania	1	Switzerland	4
USA	0	Romania	1
Switzerland	0	Colombia	2

	P	W	D	L	F	A	Pts
Romania	3	2	0	1	5	5	6
Switzerland	3	1	1	1	5	4	4
USA	3	1	1	1	3	3	4
Colombia	3	1	0	2	4	5	3

GROUP B

Cameroon	2	Sweden	2
Brazil	2	Russia	0
Brazil	3	Cameroon	0
Sweden	3	Russia	1
Russia	6	Cameroon	1
Brazil	1	Sweden	1

	P	W	D	L	F	A	Pts
Brazil	3	2	1	0	6	1	7
Sweden	3	1	2	0	6	4	5
Russia	3	1	0	2	7	6	3
Cameroon	3	0	1	2	3	11	1

GROUP C

Germany	1	Bolivia	0
Spain	2	South Korea	2
Germany	1	Spain	1
South Korea	0	Bolivia	0
Bolivia	1	Spain	3
Germany	3	South Korea	2

	P	W	D	L	F	A	Pts
Germany	3	2	1	0	5	3	7
Spain	3	1	2	0	6	4	5
South Korea	3	0	2	1	4	5	2
Bolivia	3	0	1	2	1	4	1

GROUP D

Argentina	4	Greece	0
Nigeria	3	Bulgaria	0
Argentina	2	Nigeria	1
Bulgaria	4	Greece	0
Greece	0	Nigeria	2
Argentina	0	Bulgaria	2

	P	W	D	L	F	A	Pts
Nigeria	3	2	0	1	6	2	6
Bulgaria	3	2	0	1	6	3	6
Argentina	3	2	0	1	6	3	6
Greece	3	0	0	3	0	10	0

GROUP E

Italy	0	Rep. of Ireland	1
Norway	1	Mexico	0
Italy	1	Norway	0
Mexico	2	Rep. of Ireland	1
Rep. of Ireland	0	Norway	0
Italy	1	Mexico	1

	P	W	D	L	F	A	Pts
Mexico	3	1	1	1	3	3	4
Rep. of Ireland	3	1	1	1	2	2	4
Italy	3	1	1	1	2	2	4
Norway	3	1	1	1	1	1	4

GROUP F

Belgium	1	Morocco	0
Holland	2	Saudi Arabia	1
Belgium	1	Holland	0
Saudi Arabia	2	Morocco	1
Morocco	1	Holland	2
Belgium	0	Saudi Arabia	1

	P	W	D	L	F	A	Pts
Holland	3	2	0	1	4	3	6
Saudi Arabia	3	2	0	1	4	3	6
Belgium	3	2	0	1	2	1	6
Morocco	3	0	0	3	2	5	0

SECOND ROUND

Germany	3	Belgium	2
Spain	3	Switzerland	0
Sweden	3	Saudi Arabia	1
Romania	3	Argentina	2
Holland	2	Rep. of Ireland	0
Brazil	1	USA	0
Italy	2	Nigeria	1*
Bulgaria	1(3)	Mexico	1 (1)*

* After extra time (pens)

QUARTER-FINALS

Italy	2	Spain	1
Brazil	3	Holland	2
Bulgaria	2	Germany	1
Sweden	2 (5)	Romania	2 (4)*

* After extra time (pens)

SEMI-FINALS

Brazil	1	Sweden	0
Italy	2	Bulgaria	1

THIRD-PLACE MATCH

Sweden	4	Bulgaria	0

FINAL – July 17: Rose Bowl, Pasadena

Brazil 0 (3)   Italy 0 (2)*

HT: 0-0. **Att:** 94,000. **Ref:** Puhl (Hungary)

Brazil: Taffarel, Jorginho (Cafu 20), Aldair, Marcio Santos, Branco, Mazinho, Dunga, Mauro Silva, Zinho (Viola 106), Romario, Bebeto.

Italy: Pagliuca, Mussi (Apolloni 34), Maldini, Baresi, Benarrivo, Donadoni, Berti, Albertini, D Baggio (Evani 94), R Baggio, Massaro.

Top scorer: 6 Salenko (Russia), Stoichkov (Bulgaria).

* After extra time (pens)

Brazil captain Dunga lifts the 1994 FIFA World Cup™ after Brazil beat Italy 3-2 on penalties in the Final.

France's Zinedine Zidane holds aloft the FIFA World Cup™.

1998 FRANCE

FIFA World Cup™ history came full circle as France, whose Jules Rimet had instigated the tournament, won the prize for the first time in front of their own fans in the magnificent new Stade de France. Zinedine Zidane, the son of Algerian immigrants, recovered his nerve after a first-round red card and two-game ban to head their crucial two first goals in the 3-0 final win over holders Brazil. Victory was a remarkable vindication of the French federation's academy system and the hard work of much criticised coach Aime Jacquet. Croatia marked their debut at the finals by finishing third, while centre-forward Davor Suker ended up as the tournament's six-goal top scorer. England's dream ended in the second round after yet another shoot-out defeat, this time at the hands of Argentina. Manager Glenn Hoddle's men did well to last that long after young starlet David Beckham was sent off early in the second half. Consolation was the explosive form of FIFA World Cup™ new boy Michael Owen, who stung the Argentines with one of the goals of the tournament.

GROUP A

Brazil	2	Scotland	1
Morocco	2	Norway	2
Brazil	3	Morocco	0
Scotland	1	Norway	1
Brazil	1	Norway	2
Scotland	0	Morocco	3

	P	W	D	L	F	A	Pts
Brazil	3	2	0	1	6	3	6
Norway	3	1	2	0	5	4	5
Morocco	3	1	1	1	5	5	4
Scotland	3	0	1	2	2	6	1

GROUP B

Italy	2	Chile	2
Austria	1	Cameroon	1
Chile	1	Austria	1
Italy	3	Cameroon	0
Chile	1	Cameroon	1
Italy	2	Austria	1

	P	W	D	L	F	A	Pts
Italy	3	2	1	0	7	3	7
Chile	3	0	3	0	4	4	3
Austria	3	0	2	1	3	4	2
Cameroon	3	0	2	1	2	5	2

GROUP C

Saudi Arabia	0	Denmark	1
France	3	South Africa	0
France	4	Saudi Arabia	0
South Africa	1	Denmark	1
France	2	Denmark	1
South Africa	2	Saudi Arabia	2

	P	W	D	L	F	A	Pts
France	3	3	0	0	9	1	9
Denmark	3	1	1	1	3	3	4
S. Africa	3	0	2	1	3	6	2
S. Arabia	3	0	1	2	2	7	1

GROUP D

Paraguay	0	Bulgaria	0
Spain	2	Nigeria	3
Nigeria	1	Bulgaria	0
Spain	0	Paraguay	0
Nigeria	1	Paraguay	3
Spain	6	Bulgaria	1

	P	W	D	L	F	A	Pts
Nigeria	3	2	0	1	5	5	6
Paraguay	3	1	2	0	3	1	5
Spain	3	1	1	1	8	4	4
Bulgaria	3	0	1	2	1	7	1

GROUP E

South Korea	1	Mexico	3
Holland	0	Belgium	0
Belgium	2	Mexico	2
Holland	5	South Korea	0
Belgium	1	South Korea	1
Holland	2	Mexico	2

	P	W	D	L	F	A	Pts
Holland	3	1	2	0	7	2	5
Mexico	3	1	2	0	7	5	5
Belgium	3	0	3	0	3	3	3
South Korea	3	0	1	2	2	9	1

GROUP F

Germany	2	USA	0
Yugoslavia	1	Iran	0
Germany	2	Yugoslavia	2
USA	1	Iran	2
Germany	2	Iran	0
USA	0	Yugoslavia	1

	P	W	D	L	F	A	Pts
Germany	3	2	1	0	6	2	7
Yugoslavia	3	2	1	0	4	2	7
Iran	3	1	0	2	2	4	3
USA	3	0	0	3	1	5	0

GROUP G

England	2	Tunisia	0
Romania	1	Colombia	0
Colombia	1	Tunisia	0
Romania	2	England	1
Romania	1	Tunisia	1
Colombia	0	England	2

	P	W	D	L	F	A	Pts
Romania	3	2	1	0	4	2	7
England	3	2	0	1	5	2	6
Colombia	3	1	0	2	1	3	3
Tunisia	3	0	1	2	1	4	1

GROUP H

Argentina	1	Japan	0
Jamaica	1	Croatia	3
Japan	0	Croatia	1
Argentina	5	Jamaica	0
Argentina	1	Croatia	0
Japan	1	Jamaica	2

	P	W	D	L	F	A	Pts
Argentina	3	3	0	0	7	0	9
Croatia	3	2	0	1	4	2	6
Jamaica	3	1	0	2	3	9	3
Japan	3	0	0	3	1	5	0

SECOND ROUND

Italy	1	Norway	0
Brazil	4	Chile	1
France	0 [1]	Paraguay	0 *
Nigeria	1	Denmark	4
Germany	2	Mexico	1
Holland	2	Yugoslavia	1
Romania	0	Croatia	1
Argentina	2 (4)	England	2 (3)*

* After extra time (pens) [golden goal]

QUARTER-FINALS

Italy	0 (3)	France	0 (4)*
Brazil	3	Denmark	2
Holland	2	Argentina	1
Germany	0	Croatia	3

* After extra time (pens)

SEMI-FINALS

Brazil	1 (4)	Holland	1 (2)*
France	2	Croatia	1

* After extra time (pens)

THIRD-PLACE MATCH

Holland	1	Croatia	2

FINAL – July 12: Stade de France, Paris

France 3 (Zidane 27, 45, Petit 90)   **Brazil 0**

HT: 1-0. **Att:** 75,000. **Ref:** Belqola (Morocco)

France: Barthez, Thuram, Leboeuf, Desailly, Lizarazu, Petit, Deschamps, Karembeu (Boghossian 58), Zidane, Guivarc'h (Dugarry 66), Djorkaeff (Vieira 76). **Sent off:** Desailly.

Brazil: Taffarel, Cafu, Junior Baiano, Aldair, Roberto Carlos, Dunga, Cesar Sampaio (Edmundo 75), Leonardo (Denilson 46), Rivaldo, Bebeto, Ronaldo.

Top scorer: 6 Suker (Croatia)

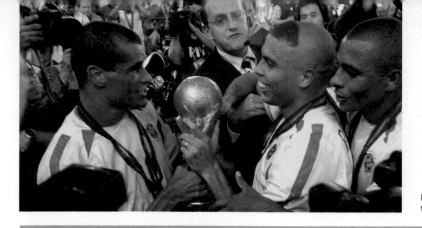

2002 SOUTH KOREA/ JAPAN

Ronaldo made amends for the 1998 upset by leading Brazil to a record-extending fifth FIFA World Cup™ win. Japan and South Korea shared the honour of hosting the first finals staged in Asia and the first to be co-hosted. Japan reached the second round, while the Koreans, under Dutch coach Guus Hiddink, reached the semi-finals before losing to Germany. By contrast, fatigue born of the increasingly stressful club season took a heavy toll on Europe's giants. Holders France collapsed in the first round without scoring a goal, Italy fell in the second round on a golden goal to the Koreans, while England tottered to a quarter-final standstill against Brazil. Ronaldinho scored a freakish winning goal against England before being sent off but returned, refreshed, for the 2-0 final defeat of the Germans. Ronaldo struck both goals and was the event's eight-goal top scorer.

GROUP A

Senegal	1	France	0
Denmark	2	Uruguay	1
France	0	Uruguay	0
Denmark	1	Senegal	1
Denmark	2	France	0
Senegal	3	Uruguay	3

	P	W	D	L	F	A	Pts
Denmark	3	2	1	0	5	2	7
Senegal	3	1	2	0	5	4	5
Uruguay	3	0	2	1	4	5	2
France	3	0	1	2	0	3	1

GROUP B

Paraguay	2	South Africa	2
Spain	3	Slovenia	1
Spain	3	Paraguay	1
South Africa	1	Slovenia	0
Spain	3	South Africa	2
Paraguay	3	Slovenia	1

	P	W	D	L	F	A	Pts
Spain	3	3	0	0	9	4	9
Paraguay	3	1	1	1	6	6	4
South Africa	3	1	1	1	5	5	4
Slovenia	3	0	0	3	2	7	0

GROUP C

Brazil	2	Turkey	1
Costa Rica	2	China	0
Brazil	4	China	0
Costa Rica	1	Turkey	1
Brazil	5	Costa Rica	2
Turkey	3	China	0

	P	W	D	L	F	A	Pts
Brazil	3	3	0	0	11	3	9
Turkey	3	1	1	1	5	3	4
Costa Rica	3	1	1	1	5	6	4
China	3	0	0	3	0	9	0

GROUP D

South Korea	2	Poland	0
USA	3	Portugal	2
South Korea	1	USA	1
Portugal	4	Poland	0
South Korea	1	Portugal	0
Poland	3	USA	1

	P	W	D	L	F	A	Pts
South Korea	3	2	1	0	4	1	7
USA	3	1	1	1	5	6	4
Portugal	3	1	0	2	6	4	3
Poland	3	1	0	2	3	7	3

GROUP E

Rep. of Ireland	1	Cameroon	1
Germany	8	Saudi Arabia	0
Germany	1	Rep. of Ireland	1
Cameroon	1	Saudi Arabia	0
Germany	2	Cameroon	0
Rep. of Ireland	3	Saudi Arabia	0

	P	W	D	L	F	A	Pts
Germany	3	2	1	0	11	1	7
Rep. Ireland	3	1	2	0	5	2	5
Cameroon	3	1	1	1	2	3	4
Saudi Arabia	3	0	0	3	0	12	0

GROUP F

England	1	Sweden	1
Argentina	1	Nigeria	0
Sweden	2	Nigeria	1
England	1	Argentina	0
Sweden	1	Argentina	1
Nigeria	0	England	0

	P	W	D	L	F	A	Pts
Sweden	3	1	2	0	4	3	5
England	3	1	2	0	2	1	5
Argentina	3	1	1	1	2	2	4
Nigeria	3	0	1	2	1	3	1

GROUP G

Mexico	1	Croatia	0
Italy	2	Ecuador	0
Croatia	2	Italy	1
Mexico	2	Ecuador	1
Mexico	1	Italy	1
Ecuador	1	Croatia	0

	P	W	D	L	F	A	Pts
Mexico	3	2	1	0	4	2	7
Italy	3	1	1	1	4	3	4
Croatia	3	1	0	2	2	3	3
Ecuador	3	1	0	2	2	4	3

GROUP H

Japan	2	Belgium	2
Russia	2	Tunisia	0
Japan	1	Russia	0
Tunisia	1	Belgium	1
Japan	2	Tunisia	0
Belgium	3	Russia	2

	P	W	D	L	F	A	Pts
Japan	3	2	1	0	5	2	7
Belgium	3	1	2	0	6	5	5
Russia	3	1	0	2	4	4	3
Tunisia	3	0	1	2	1	5	1

SECOND ROUND

Germany	1	Paraguay	0
England	3	Denmark	0
Senegal	1 [2]	Sweden	1 *
Spain	1 (3)	Rep.Ireland	1 (2)*
United States	2	Mexico	0
Brazil	2	Belgium	0
Turkey	1	Japan	0
South Korea	2	Italy	1 *

* After extra time (pens) [golden goal]

QUARTER-FINALS

Brazil	2	England	1
Germany	1	United States	0
South Korea	0 (5)	Spain	0 (4)*
Turkey	0 [1]	Senegal	0 *

* After extra time (pens) [golden goal]

SEMI-FINALS

| Germany | 1 | South Korea | 0 |
| Brazil | 1 | Turkey | 0 |

THIRD-PLACE MATCH

| Turkey | 3 | South Korea | 2 |

FINAL – June 30: International, Yokohama

Brazil 2 (Ronaldo 68, 79) **Germany 0**
HT: 0-0. **Att:** 69,029. **Ref:** Collina (Italy)
Brazil: Marcos, Cafu, Lucio, Roque Junior, Edmilson, Roberto Carlos, Gilberto Silva, Kleberson, Ronaldinho (Juninho 85), Ronaldo (Denilson 90), Rivaldo.
Germany: Kahn, Linke, Ramelow, Metzelder, Bode (Ziege 84), Schneider, Frings, Hamann, Jeremies (Asamoah 78), Neuville, Klose (Bierhoff 74).
Top scorer: 8 Ronaldo (Brazil)

Italy captain Fabio Cannavaro lifts the FIFA World Cup™.

2006 GERMANY

Italy carried off the FIFA World Cup™ for a European-country record fourth time but the final in Berlin's historic Olympic Stadium will also be remembered as the night on which the great Zinedine Zidane's career ended in disaster. Zidane, a FIFA World Cup-winner in 1998 and then a European champion in 2000 as well as World Player of the Year, was sent off in extra time for a head-butt. He thus missed the second shoot-tout in the history of the FIFA World Cup™ final. Thus it was Italy's outstanding captain and central defender Fabio Cannavaro who lifted the Cup. Germany not only put on an outstanding performance as hosts but provided a team, under manager Jurgen Klinsmann, who finished third. A quarter-final against France marked the end of Brazil's defence while England, at the same stage against Portugal, were again undone by penalties. Goal of the finals was scored by Argentina's Esteban Cambiasso against Serbia after a move involving nine players and 55 touches of the ball over 58 seconds.

GROUP A

Germany	4	Costa Rica	2
Ecuador	2	Poland	0
Germany	1	Poland	0
Ecuador	3	Costa Rica	0
Germany	3	Ecuador	0
Poland	2	Costa Rica	1

	P	W	D	L	F	A	Pts
Germany	3	3	0	0	8	2	9
Ecuador	3	2	0	1	5	3	6
Poland	3	1	0	2	2	4	3
Costa Rica	3	0	0	3	3	9	0

GROUP B

England	1	Paraguay	0
Trinidad & Tobago	0	Sweden	0
England	2	Trinidad & Tobago	0
Sweden	1	Paraguay	0
Sweden	2	England	2
Paraguay	2	Trinidad & Tobago	0

	P	W	D	L	F	A	Pts
England	3	2	1	0	5	2	7
Sweden	3	1	2	0	3	2	5
Paraguay	3	1	0	2	2	2	3
Trinidad & Tobago	3	0	1	2	0	4	1

GROUP C

Argentina	2	Ivory Coast	1
Serbia & Montenegro	0	Holland	1
Argentina	6	Serbia & Montenegro	0
Holland	2	Ivory Coast	1
Holland	0	Argentina	0
Ivory Coast	3	Serbia & Montenegro	2

	P	W	D	L	F	A	Pts
Argentina	3	2	1	0	8	1	7
Holland	3	2	1	0	3	1	7
Ivory Coast	3	1	0	2	5	6	3
Serbia & Montenegro	3	0	0	3	2	10	0

GROUP D

Mexico	3	Iran	1
Portugal	1	Angola	0
Mexico	0	Angola	0
Portugal	2	Iran	0
Portugal	2	Mexico	1
Iran	1	Angola	1

	P	W	D	L	F	A	Pts
Portugal	3	3	0	0	5	1	9
Mexico	3	1	1	1	4	3	4
Angola	3	0	2	1	1	2	2
Iran	3	0	1	2	2	6	1

GROUP E

Czech Republic	3	USA	0
Italy	2	Ghana	0
Ghana	2	Czech Republic	0
Italy	1	USA	1
Italy	2	Czech Republic	0
Ghana	2	USA	1

	P	W	D	L	F	A	Pts
Italy	3	2	1	0	5	1	7
Ghana	3	2	0	1	4	3	6
Czech Republic	3	1	0	2	3	4	3
USA	3	0	1	2	2	6	1

GROUP F

Australia	3	Japan	1
Brazil	1	Croatia	0
Croatia	0	Japan	0
Brazil	2	Australia	0
Brazil	4	Japan	1
Croatia	2	Australia	2

	P	W	D	L	F	A	Pts
Brazil	3	3	0	0	7	1	9
Australia	3	1	1	1	5	5	4
Croatia	3	0	2	1	2	3	2
Japan	3	0	1	2	2	7	1

GROUP G

South Korea	2	Togo	1
France	0	Switzerland	0
France	1	South Korea	1
Switzerland	2	Togo	0
France	2	Togo	0
Switzerland	2	South Korea	0

	P	W	D	L	F	A	Pts
Switzerland	3	2	1	0	4	0	7
France	3	1	2	0	3	1	5
South Korea	3	1	1	1	3	4	4
Togo	3	0	0	3	1	6	0

GROUP H

Spain	4	Ukraine	0
Tunisia	2	Saudi Arabia	2
Ukraine	4	Saudi Arabia	0
Spain	3	Tunisia	1
Spain	1	Saudi Arabia	0
Ukraine	1	Tunisia	0

	P	W	D	L	F	A	Pts
Spain	3	3	0	0	8	1	9
Ukraine	3	2	0	1	5	4	6
Tunisia	3	0	1	2	3	6	1
Saudi Arabia	3	0	1	2	2	7	1

SECOND ROUND

Germany	2	Sweden	0
Argentina	2	Mexico	1*
Italy	1	Australia	0
Ukraine	0 (3)	Switzerland	0 (0)*
England	1	Ecuador	0
Portugal	1	Netherlands	0
Brazil	3	Ghana	0
France	3	Spain	1

*After extra time (pens)

QUARTER-FINALS

Germany	1 (4)	Argentina	1(2)*
Italy	3	Ukraine	0
Portugal	0 (3)	England	0 (1)*
France	1	Brazil	0

*After extra time (pens)

SEMI-FINALS

| Italy | 2 | Germany | 0* |
| France | 1 | Portugal | 0 |

*After extra time

THIRD-PLACE MATCH

| Germany | 3 | Portugal | 1 |

FINAL – July 9: Olympiastadion, Berlin

Italy 1 (5) (Materazzi 19) **France 1 (3)** (Zidane 7 (pen))*
HT: 1-1. **Att:** 69,000. **Ref:** Elizondo (Argentina)
Italy: Buffon, Zambrotta, Cannavaro, Materazzi, Grosso, Gattuso, Pirlo, Camoranesi (Del Piero 86), Perrotta (De Rossi 61), Totti (Iaquinta 61), Toni.
France: Barthez, Sagnol, Thuram, Gallas, Abidal, Vieira (Diarra 56), Makélélé, Ribéry (Trezeguet 100), Zidane, Malouda, Henry (Wiltord 107). **Sent off:** Zidane.
Top scorer: 5 Klose (Germany)

*After extra time (pens)

FIFA World Cup™ Statistics

FIFA WORLD CUP™ ATTENDANCES 1930–2006

Year	Host nation	Teams	Matches	Total atts	Ave att
1930	Uruguay	13	18	434,000	24,111
1934	Italy	16	17	395,000	23,235
1938	France	15	18	483,000	26,833
1950	Brazil	13	22	1,337,000	60,773
1954	Switzerland	16	26	943,000	36,269
1958	Sweden	16	35	868,000	24,800
1962	Chile	16	32	776,000	24,250
1966	England	16	32	1,614,677	50,459
1970	Mexico	16	32	1,673,975	52,312
1974	West Germany	16	38	1,774,022	46,685
1978	Argentina	16	38	1,610,215	42,374
1982	Spain	24	52	1,856,277	35,698
1986	Mexico	24	52	2,407,431	46,297
1990	Italy	24	52	2,517,348	48,411
1994	United States	24	52	3,587,538	68,991
1998	France	32	64	2,785,100	43,517
2002	South Korea/Japan	32	64	2,722,390	42,537
2006	Germany	32	64	3,359,439	52,491

THE FIRST

GOAL
Lucien Laurent (France) v Mexico, 1930

OWN-GOAL
Ernst Loertscher (Switzerland) v Germany, 1938

HAT-TRICK
Bert Patenaude (USA) v Paraguay, 1930

EXPULSION
Mario de Las Casas (Peru) v Romania, 1930

GOALKEEPER SENT OFF
Gianluca Pagliuca (Italy) v Norway, 1994

SHOOT-OUT
West Germany v France, 3-3, 5-4 pens (1982 semi-final)

THE FASTEST

EXPULSION
Jose Batista (Uruguay) 56 seconds v Scotland, 1986

GOAL
Hakan Sukur (Turkey) 11 seconds v South Korea, 2002

THE MOST

WINS

Brazil	5
Italy	4
Germany/West Germany	3
Argentina	2
Uruguay	2
France	1
England	1

TOURNAMENTS (TEAM)

Brazil	18

TOURNAMENTS (PLAYER)

Antonio Carbajal (Mexico)	5
Lothar Matthaus (West Germany)	5

RECORD MATCH ATTENDANCE
199,854 (Brazil v Uruguay, 1950)

YOUNGEST AND OLDEST

YOUNGEST FIFA WORLD CUP™ WINNER
Pele (Brazil) 17 years 249 days (v Sweden, 1958)

YOUNGEST PLAYER
Norman Whiteside (Northern Ireland) 17 years 42 days (v Yugoslavia, 1982)

YOUNGEST SCORER
Pele (Brazil) 17 years 239 days (v Wales, 1958)

OLDEST FIFA WORLD CUP™ WINNER
Dino Zoff (Italy) 40 years 133 days (v W. Germany, 1982)

OLDEST PLAYER
Roger Milla (Cameroon) 42 years 39 days (v Russia, 1994)

OLDEST SCORER
Roger Milla (Cameroon) 42 years 39 days (v Russia, 1994)

THE HIGHEST

GOAL AGGREGATE PER GAME

Austria v Switzerland 7-5 (1954)	12
Brazil v Poland 6-5 (1938)	11
Hungary v West Germany 8-3 (1954)	11

GOALS PER TEAM PER MATCH

Hungary v El Salvador 10-1 (1982)	10
Hungary v South Korea 9-0 (1954)	9
Yugoslavia v Zaire 9-0 (1974)	9

GOALS PER TEAM PER TOURNAMENT

Hungary (1954)	27
West Germany (1954)	25
France (1958)	23

GOALS PER TOURNAMENT

Just Fontaine (France, 1958)	13
Sandor Kocsis (Hungary, 1954)	11
Gerd Muller (West Germany, 1970)	10
Ademir (Brazil, 1950),	9
Eusebio (Portugal, 1966),	9

INDIVIDUAL GOALS AGGREGATE

Ronaldo (Brazil)	15
Gerd Muller (West Germany)	14
Just Fontaine (France)	13
Pele (Brazil)	12
Sandor Kocsis (Hungary)	11
Jurgen Klinsmann (West Germany)	11

INDIVIDUAL GOALS PER GAME

Oleg Salenko (Russia)	5
Ademir (Brazil)	4
Sandor Kocsis (Hungary)	4
Just Fontaine (France)	4
Ernst Wilimowski (Poland)	4
Eusebio (Portugal)	4
Emilio Butragueno (Spain)	4
Juan Alberto Schiaffino (Uruguay)	4

GOAL SCORING

GOALS PER GAME

Year	Host nation	Matches	Goals	Ave
1930	Uruguay	18	70	3.89
1934	Italy	17	70	4.12
1938	France	18	84	4.67
1950	Brazil	22	88	4.00
1954	Switzerland	26	140	5.38
1958	Sweden	35	126	3.60
1962	Chile	32	89	2.78
1966	England	32	89	2.78
1970	Mexico	32	95	2.97
1974	West Germany	38	97	2.55
1978	Argentina	38	102	2.68
1982	Spain	52	146	2.81
1986	Mexico	52	132	2.54
1990	Italy	52	115	2.21
1994	United States	52	141	2.71
1998	France	64	171	2.67
2002	South Korea/Japan	64	161	2.52
2006	Germany	64	147	2.29

The publishers would like to thank the following sources for their kind permission to reproduce the pictures in this book. The page numbers for each of the photographs are listed below, giving the page on which they appear in the book and any location indicator (C-centre, T-top, B-bottom, L-left, R-right).

Getty Images: /AFP: 17B; /Gallo Images: 18C; /Alexander Joe/AFP: 17T; /Richard Rad/Latin Content: 30, 31

Press Association Images: /AP: 57, 62BR, 110-111; /Barry Aldworth/Sports Inc: 109; /Hassan Ammar/AP: 10; /Matthew Ashton/ Empics Sport: 96BL; /Olivier Asselin/AP: 26; /Frank Augstein/AP: 50BL; /David Azia/AP: 8-9, /Darko Bandic/AP: 22-23; /Gavin Barker/ Sports Inc: 20, 47, 67, 85, 106; /Luigi Bennett/Sports Inc: 21; /Fabian Bimmer/AP: 70BL; /Rebecca Blackwell/AP: 89; /Abdeljalil Bounhar/AP: 74BR; /Luca Bruno/AP: 90BR; /Lynne Cameron/PA Archive: 68BL, 69; /Barry Coombs/Empics Sport: 70BR, 71, 73, 77, 86BR, 94BL, 95; /Claudio Cruz/AP: 38BL; /Andres Cuenca/AP: 40BR; /DPA: 122; /David Davies/PA Wire: 18B; /Adam Davy/Empics Sport: 11, 14, 16T, 17C, 36BR, 37, 51, 55, 66BR, 72BR, 84BR, 92BR, 93, 94BR; /Sean Dempsey/PA Archive: 52BR, 53; /Mike Egerton/ Empics Sport: 4, 28, 63, 90BL, 103, 125; /Empics Sport: 27, 48BL, 48BR, 49, 91, 112; /Dominic Favre/AP: 108; /Esteban Felix/AP: 97; /Nigel French/Empics Sport: 98BL, 98BR; /Carlo Fumagalli/AP: 120; /Clive Gee/PA Archive: 46BL, 46BR; /Petros Giannakouris/ AP: 50BR; /Joe Giddens/Empics Sport: 36BL, 74BL, 82BL, 82BR; /Nicolas Gouhier/ABACA: 42BL; /Themba Hadebe/AP: 19T; /Owen Humphreys/PA Wire: 6; /Srdjan Ilic/AP: 64BL; /Matthew Impey/Empics Sport: 66BL; /Itsuo Inouye/AP: 72BL; /Silvia Izquierdo/AP: 99; /Hasan Jamali/AP: 81; /Georgios Kefalas/AP: 76BR; /Peter Kneffel/DPA: 60BR; /Lee Jin-Man/AP: 86BL, 87; /Fernando Llano/AP: 41; /Daniel Luna/AP: 40BL; /Sydney Mahlangu/Sports Inc: 18T, 80BL; /Tony Marshall/Empics Sport: 34-35, 38BR, 39, 58BL, 59, 64BR, 79, 96BR; /Steeve McMay/ABACA: 43; /Martin Meissner/AP: 24, 92BL, 102; /Sabelo Mngoma/Sports Inc: 16B; /Peter Morrison/AP: 62BL; /Stuart Morton/ABACA: 56BR; /Andre Penner/AP: 84BL; /Ph Perusseau/Panoramic: 123; /Gabriel Piko/PikoPress: 7, 107, 124; / Daniel Piris/AP: 78BL, 78BR; /Natacha Pisarenko/AP: 44BL; /Stephen Pond/Empics Sport: 44BR, 56BL, 61; /Nick Potts: 76BL; /Dean Purcell/AP: 80BR; /Guillaume Ramon/ABACA: 42BR; /Dusan Ranic/AP: 88BR; /Martin Rickett/PA Archive: 52BL; /Peter Robinson/ Empics Sport: 118, 119, 121; /Joerg Sarbach/AP: 105; /Ross Setford/AP: 25, 29; /Shajor/PikoPress: 45; /Sven Simon: 116; /Neal Simpson/Empics Sport: 83; /Jon Super/AP: 60BL; /J-Paul Thomas/Panoramic: 88BL; /Paul Thomas/AP: 12; /Erik Vandenbuch/ABACA: 54BL, 54BR; /Marco Vasini/AP: 58BR; /Claudio Villa/Grazia Neri: 104; /Darko Vojinovic/AP: 65; /John Walton/Empics Sport: 68BR, 75; /Bernd Weissbrod/DPA: 16C; /Ryan Wilkisky/Sports Inc: 19B; /Wilfried Witters: 100-101

Every effort has been made to acknowledge correctly and contact the source and/or copyright holder of each picture and Carlton Books Limited apologises for any unintentional errors or omissions that will be corrected in future editions of this book.

TOP SCORER(S) PER TOURNAMENT

Year	Host nation	Top scorer	Goals
1930	Uruguay	Guillermo Stabile (Argentina)	8
1934	Italy	Oldrich Nejedly (Czechoslovakia)	5
1938	France	Leonidas (Brazil)	7
1950	Brazil	Ademir (Brazil)	9
1954	Switzerland	Sandor Kocsis (Hungary)	11
1958	Sweden	Just Fontaine (France)	13
1962	Chile	Garrincha (Brazil), Vava (Brazil)	4
		Leonel Sanchez (Chile)	4
		Drazan Jerkovic (Yugoslavia)	4
		Florian Albert (Hungary)	4
		Valentin Ivanov (Soviet Union)	4
1966	England	Eusebio (Portugal)	9
1970	Mexico	Gerd Muller (West Germany)	10
1974	West Germany	Grzegorz Lato (Poland)	7
1978	Argentina	Mario Kempes (Argentina)	6
1982	Spain	Paolo Rossi (Italy)	6
1986	Mexico	Gary Lineker (England)	6
1990	Italy	Salvatore Schillaci (Italy)	6
1994	United States	Oleg Salenko (Russia)	6
		Hristo Stoichkov (Bulgaria)	6
1998	France	Davor Suker (Croatia)	6
2002	South Korea/Japan	Ronaldo (Brazil)	8
2006	Germany	Miroslav Klose (Germany)	5

LANDMARK GOALS

No.	Player	Against	Year
1	Lucien Laurent (France)	Mexico	1930
100	Angelo Schiavio (Italy)	United States	1934
200	Harry Andersson (Sweden)	Cuba	1938
300	Chico (Brazil)	Spain	1950
400	Max Morlock (West Germany)	Turkey	1954
500	Bobby Collins (Scotland)	Paraguay	1958
600	Drazan Jerkovic (Yugoslavia)	Uruguay	1962
700	Pak Seung Zing (North Korea)	Chile	1966
800	Gerd Muller (West Germany)	Bulgaria	1970
900	Hector Yazalde (Argentina)	Haiti	1974
1000	Rob Rensenbrink (Holland)	Scotland	1978
1100	Sergei Baltacha (Soviet Union)	New Zealand	1982
1200	Jean-Pierre Papin (France)	Canada	1986
1300	Gary Lineker (England)	Paraguay	1986
1400	Johnny Ekstrom (Sweden)	Costa Rica	1990
1500	Claudio Caniggia (Argentina)	Nigeria	1994
1600	Pierre Issa (own-goal for France)	South Africa	1998
1700	Slobodan Komljenovic (Yugoslavia)	United States	1998
1800	Beto (Portugal)	United States	2002
1900	Christian Vieri (Italy)	South Korea	2002
2000	Markus Allback (Sweden)	England	2006

SHOOT-OUT RECORD PER TEAM

Year	Host	Round	Match	Score
1982	Spain	Semi-final	West Germany v France	3-3, 5-4 pens
1986	Mexico	Quarter-final	France v Brazil	1-1, 4-3 pens
		Quarter-final	West Germany v Mexico	0-0, 4-1 pens
		Quarter-final	Belgium v Spain	1-1, 5-4 pens
1990	Italy	2nd round	Rep. of Ireland v Romania	0-0, 5-4 pens
		2nd round	Argentina v Yugoslavia	0-0, 3-2 pens
		Semi-final	Argentina v Italy	1-1, 4-3 pens
		Semi-final	West Germany v England	1-1, 4-3 pens
1994	USA	2nd round	Bulgaria v Mexico	1-1, 3-1 pens
		Quarter-final	Sweden v Romania	1-1, 5-4 pens
		Final	Brazil v Italy	0-0, 3-2 pens
1998	France	2nd round	Argentina v England	2-2, 4-3 pens
		Quarter-final	France v Italy	0-0, 4-3 pens
		Semi-final	Brazil v Holland	1-1, 4-2 pens
2002	S Korea	2nd round	Spain v Rep of Ireland	1-1, 3-2 pens
		Quarter-final	South Korea v Spain	0-0, 5-3 pens
2006	Germany	2nd round	Ukraine v Switzerland	0-0, 3-0 pens
		Quarter-final	Germany v Argentina	1-1, 4-2 pens
		Quarter-final	Portugal v England	0-0, 3-1 pens
		Final	Italy v France	1-1, 5-3 pens

DISCIPLINE

EXPULSIONS PER TOURNAMENT

Year	Host nation	No
1930	Uruguay	1
1934	Italy	1
1938	France	4
1950	Brazil	0
1954	Switzerland	3
1958	Sweden	3
1962	Chile	6
1966	England	5
1970	Mexico	0
1974	West Germany	5
1978	Argentina	3
1982	Spain	5
1986	Mexico	8
1990	Italy	16
1994	United States	15
1998	France	22
2002	South Korea/Japan	17
2006	Germany	28

EXPULSIONS PER TEAM

Argentina	10
Brazil	9
Cameroon	7
Italy	7
Czechoslovakia	6
Germany/West Germany	6
Holland	6
Mexico	6
Uruguay	6
France	5
Hungary	5
Portugal	4
United States	4
Bulgaria	3
Croatia	3
Denmark	3
England	3
Soviet Union	3
Sweden	3
Australia	2
Belgium	2
Bolivia	2
Chile	2
Paraguay	2
Serbia	2
South Korea	2
Turkey	2
Yugoslavia	2
Angola, Austria, Canada, China, Ghana, Honduras, Iraq, Ivory Coast, Jamaica, Northern Ireland, Peru, Poland, Romania, Saudi Arabia, Scotland, Senegal, Slovenia, South Africa, Spain, Togo, Trinidad & Tobago, Tunisia, Ukraine, United Arab Emirates, Zaire	1

PENALTY SHOOT-OUTS

SHOOT-OUT RECORD PER TEAM

Team	Won	Lost
West Germany	4	0
Argentina	3	1
Brazil	2	1
Bulgaria	1	0
Belgium	1	0
Portugal	1	0
South Korea	1	0
Sweden	1	0
Ukraine	1	0
France	2	2
Rep of Ireland	1	1
Spain	1	2
Holland	0	1
Switzerland	0	1
Yugoslavia	0	1
Mexico	0	2
Romania	0	2
Italy	1	3
England	0	3